EARLY OPERA IN AMERICA

ROOTS AND SOURCES OF THE AMERICAN THEATRE

General Editor: Prof. Richard Moody, Indiana University

SONNECK, Oscar . . . . Early Opera in America

CARSON, William, G.B. . . . . . . Managers In Distress:
                               The St. Louis Stage, 1840-1844

LEMAN, Walter, M. . . . . Memories of An Old Actor.
                               With lengthy introduction by Prof. Garff Wilson
                               (Univ. of Calif.) and new index, and John H.
                               McCabe's Historical Essay on the Drama In California.

LUDLOW, Noah Miller . . . . . . Dramatic Life as I Found It.
                               With a lengthy introduction by Prof. Francis Hodge
                               (Univ. of Texas) and new index by Prof. Napier Wilt
                               (Univ. of Texas)

MOSES, Montrose, J. (ed.) . . . . Representative Plays By American Dramatists, 3 vols.
                               Vol. 1, 1765-1819
                               Vol. 2, 1815-1858
                               Vol. 3, 1856-1917

BROWN, Thomas Allston . . . . History of the New York Stage
                               From The First Performance In 1732 To 1901.
                               Three Volumes.

MOSES, Montrose, J. . . . . The American Dramatist. Revised edition.

EARLY OPERA IN AMERICA

By

O. G. SONNECK

Chief of the Division of Music
Library of Congress

Author of
"Early Concert-Life in America," etc.

Benjamin Blom
New York

Printed in U.S.A. by
NOBLE OFFSET PRINTERS, INC.
NEW YORK 3, N. Y.

PREFATORY NOTE

This book was written for serial publication in the "New Music Review." The first part appeared there from June to August, 1907 and is here reprinted, practically intact, with the kind permission of the H. W. Gray Co. Of the other part merely a summary could be published by the "New Music Review" from August to October, 1908. The book had grown too bulky for magazine purposes, notwithstanding a merciless pruning of my material and a persistent effort at condensation, illustrated, for instance, by the somewhat unusual tabular form of dry but indispensable statistics of performances. That the book is written with a somewhat lighter touch than my other books, explains itself for similar reasons.

Had this survey of Early Opera in America originally not been intended for serial publication, which forbade instructive and perhaps entertaining but not absolutely necessary digressions into general operatic history, it would easily have assumed the proportions of my pendant book on "Early Concert-Life in America." Nothing essential, I believe, has been discarded; and I hope that the book will serve the twofold purpose of laying bare the roots of opera in America and of throwing light on the customs and manners of olden times.

The above paragraphs were written in September, 1910. Since then pressing duties absolutely forbade the revision of the manuscript with reference to recent literature that may shed additional light on our early operatic history. To be perfectly frank, I had neither the time nor the inclination to continue systematically to search for such data. Important new data may have appeared elsewhere and they may affect our knowledge of early opera in America in detail, but I hardly believe that they will affect the main historical currents, as here investigated.

To this perhaps dangerous confession I add the regret that my knowledge of eighteenth-century English opera seven years ago, when this book was written, was not what it is to-day. Not that I lay claim to deep research since then in a woefully neglected field of musical history; but during these seven years my duties as a musical librarian brought me into frequent contact with much historical information that might have been utilized advantageously in this book, if I could have done so without recasting the manuscript. Those of my friends who know the history of my book, before it attracted the attention of its present publishers, will appreciate the deterring influences against any attempt to bestow much additional labor on a book, almost cast aside by me as "hopeless."

O. G. SONNECK

Washington, D. C., May 15, 1914

CONTENTS

LIST OF ILLUSTRATIONS

PART I

PRE-REVOLUTIONARY OPERA

EARLY OPERA IN AMERICA

PART I

PRE-REVOLUTIONARY OPERA

Until the close of the eighteenth century opera played a secondary part in the theatrical affairs of our country, very much in the same manner as it still does in the small provincial towns of the European continent. But, whereas there the repertory is not wholly restricted to the historical descendants of the old Singspiele, operettas and the like (plays interspersed with songs, etc.), the Americans of the eighteenth century were treated almost exclusively to ballad-operas, using this term here, for want of a better one, not only for such English operas in which popular ballads, airs, folk-songs were pressed into service, but for all light English operas in which the plot is carried on in spoken dialogue instead of by recitative. So closely are the vicissitudes of early opera in America interwoven with the early history of the American theatre in general that the historian of the latter incidentally will contribute perceptibly to a history of the beginnings of opera in our country. If this historian brings thoroughness to his difficult task, then the musical historian, after carefully and independently digging through the mass of contemporary sources, will find it very much easier to treat the musical side of the historical structure from a more musical standpoint, to remove unmusical misconceptions and to make corrections and additions.

This task of writing a "History of the American Theatre" has been accomplished by George A. Seilhamer in three bulky volumes, carrying theatrical events from

3

1749 down to 1797. His work is truly monumental and so astonishingly full of information that merely to extract and copy the musical data would mean to have compiled a fairly exhaustive monograph on our early opera, opera singers, opera houses, and so forth. Yet, though Mr. Seilhamer's *magnum opus* appeared almost twenty years ago, very few musical historians have, to this day, taken cognizance of it! Whoever cares to inform himself or write on early opera in America must study Seilhamer, be it only to produce a popular second-hand compilation. Obviously, a second-hand compilation from Seilhamer this book of mine is not. Though it owes much to Seilhamer's industrious research and though its sources are often necessarily identical with his, yet this book just as often goes beyond his sources and is really the ultimate result of independent research. Also, it digests the more recent serious contributions to the history of the American stage, and deals impartially with those earlier historians against whom Mr. Seilhamer in the heat of conflict has pressed his points too polemically. I have principally William Dunlap in mind, the famous author of the first important "History of the American Theatre." In fact, the Dunlap Society was not slow in coming to the rescue of their patron, whom Seilhamer, at times, attacks too savagely. Of course, Mr. Seilhamer's own work is not perfect, and especially did he not show his usual lucky hand when gathering together the obscure data on the beginnings of the theatre in America, though he knew a good deal more about them than Dunlap.

Mr. Seilhamer had the misfortune to overlook a paper on the "First Theatre in America," written, read and published by Mr. Charles P. Daly in the sixties of the last century. This paper was reprinted with a supplement by the Dunlap Society in 1896, and is the chief source on the introduction of drama into America. In the supplement attention was drawn to "a small quarto volume, now

FRONTISPIECE OF
ANTHONY ASTON'S "THE FOOL'S OPERA"
(*circa* 1730)

excessively rare, published in the eighteenth century by Anthony Aston, or, as he was generally known, Tony Aston, who has been an actor in the West Indies and afterward came to Virginia and New York, who, according to his own statement, acted in the city of New York in 1702." In other words, Mr. McKee, of New York, the possessor of this rarity—only one copy seems to be extant in the United States[1]—held, or rather believed that he held, in his hands the means for dating the beginning of the American theatre about fifty years earlier than most historians. Mr. Daly contented himself with the hint as quoted, because Mr. McKee was expected to print a paper on Aston and his career. His death interfered, and the book passed into other hands for the handsome sum of eighty-one dollars. As this copy of Aston's "volume" was not generally accessible, we were left somewhat in the dark regarding its contents. Yet from time to time further hints, and even excerpts, appeared in the press, and it will be seen how easily one could date, without having seen the book itself and relying upon the accuracy of such hints, not only the introduction of the drama, but also of opera, in America as early as New York, A. D. 1702. I myself plead guilty of having gone so far as to write of *unmistakable* signs. It is about time that the matter be settled once for ever.

The title of the "small quarto volume"—really a duodecimo of nineteen pages, as I convinced myself at the British Museum—reads:

"The Fool's Opera; or, The Taste of the Age. Written by Mat Medley and performed by His Company in Oxford. To which is prefix'd [*sic!*] A Sketch of the Author's Life, Written by Himself.

"London: Printed for T. Payne. . . "

The pseudonym Mat. Medley is not puzzling, as on p. 15 the heading appears: "A Sketch of the Life . . . of Mr. Anthony Aston, commonly call'd Tony Aston.

[1] Another copy now in the Library of Congress.

Written by himself," and furthermore, the very droll narrative is signed "Your humble Servant, A. Aston." It was intended merely as a "cursory touch" of his life, and I do not know if he ever extended his autobiography beyond the three pages in this sketch. However, Tony Aston proceeds *"ad rem* at once," addressing "my merry hearts" thus:

> You are to know me, as a Gentleman, Lawyer, Poet, Actor, Soldier, Sailor, Exciseman, Publican; in England, Scotland, Ireland, *New York, East and West Jersey, Maryland, Virginia* (*on both sides Cheesapeek*), *North and South Carolina, South Florida*, Bahamas, Jamaica, Hispaniola, and often a Coaster by all the same.

That Tony was the son of a lawyer in Staffordshire, that his mother was Irish, that he indulged in "innocent pranks and mercurial disposition," that he drifted from making verses and reading plays into acting them and writing some himself, does not concern us here, nor how he was knocked about in his travels, except in so far as his narrative relates to his theatrical experiences in America—and these were very few! He arrived *quasi* accidentally in the "beginning of Queen Anne's reign" at Port Royal Harbour, where Governor Moore anchored with a fleet about to start on his unsuccessful expedition against St. Augustine. Aston accompanied Moore, and goes on to say:

> "Well, we arrived in Charles-Town, full of Lice, Shame, Poverty, Nakedness and Hunger:—I turn'd Player and Poet, and wrote one Play on the Subject of the Country."

Not a further syllable on acting until he reached New York:

> "There I lighted on my old Acquaintance Jack Charlton, Fencing Master—and counsellor Reignieur, sometime of Lincolns-Inn, supply'd me with business— . . . *after acting, writing, courting, fighting that Winter* . . . my kind Captain Davis . . . . gave me free passage for Virginia, where the noble Governor Nicholson

treated me handsomely till the fleet under Commodore Evans
. . . convoy'd above 500 sail out of the Capes. The generous
Captain Pulman . . . gave me my passage Home. . . .
We arriv'd in the Downs in August—up to London . . .

No other theatrical references appear in the autobio-
graphical sketch, and those quoted are meagre enough.
Yet one point is now, for the first time, established
beyond a doubt: If the honor of having introduced plays
in America belongs to Tony Aston, then he did so at
Charleston, S. C., and not at New York. And when? Mr.
Daly, and, with him others, say 1702, but this, too, is
incorrect. Governor Moore started on his expedition in
September, 1702, and returned to Charleston in January,
1703. Consequently Aston played at Charleston in
1703, and at New York during the winter of 1703-4!
This, then, is the accurate chronological and local basis
for the next query: Did his repertory, and that of the
other strolling players, include operas of any description?
On the title-page of 'The Fool's Opera' no date appears, and without having seen the libretto, and relying
upon the several rather inaccurate hints, one might be
induced to answer in the affirmative, as far as 'The
Fool's Opera' is concerned. A cross-examination of the
libretto, however, destroys that possibility. Aston uses
the pseudonym Mat. Medley, and it is significant that he
did not set up his "medley," evidently a kind of theatrical
entertainment, until having "acted up and down England,
Scotland, Ireland" after his return from America. Furthermore, the libretto is followed on pp. 12-13 by "A
Ballad call'd a Dissertation on the Beggar's Opera,"
first performed, as everybody knows, in 1728. For this
reason the authorities at the British Museum added to
their copy after the imprint: [1730?]. This approximate
date can apply only, of course, to this particular edition,
and arguing that it is a rather queer proceeding to offset
the effectiveness of a pseudonym by unveiling one's
real name twice a few pages further on, the point may be

raised that perhaps the libretto of 'The Fool's Opera' was published originally, which means previously, without the *cursory touch* and the *dissertation* on the Beggar's Opera, or, at any rate, that it was written previous to the year 1730. Still, after having exhausted all tricks of bibliographical distinction, it is safe to say that the Fool's Opera was neither written nor performed by Aston in America. At all events, it was not the play Aston delivered himself of at Charleston "on the subject of the country," as the libretto contains no reference to America. Nor does his "Pastora, or, the Coy Shepherdess. An Opera," performed 1712 and also preserved at the British Museum. Consequently these two operas drop out and the whole delicate problem turns around the query, Can Aston possibly have performed other operas in America during the years 1703 and 1704 at Charleston and New York?

Probably not, but to deny the possibility would be rather incautious. The Italian operas of that age, with their costly machinery and the "buzzing and squeaking Trilladoes," as D'Urfey put it, may be eliminated, as also English operas, set after the Italian manner with recitative instead of spoken dialogue, *e. g.*, D'Avenant's 'Siege of Rhodes,' with music by Henry Lawes and others, or Purcell's 'Dido and Æneas.' Just as improbable is Aston's meddling with the English semi-operas, as Burney called them for their lack of recitative, *e. g.*, Matthew Locke's 'Psyche' or Purcell's 'King Arthur.' What remains? English operas, which we in America in distinction from grand operas would style light or comic operas, preferably the latter, having to deal with a Mat. Medley. But here we touch the weak spot in the history of English opera. Walking leisurely in the shadow of Burney's ghost, who was loath to concede the title of opera to any but the grand Italian operas with their Trilladoes, machines, humbug and recitative, and almost invariably dating the beginning of light or comic English opera from the Beggar's Opera, the historians have neglected to trace the forerunners of Gay-Pepusch's masterpiece. I, for one, am of the opinion that the musical novelty of the comic Beggar's Opera, if it really was a novelty, which I sincerely doubt, consisted mainly in the use of popular ballads instead of songs made to order, and that for reasons of parody. In other words, the ballad-operas proper constituted only one special branch of early English comic opera. Leaving aside the anti-masques invented by Ben Jonson as parodies of the masques in 1609, how about Aston's 'Medley,' his 'Pastora,' Carey's 'Contrivances' (1715), D'Urfey's "The Two Queens of Brentford. A musical farce or comical opera" (rehearsed but not acted, and published 1721), in which grand opera is parodied by the juxtaposition of stilted recitative and "Scotch songs," and more particularly D'Urfey's 'The Wonders in the Sun' (performed 1706), in which, as Burney says, *the songs were all set to ballad tunes of a true English growth?*[1] Here is, in my humble opinion, a practically unexplored field. If research brings to light comic operas of this stamp that were written before 1702, and which Tony Aston may have known, then no arguments will be strong enough to destroy the possibility that such musical farces were included in his American repertory, and not until it has been conclusively proven that such works did not exist can the possibility of the introduction of English opera in America in 1703 be shelved.

The same line of reasoning prevails with increasing force as the years go by before an opera is positively mentioned by name as having been performed on American soil. If, within that period, the existence of theatres in America, theatrical companies and theatrical performances can be traced, though such of operas be not

---

[1] He forgot that for the dialogue "Pray now, John," in Act III, music by Lully was used. 'The Contrivances' was not a ballad-opera in the strict sense, since the piece was written and composed by Henry Carey.

mentioned; and if, within that period, English operas are known to us which reasonably came within the performing capacity of Thespians in America, then the possibility, at least, cannot be refuted that such operas were performed in America. Unfortunately, only extremely few data are available to strengthen this possibility.[1]

The first theatrical reference after Tony Aston's return to England appears in a letter by Judge Sewall of Boston, dated March 2, 1714, in which he protests against the acting of a play at the Council Chamber. As this attempt to introduce plays in Boston was suppressed not less promptly than the one in 1686, of which Increase Mather wrote in his "Testimony against profane and superstitious customs," it is quite unnecessary to conjecture music into the ill-fated play. In fact, Boston remained a negligible quantity in matters theatrical and operatic until towards the end of the century; this was owing to the stringent act passed against "public stage-plays, interludes and other theatrical entertainments" in 1750 after two young Englishmen, assisted by some volunteer comrades, had horrified the Hub with a performance of Otway's 'Orphan.'

Different views on life in general and on the pleasures of life in particular prevailed at Williamsburg, the capital of Virginia. There, as we know from Jones's "Present State of Virginia," published at London in 1724, a *Play-House* existed near the Market Place as early as 1722. Indeed, it might have been in existence in 1718, when Governor Spottiswood expressed his indignation at the refusal of some of the members of the House of Assembly to "solemnize His Majesty's Birthday" at his house or "go to the play which was acted on the occasion."

1 To avoid crowding the pages with foot-notes giving my sources, I desire it to be understood that all my data are based either on the books dealing with the American theatre and accessible to everybody, or on my own independent researches covering the same ground. When necessary, the source will be mentioned in the text. This rule will apply particularly if I have reason to contradict the statements of Daly, Seilhamer, Durang, Ford, Dunlap Clapp, Ireland, Ritter, Armstrong, etc.

Further than this we know nothing about the Play House at Williamsburg, probably the first erected in America, and this is not surprising, as no newspaper was printed in Virginia until 1732. That the house still stood in 1736 appears from the *Virginia Gazette* for September 3, 10, when performances of Addison's "Cato" and three comedies by the "young gentlemen of the college" and "by the gentlemen and ladies of this country" were advertised.

We are equally in the dark concerning the repertory of the company that walked the boards of "the New Theatre in the building of the Hon. Rip Van Dam, Esq.," at New York, opened, as we know from the *New England and Boston Gazette* of January I, 1733, on December 11, 1732, with George Farquhar's "Recruiting Officer," in which the part of Worthy was acted "by the ingenious Mr. Thos. Heady, barber and peruque maker to his Honor." There seems to have been a temporary interruption in the career of this *new* theatre (which does not necessarily imply that an older one had existed), for a manuscript prologue by Archibald Home has been preserved "intended for the second opening of the theatre at New York, anno 1739." If the "Long Room" of Mr. Henry Holt, the dancing master, was identical with the New Theatre in Rip Van Dam's building, then the theatre actually had its second opening. At any rate, it appears from the *New York Weekly Journal*, February 5, 1739, that on Monday the 12th was to be performed at Holt's

"A New Pantomime Entertainment in Grotesque Characters, call'd the 'Adventures of Harlequin and Scaramouch, or, The Spaniard Trick'd.' To which will be added an Optick."

Now it should be remembered that by this time 'The Beggar's Opera,' 'The Devil to Pay,' 'Flora,' and a host of other ballad-operas had come to light abroad; and, as the intercourse between London and the Colonies was regular, as moreover the comedians probably had drifted to America with the tide of immigration, and as a pantomime was given which necessarily called for music, there is nothing to prevent us from assuming that such ballad-operas were performed at New York from 1732 on. On the contrary, it is probable, for why should operas not have been given in those days at New York, if they were performed about the same time at Charleston, S. C.? And now, at last, we gain *terra firma*.

> . . . we presume to usher in those Arts
> Which oft have warm'd the best and bravest Hearts.
> Faint our Endeavours, wide are our essays,
> We strive to please, but can't pretend to Praise;
> Forgiving Smiles o'er pay the grateful task,
> Those all we hope and all we humbly ask.

With these, the closing words of the Prologue, was ushered in the first theatrical season at Charleston, S. C., on January 24, 1735, at the Courtroom. Otway's 'Orphan' was the piece. By perusing the exceptionally fine files of the *South Carolina Gazette* at the Charleston Library Society we are enabled to determine that at least five performances took place until March 25. The third, on February 4, presented a double bill, the 'Orphan' being followed by 'The Adventures of Harlequin and Scaramouch.' In the fourth, on February 18, 1735, this pantomime was honored by being coupled as afterpiece with the first opera advertised by title for performance on American soil. This advertisement, historically so important, runs thus in the *South Carolina Gazette*, February 8, 1735:

> On Tuesday the 18th inst. will be presented at the Courtroom the opera of 'Flora, or Hob in the Well,' with the Dance of the two Pierrots, and a new Pantomime entertainment, called the Adventures of Harlequin Scaramouch . . .
> Tickets to be had at Mr. Shepheard's in Broad street at 40/ each. To begin at 6 o'clock precisely.

No cast is mentioned, nor do the advertisements of the next season yield more definite information. In May, 1735, "any gentlemen that are dispos'd to encourage the exhibition of plays next winter" had been invited to apply for shares in the subscription. The fund raised evidently was sufficient for defraying expenses, as the second season opened on February 12, 1736, and lasted until the middle of March. A third, equally short series, which seems to have escaped other historians, began on November 11 and came to an end in December of the same year. The performances took place at the "New Theatre in Queen street," fitted up with "Pitt and Boxes at 25/; Gallery 15/". Of ballad-operas on the repertory of the anonymous company the *Gazette* mentions 'The Devil to Pay,' presented on March 16 and 23, 1736, and 'Flora,' on November 23, 1736. The performances began at an hour now reserved by English-speaking people for an indulgence in tea, then considered a more objectionable drink than Madeira, namely 5 P. M., and of the several odd managerial details one will not fail to amuse. It was announced on February 7, that

. . . the Doors will be open'd all the afternoon. The Subscribers are desired to send to the Stagedoor in the forenoon to bespeak places, otherwise it will be too late.

With these three series the promising introduction of drama and opera came to grief at Charleston for a number of years. The doors of the New Theatre were opened on May 26, 1737, for the entertainment of the "Ancient and Honourable Society of Free and Accepted Masons," when 'The Recruiting Officer' was given and Masonic songs were sung on the stage, but after that the theatre was turned over to the several dancing-masters for balls and assemblies.

No further references to theatrical affairs appear in the old sources until 1749. To be sure, "an agreeable comedy or tragedy" was to be performed every evening at Philadelphia from December 30, 1742, on, "at the Sign of the Coach and Horse, against the State House" (*Pennsylvania Gazette*, December 30); but these were acted "by changeable figures of two feet high," and "Punch Opera, Bateman or the Unhappy Marriage," given in September, 1747, at New York, "late from Philadelphia" (*New York Weekly Post Boy*, August 31), and James Wyatt's "Punch Company of Comedians," which entertained New Yorkers in November, 1749 (*New York Gazette*, October 30), clearly belonged to the same category of puppet-shows. Still, if James Wyatt was as spirited, witty and musical as some of his colleagues in Italy are, these affairs must have been quite entertaining.

While his changeable figures thus were kept busy, actors of flesh and blood had invaded Philadelphia. A Mr. John Smith entered in his MS. journal under date of "Sixth Month, 22d, 1749," a performance of Addison's 'Cato' at Philadelphia. We know not if this was the first play night, but it probably was not the last, as otherwise the remonstrance of the Recorder of the corporation of the city of Philadelphia in the minutes of January 8, 1750, would be without a point. The substance of his report, quoted by Durang, is this, that

. . . certain persons had lately taken upon them to act plays in this city, and as he was informed intended to make a frequent practice thereof, which, it was feared, would be attended with very mischievous effects.

To this the Board agreed and requested

. . . the Magistrates to take the most effectual measures for suppressing this disorder by sending for the actors and binding them to their good behaviour or by such other means as they should judge most proper.

The magistrates preferred the other means. The company evacuated William Plumstead's warehouse in

King street, where they had put up a theatre, and hastened to New York. The *New York Gazette* on February 26, 1750, duly recorded the arrival "last week of a company of comedians from Philadelphia," and as the newspapers of New York continued to open their columns to the actors, or rather as Messrs. Kean and Murray, the managers of the company, regularly advertised their weekly performances, we are enabled to form an adequately correct opinion of their activity.

They fitted up "one of the buildings lately belonging to the Hon. Rip Van Dam, Esq.," and called it "Theatre in Nassau Street." It was opened "by his Excellency's permission" on March 5, 1750, with Cibber's alteration of the "Historical Tragedy of King Richard III.," closed on July 23, reopened on September 13, and closed again after a series of the usual time-honored benefits for the individual actors, on July 8, 1751. The repertory contained about a dozen plays and an equal number of farces. The latter were usually performed as afterpieces, and among these the ballad-operas figured quite prominently. Ascertaining, as far as still possible, the dates of performance, the following operas were selected to delight the New Yorkers:

Fielding's 'Mock Doctor' (1750, April 30; 1751, March 11).
'The Beggar's Opera' (1750, December 3, 10; 1751, January 14, February 18, May 13).
Hill's 'The Devil to Pay' (1751, January 8, 28, February 4).
Cibber's 'Damon and Phillida' (1751, February 18, 25, March 5, May 6, July 8).
Fielding's 'Virgin Unmask'd' (1751, April 22, 29, May 13).
'Flora, or Hob in the Well' (1751, May 20, 27).
'Colin and Phœbe,' a pastoral sketch (1751, January 8).

Between the acts, or between the plays and afterpieces, "entertainments of singing" were given, *e. g.*, on February 25, 1751, the "favourite dialogue called 'Jockey and Jenny,' to be sung by Mr. Woodham and

Mrs. Taylor"; on January 14, an "oratorio," by Mr. Kean, *alias* probably a sacred song; and on April 29 the patriotic ode "Briton's Charter." From the advertisements of *benefits* we are enabled to glean the names of the principal performers: Messrs. Thomas Kean, Walter Murray, Charles Somerset Woodham, Tremain, Scott; Mrs. Taylor, Miss Osborne and Miss Nancy George. The principal vocalists seem to have been Mr. Kean, Mr. Woodham and Mrs. Taylor.

The path of these acting vagabonds, for such they were in the estimation of the eighteenth century, was not exactly strewn with roses. Mr. Kean in 1751 was almost on the point of taking to his original profession of writing, a Mr. Jago (*nomen est omen*) needed a benefit badly, being "just come out of prison," and a Mrs. Davis was granted one "to buy off her time," this probably meaning that she was unfortunate enough to be a Redemptioner, or practically a slave. Even filled to its capacity, the theatre cannot have been a gold mine, for we know from answers made to certain reflections on the managers that the number of tickets printed was "161 Pit, 10 Boxes and 121 Gallery"; and as the price of admission— no money was taken at the doors—was "Box, 5/; Pit, 4/; Gallery, 2/" it is easy to figure out that the house held 936/ or $234. How much of the receipts went to the orchestra it would be difficult to state, because no musicians are mentioned in the papers. Though half a dozen fiddlers, etc., could easily have been picked up in New York, presumably Messrs. Murray and Kean contented themselves with a harpsichord for the accompaniment of the musical numbers. How remote the whole affair still was from these our own days of *all modern improvements* is illustrated by the delightful announcement which appeared in one of the papers:

The house, being new-floored, is made warm and comfortable, besides which Gentlemen and Ladies may cause their stoves to be brought.

Neither this privilege—quite in keeping, by the way, with the custom of that age—nor Messrs. Kean and Murray's rather ambitious dramatic repertory appears to have attracted crowds to the Nassau Street Theatre. Otherwise the managers would have settled at New York instead of trying their luck in the South.

From Burke's "History of Virginia" we know that Acting Governor Richard Lee gave permission in 1751 to "the New York Company of Comedians . . . to build a theatre in Williamsburg," and the lamented Paul Leicester Ford gathered from the *Virginia Gazette* into his interesting monograph on "Washington and the Theatre" the several facts pertaining to this enterprise. It would seem that, as in New York, they had first sought to fit up a room suitable for a *Play House*— evidently the first theatre was no longer available; but they had to desist and boldly proposed the erection of a real theatre by way of subscription. This appeal met with favor, and during the winter of 1751 to 1752 a series of performances took place at Williamsburg, where life was gay and money plentiful. In May the company played at Hobb's Hole, and I leave it to others to locate this suspicious sounding community on a map of Virginia. They then proceeded to Fredericksburg "to play during the continuance of June Fair," and it was in the course of this tour that George Washington, according to his ledger for June 2, 1752, loaned his younger brother Samuel "by cash at the play house 1/ 3*d.*," so that they might attend the performance together—the first play the theatre-loving George saw on Virginian soil.

Though Mr. Ford does not mention any operatic entertainments, it is safe to say that such were not missing, for the managers certainly cannot have considered Virginia less musically inclined than Maryland, where they arrived the middle of June. The "Company of Comedians from Virginia" opened the "New Theatre in

Annapolis" on June 22, 1752, with the best drawing card of that age: Gay-Pepusch's 'Beggar's Opera,' and, according to the extant files of the *Maryland Gazette*, followed this up with performances of the 'Virgin Unmask'd' (July 13), the 'Mock Doctor' (July 21), 'Damon and Phillida' (July 27), and the 'Devil to Pay' (July 31).

At the beginning of the season the managers had mapped out a tour to Upper Marlborough and to two places with the euphonious names of Piscataway and Port Tobacco. On July 2 they then notified the public of Annapolis:

"As the Company have now got their Hands, Cloaths, etc., compleat, they now confirm their Resolution of going to Upper Marlborough as soon as ever Encouragement fails here."

Encouragement failed by the end of July, and our "Company of Comedians from Annapolis" opened "The New Theatre at Upper Marlborough" on August 20, and again with the "Beggar's Opera." This classic seems to have been a special favorite at Upper Marlborough and, ludicrous though this may be, we have to look to Upper Marlborough for the place where, for the first time in the history of opera in America, the employment of an orchestra is recorded. Trusting the *Maryland Gazette* of August 27, there was to be at the request of the Ancient and Honourable Society of Free and Accepted Masons on September 14, 1752, a performance of

"The 'Beggar's Opera': With Instrumental Music to each Air, given by a Set of Private Gentlemen."

Tempi passati! And perhaps we should feel thankful, or can the gentle reader imagine 'Salome' being entrusted to a set of private gentlemen?

Not all of Kean and Murray's original constituents had gone South with them. A few remained in New York and made part of "a new company of comedians" that occupied the Nassau Street Theatre during the winter of

1751-52, without much success. The short-lived career of this company deserves attention for two reasons only; first, because it introduced, on March 2, Carey's "Honest Yorkshireman" (partly a ballad-opera, partly composed by him) to America, and second, because it was headed by Robert Upton, the rather unscrupulous advance agent of a company which was to raise the American theatre to a comparatively high level, namely, Hallam's London Company of Comedians, which started its American career late in 1752 at Williamsburg, Va. The history of this company, subsequently known as the American Company and still later as the Old American Company, is a twice told tale, but it never has been told from the musical standpoint.

The capitalist and backer of the London Company of Comedians was William Hallam. He little thought that, when he sent Robert Upton well supplied with funds to New York to survey the field, erect a theatre and prepare the path of the company, it would be the last he saw of this gentleman. Upton's perfidy is well set forth in a *card* entitled "The case of the London Company of Comedians, lately arrived from Virginia," in the *New York Mercury*, July 2, 1753. But William Hallam was not so easily deterred and, prompted by the persuasive powers of several gentlemen in London and Virginia Captains, shipped the company with his brother Lewis as manager to the Colonies. They arrived in Virginia the end of June, proceeded to Williamsburg, obtained the Governor's permission to entirely alter the old Play-House "to a regular theatre, fit for the reception of ladies and gentlemen and the execution of their own performances," and informed the public through the medium of the *Virginia Gazette* that they would open on September 15, 1752, with 'The Merchant of Venice' and the farce of 'The Anatomist.' Unfortunately, the *Virginia Gazette* has not withstood the ravages of time, war and carelessness, and its extant files yield hardly any further information.   Lewis Hallam's card, however, tells us that the company stayed eleven months at Williamsburg, where they "performed with universal applause and met with the greatest encouragement." John Esten Cooke's entertaining novel, "Virginia Comedians," in which the Hallams hold the centre of the stage, is, therefore, full of poetic and historic license, yet it must be admitted that the author has succeeded in fixing the *milieu*—and, after all, what more do we expect of a historical novel?   On the whole, he made the best of his scarce historical data, and if I remember correctly even introduced the harpsichordist of the company at Williamsburg, Peter Pelham.   He had not been imported with the others, but, as readers of my book on "Early Concert Life in America" may remember, hailed from Boston as son of the engraver and dancing-master Peter Pelham, Sr., and had drifted down to Virginia as music-master in the forties.

Having been told that they "were really expected" at New York and would find "a very fine Play-House Building" there, the London Company moved to New York in the summer of 1753, armed with a certificate of Governor Dinwiddie recommending, as Ireland put it, the comedians as actors and testifying to the correctness of their conduct as men.   Such a true bill of moral health was necessary, for, at first, the authorities entertained some grave doubts as to the advisability of welcoming the actors.   This difficulty removed, Lewis Hallam saw himself confronted by the necessity of tearing the old theatre in Nassau street down and erecting "a very fine, large and commodious New Theatre" on the same spot which would be more in keeping with his ambitions and dignity.   And all this happened between June and September 13, 1753, the opening night "by his Excellency's authority."   Certainly the world's record up to that time for building a brand new theatre!   The performances were advertised for Mondays, Wednesdays and Fridays;

and now the historian is confronted with his difficulties, as the newspapers were printed on Mondays only and consequently contain the announcements of one-third only of Lewis Hallam's activity. The season lasted until March 25, 1754, and during these six months at least twenty-one different plays and twelve farces, inclusive of the ballad-operas, are known to have been performed, and if one considers how the company must have been handicapped at first, this record becomes all the more remarkable, even for a good company such as the London Company undoubtedly was.

So far as opera is concerned, the repertory did not go beyond that already known to New Yorkers, but the difference, of course, was made up in quality. On September 13, 1753, the opening night, the ballad-farce 'Damon and Phillida' was given as afterpiece to "The Conscious Lovers," and then followed, always remembering the Monday weeklies, on

1753, Oct. 8: Virgin Unmasked.
     Nov. 5: Flora; or, Hob in the Well.
         12: Devil to Pay.
         19: Beggar's Opera.
     Dec. 10: Harlequin Collector; or, The Miller Deceived. (A so-called speaking pantomime.)
         26: Damon and Phillida.
1754, Jan. 14: Damon and Phillida.
         21: Devil to Pay.
     Feb. 18: Harlequin *Skeleton;* or, The Miller Deceived.
         25: Virgin Unmasked.
     Mar. 4: Harlequin Skeleton.
         18: Beggar's Opera.
         —: Devil to Pay.
         25: "A new pantomime." (The name is not mentioned.)

Lewis Hallam introduced the custom of announcing the full casts. It is unnecessary to quote them all, the more so as they may be found in Ireland and Seilhamer; but two may also find a place here, that of 'Damon and Phillida,' on September 13, 1753, because it presumably was the first full opera-cast ever printed in America, and that of the 'Beggar's Opera,' on November 19, as it will display the strength and supply of histrionic talent of the London Company of Comedians.

Damon and Phillida

Damon	By	Mr. Adcock
Arcas		Mr. Bell
Mopsus		Mr. Hallam
Aegon		Mr. Rigby
Corydòn		Mr. Clarkson
Cymon		Mr. Miller
Phillida		Mrs. Becceley

Beggar's Opera

Peachum	By	Mr. Hallam
Locket		Mr. Malone
Macheath		Mr. Adcock
Filch		Mr. Miller
Mat o' th' Mint		Mr. Bell
Wat Dreary		Mr. Singleton
Nimming Ned		Mr. Hullet
Mrs. Peachum		Mrs. Adcock
Polly		Mrs. Becceley
Lucy		Mrs. Clarkson
Mrs. Coaxer		Miss Hallam
Diana Trapez		Mrs. Adcock
Mrs. Vixen		Mrs. Rigby
Jenny Diver		Mrs. Love
Molly Brazin		Mrs. Clarkson

Great as Lewis Hallam's contempt was for his "theatrical predecessors" in America, he did not deviate from their custom of entertaining the audience with dancing and singing between the acts. Here are two specimens of these sandwiched musicales, since grown to be a veritable nuisance. On March 11, Hallam presented between the acts

A Punch's Dance, by Master A. Hallam.
A Tambourin Dance, by Mrs. Hulet.

As Chloe Came into the Room, Sung by Master L. Hallam;
and
The Reasonable Lover.
End of the Play, a Hornpipe, by Mr. Hulet.
The Quaker's Sermon on the violin; and a *Solo* on the
Hautboy, by Mr. Love.

The names of William C. Hulett[1] and Charles Love confront us immediately with the problem of the orchestra employed by the company. Dunlap, when describing how the Old American Company was forced in the nineties to fall in line with Wignell and Reinagle's company by improving their orchestra, writes of the "one Mr. Pelham and his harpsichord, or, the single fiddle of Mr. Hewlett," during the early career of the company. Possibly these two gentlemen did murder, *à quatre mains*, the operas at Williamsburg, but the very fact that Pelham did not join the company at New York and that Dunlap does not mention Charles Love in connection with the London Company makes his off-hand statement suspicious. It is clear that Charles Love, "musician from London," husband of Mrs. Love and teacher of half a dozen instruments, *but not of the harpsichord* (*N. Y. Mercury*, July 2, 1753), was connected with Hallam's company as violinist or oboist, or both. The newspapers also bear testimony to the fact that William C. Hulett, while perhaps engaged principally as dancer—he remained the most fashionable dancing-master at New York for many years—played the violin, as did all dancing-masters, and well enough to lead in concerts. But with one or two fiddles, or one fiddle and one oboe, even ballad-operas could not very well be executed, and at least, in addition, a harpsichord was needed. Is it not reasonable to suppose that Lewis Hallam did not import the half dozen instrumentalists he needed, because he expected to find enough at New

---

[1] I state here in passing that quoted matter is spelled as found in my sources, but that in the text names, etc., are given in the form which I have reason to believe is correct.

York? If he did entertain such expectations, my book on "Early Concert Life in America" will have proved that he was not mistaken. Bearing in mind that about this time New York and other American cities were becoming used to performances of the best music of the time by orchestras, possibly smaller than the small orchestras used abroad, but sufficiently large to render overtures, concerti grossi, and symphonies, it may seriously be doubted whether Lewis Hallam would have dared to treat New York to the ballad-operas with "the single fiddle of Mr. Hewlett."

On the surface, the item "To Music: Messrs. Harrison & Van Dienval, £3 12/," on the account published after the performance of January 25, 1762, for the benefit of the poor, would seem to interfere with this opinion, but it stands to reason that Thomas Harrison (organist of Trinity Church, by the way!) and Alexander Van Dienval did not receive 36/ each for one night's exertion. Rather am I inclined to interpret the item thus: They received the sum for themselves and whoever else they engaged to play under them, somewhat in the same manner as the arrangement between concert-master and manager nowadays.

Granting that possibly at first only a miniature orchestra may have been employed, perhaps at the very beginning only a harpsichordist and one fiddler, it did not take many years before the scores were treated more respectfully, and it might be well to prove this here by two quotations from the old newspapers. On September 24,1767, the *Pennsylvania Journal* distinctly mentions the "band of music" which was to play the music between the acts, and in the advance notice of Milton's 'Comus' in the same newspaper on March 8, 1770, it is said: "The orchestra to be conducted by Mr. Hallam." Finally, it should not be forgotten that in those days provincial orchestras were often made up of professional musicians *plus* "gentlemen performers" who sat in the orchestra for their own enjoyment and, of course, received no payment. Of this custom traces are also to be found in America, and a notice in the *Pennsylvania Gazette* of November 30, 1769, illustrates the point with a vengeance:

"For the future, the days of performance will be Tuesday and Friday. The Orchestra, on Opera Nights, will be assisted by some musical Persons, who, as they have no View but to contribute to the Entertainment of the Public, certainly claim a Protection from any Manner of Insult."

What prompted Lewis Hallam to risk the very existence of his company by "intending for Philadelphia" is a mystery. That he anticipated stubborn opposition there is clear, otherwise he would not have sent his colleague, Malone, the possessor "of a tongue that could wheedle with the devil" (Durang), and William C. Hulett there as his ambassadors to Governor Hamilton. But the number of such influential persons who pleaded in favor of the theatre was so strong as finally to break the opposition and Hallam received leave to give twenty-four performances on condition that nothing indecent or immoral should be presented. So it happened that Plumstead's warehouse again saw a theatrical season. The first performance took place on April 15, 1754, the last on June 27. Exceedingly little is to be gleaned from the papers on this limited season of two months. On June 17 'Harlequin Collector' was given, and it is also said that 'Flora' was considered moral and decent enough to be presented, but beyond this the history of opera in Philadelphia possibly will never be enriched by further data. If the opponents of the theatre, as Durang tells us, went so far as to send one of the unfriendly petitioners as a spy to the opening performance —the result being a great tumult in the pit and the bodily ejection of the gentleman—it is clear that this Philadelphia season ended in failure. So much so that

Lewis Hallam betook himself and his company by way of Charleston (where he performed in October and November, 1754) to Jamaica.   There he died a year later, and the company disbanded.

Hallam's widow married a gentleman by the name of David Douglass, and forthwith drama in America received a new lease of life.   A skilled actor and a man of great business acumen and administrative ability, Douglass controlled theatrical destinies in our country from 1758 on, until the impending War of the Revolution forced him to leave the continent and return to Jamaica, where he became a judge; he died there in 1786.

Douglass arrived at New York in 1758.   In the meantime, the Nassau Street Theatre had been converted into a place of worship and consequently Hallam's successor saw himself obliged to look for a suitable place for the erection of a theatre.   He selected Cruger's wharf, and after having, by some clever diplomacy, softened the anti-theatrical hearts of the magistrates, he opened, on December 28, 1758, with 'Jane Shore' and the ballad-farce of the 'Mock Doctor.'   Of this first night the *New York Mercury* condescended to remark, on January 1, 1759, that the company "acted with great applause, to a most crowded audience."   It might be of interest to quote from the announcement of the three nights in the first week of January a few managerial details that are characteristic of the age:

> Tickets to be had at the Printing-office in Hanover Square, at the Coffee House, and at the Fountain Tavern, and nowhere else.
>
> The Doors for the Gallery will be opened at Four o'clock, but the Pit and the Boxes, that the Ladies may be well accommodated with seats—not till Five—and the Play begins precisely at Six.
>
> Box, 8 shillings. Pit, 5 shillings. Gallery, 2 shillings.
>
> N. B.—No more tickets will be given out than the House will hold. And positively no money taken at the Door.

Occasionally, Mr. Douglass made an exception to this last rule, and in course of time it permanently gave way

to the more modern and sensible institution of selling
tickets not only in advance by deputy, but also at the
door, or rather at the ticket window, shortly before
the performance. Another strange custom, however,
was expedited to speedier oblivion. In those days,
gentlemen, sportive and otherwise, not only had free
access behind the scenes, but were in the habit of crowding the stage proper during performance and conversing
with the actresses while they were waiting for their lines,
and in this respect the well-known, delightful scene in
Cooke's "Virginian Comedians" is by no means exaggerated. As long as the audience submitted to the
nuisance, managers were, of course, loath to stop it, but
by 1761 Mr. Douglass had received several complaints,
and he then took it "as a particular favour if no gentleman will be offended that he be absolutely refused ad-
mittance at the Stage Door, unless he has previously
secured himself a place in either the Stage or Upper
Boxes." Gradually this polite request was heeded and
the vicious custom became obsolete. The prerogatives
of the gallery-gods were of a different nature. Unruly
to this day, their manners in the eighteenth century
kept the managers and the ladies in the boxes and pit
in constant fear lest some missiles should follow the
laws of gravitation with a vengeance. But if Douglass
found it necessary in May, 1762, to offer a

Pistole Reward—To whoever can discover the person who was
so very rude as to throw Eggs from the Gallery upon the Stage, last
Monday, by which the Cloaths of some Ladies and Gentlemen were
spoiled and the performance in some measure interrupted

it must not be imagined that such things happened in
the Colonies only. They happen, as everybody knows,
even to-day, and preferably in college towns.

Douglass's first season at New York lasted until
February 7, 1759, including on this evening 'Damon and
Phillida.' He then proceeded to Philadelphia, having
obtained Governor Denny's authority to build a wooden

theatre on "Society Hill" in the Southern Liberties, and to give performances before his inroad on the morality of the good citizens of Philadelphia became known. But once known, the Quakers, the German Lutherans, the Presbyterians, were up in arms against "the idle persons and strollers [who] have come into this Province from foreign parts in the character of players." A blue Law against Plays was enacted on May 31, 1759, condemning every "person and persons whatsoever" who should transgress this law from and after the first of January, 1760, to a fine of "five hundred pounds lawful money." Governor Denny, anxious to keep faith with Douglass, could do nothing except filibuster until the middle of June. On June 20 he was forced to sanction the antediluvian measure, but the King had sense enough to set it aside in Council, September 2, 1760.

Douglass hastened to make the best of his embarrassing position as long as he could, and gladly agreed to Governor Denny's stipulation that one night be given for the benefit of the Pennyslvania Hospital. He began operations on June 25, 1759, and wound up (with debts amounting to several hundred pounds *lawful* money), on December 28, with the charity benefit. But Douglass was even more generous than the Governor expected him to be, for on December 27 he gave a benefit performance "towards raising a Fund for the purchasing of an Organ to the College Hall and instructing the Charity Children in Psalmody," which was ushered in by Francis Hopkinson's "Prologue in Praise of Music: Spoken by Mr. Hallam." And here may be the proper place to remark that the several elaborately prepared and minutely reported performances of Arne's "Masque of Alfred" at the College Hall in January, 1757, with omissions, alterations and additions—Hopkinson probably contributing the additional music—were given merely in concert garb as an "Oratorial Exercise" for and by the young gentlemen of the college.

It will be seen from the following list of performances that Douglass added nothing to the operatic repertory of his predecessors. He presented on

1759, June 25: Virgin Unmasked.
     July 6: Honest Yorkshireman.
         13: Mock Doctor.
     Aug. 17: Harlequin Collector.
       —: Beggar's Opera.
         24: Beggar's Opera.
     Nov. 9: Beggar's Opera.
     Dec. 7: Virgin Unmasked.
         21: Harlequin Collector.

The reorganization of the London Company had brought about a material change in its personnel. The difference will appear immediately from the casts for the double bill on November 9:

Beggar's Opera

Macheath	By Mr. Harman
Peachum	Mr. Tomlinson
Moll Brazen	Mr. Douglass
Lockit	Mr. Scott
Mat o' the Mint	Mr. Reed
Beggar	Mr. Morris
Player	Mr. Douglass
Jemmy Twitcher	Mr. Allyn
Filch	Mr. A. Hallam
Harry Paddington	Mr. Horne
Polly	Mrs. Love
Mrs. Peachum	Mrs. Harman
Diana Trapez	Mrs. Harman
Mrs. Coaxer	Mrs. Douglass
Mrs. Slammekin	Mrs. Tomlinson

Harlequin Collector

Harlequin	Mr. Hallam
Miller	Mr. Allyn
Clown	Mr. Douglass
Conjuror	Mr. Harman
Doctor	Mr. Tomlinson
Columbine	Mrs. Douglass

Most of the actors remained true to Douglass down to the Revolution. The Harlequin Mr. Hallam was Lewis Hallam, the younger, then eighteen years of age, destined in after years to become one of Douglass's successors in every respect. Next in importance was Owen Morris, who lived to be the dean of the company at the end of the century. He died in 1809 at the patriarchal age of ninety years. Mrs. Love evidently was regarded as the star *soubrette.* Her husband Charles, however, no longer seconded her vocal triumphs, nor did he preach "The Quaker's Sermon" on the violin to the Quakers, as by 1757 (see *Pennsylvania Gazette,* December 27) he was wanted in Virginia for running away from a Mr. Philipp Ludwell Lee with a "small white horse" and "a very good bassoon." He was then "a tall, thin Mann, about sixty of age."

Ostracized by Philadelphia, Douglass experimented with Annapolis. He had no difficulty in obtaining permission to erect a theatre there, and while the building was in course of construction the company invaded Chester-Town. The Annapolis theatre was opened on March 3, 1760, and the *Maryland Gazette* took notice of the event with this amusing bit of local patriotism:

"The applause which attended the whole representation did less Honour to the abilities of the actors than to the Taste of their auditors."

When the season closed in May, the same newspaper made a departure in American journalism by printing the full list of the plays performed, and thus we are enabled also to put on record the ballad-operas which gave Annapolis an opportunity to show the taste of the auditors:

1760,	Mar. 8, 24:	Mock Doctor.
	29:	Damon and Phillida.
	April 8:	Honest Yorkshireman.
	9, 10:	Devil to Pay.
	12:	Mock Doctor.

April 14: Flora.
    16: Devil to Pay.
17, 24: Honest Yorkshireman.
May 5: Virgin Unmasked.

For the first time, it would seem, in the history of the American Theatre, the 'Beggar's Opera' had been slighted!

Douglass then moved his "Wandering Theatre" (as it was called on the last night, in a bombastic "Address to the Ladies" containing amongst other things a spicy contrast between the "Gallic beauty" of France's "painted dames" and "English charms") to Upper Marlborough, where on May 26 'The Virgin Unmasked,' and on June 16 'The Devil to Pay,' were sung. In the winter following, the company turned up at Williamsburg. To no other company can George Washington's entries "by play tickets at sundry times [£] 7.10.3." on October 8, 1760, and similarly in March, 1761, possibly have reference. But we need no circumstantial evidence of this kind, for Douglass, after having "performed in this colony for near a twelve-month," took with him a recommendation signed by the Governor, Council and one hundred of the principal gentlemen of Virginia, and this certificate he printed in the *Newport* (R. I.) *Mercury* of August 11, 1761, when announcing his intention "to entertain the town for a short time with theatrical performances." To conciliate the enemies of the theatre—we must remember Mr. David Douglass had ventured into New England—he resorted to performances under the disguise of "Moral Dialogues," a foretaste of the tricks of the managers shortly after the Revolutionary War. From Newport the company returned to New York in the winter of 1761-1762, again visited Newport in 1762, proceeded to Providence, R. I., and then invaded Philadelphia for a second time. It is unnecessary to dwell on these New England experiments. Those interested may be referred to George O. Willard's "History of the Providence Stage."

Cured by previous experiences, Douglass did not go to New York during the winter of 1761-1762 before having the permission of the proper authorities in his pocket. This, however, was only one of his problems. Theatre-building was another, to an extent which would fill even Oscar Hammerstein with envy. The house on Cruger's Wharf had been abandoned and a new theatre was erected in Chapel Street at an estimated cost of $1,625. Originally, Douglass received leave only for sixteen performances, but such was the resourcefulness of this remarkable man that he forced a season of five months on the authorities. It did not enrich the history of opera in America, but as a matter of permanent record the few data that are obtainable from the newspapers follow here:

1761,	Nov.	26:	Honest Yorkshireman.
	Dec.	1:	Damon and Phillida.
		18:	Flora.
		21:	Devil to Pay.
1762,	Jan.	1:	Beggar's Opera.
		7:	Honest Yorkshireman.
		20:	Harlequin Collector.
	Feb.	4:	Virgin Unmasked.
		10, 15:	Damon and Phillida.
		18:	Harlequin Collector.
	Mar.	15:	Harlequin Collector.
		22:	Flora.
	Apr.	12:	Devil to Pay.
		19:	Mock Doctor.
		26:	Honest Yorkshireman.

During these five months the opposition against the theatre had become violent and a newspaper war *pro et contra* was waged in miniature. Indeed, when Thomas Harrison, the organist of Trinity Church, in December, 1761, lost "a lady's hoop-ring" coming from the play, and another person a few days later a valuable letter-case at the Play-House itself, the theatre in Chapel Street seems to have come into disrepute. Under the circumstances, David Douglass found it useless to struggle against the tide, so he left New York not to return for several years. Fortunately so for him, since we know from Dunlap that in 1764 or 1766 the New York mob was so incensed against theatres and everything connected with them that they brutally wrecked the Chapel Street Theatre.

Between 1762 and 1766 other historians record a hiatus in Douglass's career or claim, like Durang, that the company embarked for the West Indies. These statements are only partly true. George Washington's ledger proves that he frequented the Play-House at Williamsburg in November, 1762, and in the spring of 1763. This would have given a clue, and by consulting in the *Providence* (R. I.) *Gazette* of December 31, 1763, a communication from "Charlestown, in S. Carolina, Nov. 3," it would have been noticed that

"A Company of Comedians arrived here last Monday from Virginia who are called the American Company, and were formerly under the direction of Mr. Lewis Hallam, 'till his death.' Amongst the principal performers, we hear, are Mr. David Douglass. . . . A theatre is already contracted for, 75 feet by 35, to be erected near where that of Messrs. Holliday and comp. formerly stood, and intended to be opened the 5th of December next."

It was indeed opened and performances took place in this "New Theatre in Queen-street" by the American Company until April, 1764, as the extant files of the *South Carolina Gazette* will prove. What Douglass did after this until he, as we also learn from the *South Carolina Gazette* of October 30, 1766, returned from London, I do not know. Nor does this hiatus matter much in view of the fact that he brought with him

. . . a most excellent set of scenes done by Mr. Doll, principal scene-painter to Covent Garden House, and collected some very eminent performers from both the theatres in London, particularly in the *Singing Way*, so that the English *Comic Opera*, a species of entertainment that has never yet appeared properly on this side of the water, is likely to be performed here this winter to advantage.

Not content with reorganizing his forces, Douglass was bent upon conquering Philadelphia to his cause in spite of Quakers, Lutherans and Presbyterians. He put up a new theatre, and this house, substantial though ugly, known as the Southwark Theatre in South Street, continued to be used for theatrical exhibitions until the beginning of the nineteenth century. Later it was converted into a warehouse, but was partly destroyed by an incendiary attempt in 1821. Fortunately for the American Company, John Penn, a lover of music, governed the Commonwealth, and though an elaborate Remonstrance against the designs of Douglass was submitted to him, he did not pay much attention to it. Not being further molested, the American Company opened the Southwark Theatre in November, 1766. These performances were preceded in May and June of the same year "by authority" of Governor Penn by some sham theatricals at the Academy, *alias* the Assembly Room in Lodge Alley. The plays and operas were not acted, but "read," as appears from the announcements, and in the case of operas was added, "all the songs will be sung accompanied by instrumental musick." In this ludicrous concert garb were presented, on June 5, 1766, 'Damon and Phillida'; June 13, the 'Beggar's Opera'; and on June 19, Dr. Arne's pasticcio 'Love in a Village' —of course, with the usual musical incidentals, as for instance, at the end of 'Damon and Phillida,' "Water Parted from the Sea," from Arne's 'Artaxerxes.'

Some confusion seems to linger about the date of the opening of the Southwark Theatre. Durang, Seilhamer and others give it as November 21, but I find in the *Pennsylvania Journal* of October 31 that the theatre "will be opened on Monday the tenth of November," no further particulars being mentioned, and again on

November 6 a performance was advertised for November 12, but, as on November 13 the identical program was announced for the following night with the "musical entertainment of 'Thomas and Sally, or, the Sailor's Return,' " it stands to reason that the performance was postponed to November 14. Perhaps it will be best to let the chronological record precede the comments and a few interesting data that have come down to us:

1766, Nov. 14: *Thomas and Sally.*
          26: Beggar's Opera.
    Dec. 19: Devil to Pay.
1767, Jan. 9: Mock Doctor.
          16: Devil to Pay.
    Feb. 16: Damon and Phillida.
          20: Thomas and Sally.
          27: Damon and Phillida.
  Mar. 3, 9: Harlequin Collector.
          19: *Love in a Village.* (Announced as "the fourth night." Consequently three performances must have preceded this.)
          23: Harlequin Collector.
  Apr. 2, 9: The *Witches;* or, Harlequin Restored.
    20, 24: *Contrivances.*
          27: Devil to Pay.
    May 1: Flora.
          28: Love in a Village.
    June 4: The *Chaplet* ("never performed here").
         8: Contrivances.
        18: Flora.

(Plays such as 'Theodosius,' 'Lethe,' 'Romeo and Juliet,' or 'Macbeth,' which were interspersed with dirges, marches, songs, etc., are passed over in this study in order not to crowd the narrative with foreign matter.)

During the summer of 1767, while Mr. Douglass was again busy building a theatre, this time at New York, the Southwark Theatre saw another brief season. It lasted from September 24 to November 23, and the musical entertainments presented were these:

1767, Oct. 9: Harlequin Restored. (Also called "The Witches.")
         23: Harlequin Collector.

1767,   Oct. 26:   Love in a Village.
            30:   Devil to Pay.
        Nov. 13:   Chaplet.

In the lists given above, the works printed in italics were novelties for America, and at last the threadbare repertory of the last thirty years had been interwoven with new material. Considering the vogue abroad of Carey's 'Contrivances' (1715) or Boyce's 'Chaplet' (1749), it is surprising that these operas were not imported sooner. On the other hand, the arrival of Arne's 'Thomas and Sally' and 'Love in a Village' in America occurred at a comparatively early date, as the former was brought out in London in 1760 and the latter in 1762. Thereafter the operatic intercourse between England and America remained pretty lively, everything considered, and from 1766 on, with occasional relapses, the operatic repertory grew steadily. A demand for these works in the "singing way" certainly was in the air, otherwise book dealers like Bradford hardly would have regularly included in their bargain lists numerous opera librettos, and from selling European editions to publishing American was but one step.

In order to keep the reader in touch with the principal stars, big and small, who adorned the American stage in those days, I give the original casts of 'Thomas and Sally' and 'Love in a Village.'

Thomas and Sally

Dorcas	Miss Cheer
Sally	Miss Wainwright
Squire	Mr. Woolls
Sailor	Mr. Wall

Love in a Village

Justice Woodcock	Mr. Douglass
Hawthorn	Mr. Woolls
Sir William Meadows	Mr. Morris
Young Meadows	Mr. Wall

Eustace	. . . . . .	Mr. Allyn
Hodge	. . . . . .	Mr. Hallam
Lucinda	. . . . . .	Miss Hallam
Mrs. Deborah Woodcock	. . .	Mrs. Douglass
Margery	. . . . . .	Mrs. Harman

Of the newcomers, Margaret Cheer was considered the most talented and most versatile, and it was a distinct loss to the American public, though a decided gain to herself, that she married in August, 1768, Lord Rosehill in Maryland—the first and the last instance during the eighteenth century that an actress married a title on American soil. Her successor became, in course of time, Miss Maria Storer, sister of the less important Fanny Storer. Subsequently the last wife of John Henry, who had the chronic marrying habit, Maria Storer is said by Dunlap to have "possessed both beauty and talent, and until the year 1792 was the best public singer America had known." She was immensely popular in spite of her frequently silly and capricious conduct. She retired from the stage in 1794, and followed her husband to Rhode Island. His death in 1795 so preyed upon her mind that she died a lunatic at Philadelphia in the same year. She made her first bow to an American audience on January 8, 1768, at New York. Fanny Storer afterwards became Mrs. Mechtler, and as such she appears very often on the play-bills in the nineties. Mrs. Catharine Maria Harman was a grand-daughter of Colley Cibber, and principally played old ladies. She died in 1773.

Two of the other artists, Miss Wainwright and Stephen Woolls (the leading singer of the company, who died in New York in 1799), are said by Durang to have been pupils of Dr. Arne. If true, this relation cannot have failed to infuse a proper tradition into the interpretation of Arne's operas. Indeed, the first critical notice on opera printed in America would have us believe that the American performances of 'Love in a Village' fell not far below those in London.   Said the critic in the *Penn-sylvania Gazette*, January, 1767:

> I must beg leave to inform the public that the pleasing 'Love in a Village' is done here beyond expectation, and must give real delight to every person void of ill-nature. Miss Wainwright is a very good singer, and her action exceeds the famous Miss Brent. Mr. Hallam exceeds everything in the character of Hodge, and Mr. Woolls almost equals Beard in Hawthorne. Miss Hallam deserves universal applause and encouragement. I could wish to see the house better filled whenever this justly applauded entertainment is exhibited.

Mr. Woölls was a special favorite with the public in the "entertainments between the acts," and for a long time to come these were not left, as nowadays, to the "band of music," of which, contrary to the rule, special mention was made in the *Pennyslvania Journal* of September 24, 1767, but to the most popular vocalists. These *quasi* concerts were frequently mentioned, but not always so minutely as in the announcement of the *Pennsylvania Journal*, June 4, where we read this attractive program:

> End of Act I., God save the King, by Mr. Woolls and Miss Wainwright.   End of Act II., 'The Spinning Wheel,' by Miss Wainwright. End of Act III., a Duet, written on the Marriage of the Princess Augusta and the Prince of Brunswick, composed by Dr. Arne, and sung before their Majesties.   End of Act IV., 'Lovely Nancy,' by Miss Wainwright.   After the Play, dancing by Mr. Matthews.

The year of 1767, besides proving Douglass's promise of more English comic opera to be sincere, came pretty near being the birth-year of American opera, or, to put it less extravagantly, of opera made in America.   For April 20 was announced the first performance of "a new Comic Opera, called the 'Disappointment, or, the Force of Credulity,'" but on April 16 the *Pennsylvania Gazette* suddenly notified the public that "'The Disappointment' (that was advertised for Monday), as it contains personal reflections, in unfit for the stage."

Plac. No, indeed, indeed, indeed I won't, my dear
Cooney.

Rac. Well den, I'll not keep my dear pet in fufpenfe
any longer, but you muſt buſs me, when I ſay any ting
dat pleſes you.

Plac. Well, ſo I will then.

Rac. Well den——Mr. Hum has receib'd a letter from
his fiſter in England, wid an account of two or ree
hundred touſand pound, dat was buried by old Blackbeard de pirate ; wid de draught where it is hid——and we
know de bery ſpot (*She kiſſes him*) and I'll gib you £.500
a year for pin-money ; (*Kiſſes*) and we'll ride in de coach
togeder ; (*Kiſſes*) and we'll go to de play togeder (*Kiſſes*)
and den we'll come home and go to bed togeder (*Kiſſes*)
and den we'll—— a you little rogue you. (*Kiſſes again.*)

Plac. And do you really think you'll find it ?——Why,
if you knew where all the treaſure in the world was bu-
ry'd, you'd never obtain it without a conjurer.

Rac. Yes, my dear, but we hab a conjurer—we'b
got Mr. Rattletrap ; he underſtands 'ſtrology and de
magic-art, better den any man in de guberment—and
dis night we intend to make de tryal— and I muſt go
dis inſtant, and ſettle de place of meeting.

Plac. Can you leave me ſo ſoon, my dear Cooney ?

Raccoon *ſings.*

AIR IV. Yankee Doodle.

O! how joyful ſhall I be,
When I get de money,
I will bring it all to dee ;
O! my diddling honey.

(*Exit, ſinging they chorus,* yankee doodle, *&c.*

Plac. By'e, b'ye Cooney ——There he goes, and
good luck attend him—poor old fool ; he thinks I have a
prodigious fondneſs for him—and ſo I have for his better
part, that's his money—He has been deficient in payment
for ſometime paſt ; but he thinks he makes that up with
ſoft language ; for he calls me his pet, his dove, his poor
ting, and a thouſand ſuch ſoft names ; and I keep pace
with him, as well as I can ; for I call him Cooney,
cock-a-pidgeon, ſugar-plumb, cock-a-dandy, and all
the

A PAGE FROM
ANDREW BARTON'S "THE DISAPPOINTMENT," 1767
The first ballad-opera libretto printed in America

Those who had not been taken into the secret had not long to wait to satisfy their curiosity, as a few days later the Philadelphia papers advertised for sale:

The 'Disappointment, or, the Force of Credulity,' a new American Comic Opera of two Acts. By Andrew Barton, Esq. [verses]. New York: Printed in the year MDCCLXVII.

Such is the title of the first American opera libretto, rehearsed but never performed, of which several copies are extant in American libraries. It is not difficult to see why pressure was brought to bear on Mr. Douglass to withdraw the piece. Had this ballad-opera been performed, certain well-known Philadelphians, who were industriously searching for the hidden treasures of the pirate Captain Blackbeard, would have become the butt of public ridicule.[1] Coarse, and at times obscene, as this libretto is in its language, it is also full of genuine wit, and the plot is developed with surprising instinct for theatrical effectiveness. I must content myself here with these few hints. Those interested in 'The Disappointment' will find a full description and history of the libretto in my study on "Early American Operas," in the Sammelbände of the I. M. S., 1904-5.

Immediately after the Southwark Theatre closed its doors, the American Company moved to New York, where, in the meantime, Douglass's John Street Theatre, a frame building painted red and holding about eight hundred dollars, had been finished. The season lasted from December 7, 1767, to June 2, 1768, comprising the following opera nights:

1767,	Dec. 21:	Thomas and Sally.
1768,	Jan. 11:	Love in a Village.
	—:	Contrivances.
	15, 18:	Witches.
	25:	Flora.

[1] John Macpherson in his letter to William Patterson, May 30, 1767, discloses the identity of "the actors of this real farce," but unfortunately he does not help us to decide the vexed question whether or not the author's name, Andrew Barton, was an assumed name. (Comp. *Pa. Mag. of Hist.*, v. 23, 1899, p. 52.)

1768, Jan. 28: Damon and Phillida.
      Feb. 1: Devil to Pay.
          8: Love in a Village.
      11, 22: Harlequin Collector.
        29: Honest Yorkshireman.
    Mar. 14: Chaplet.
       19: Witches.
       21: Honest Yorkshireman.
    Apr. 4: Witches.
        8: Harlequin Collector.
    May 16: Thomas and Sally.
       19: Love in a Village.
       26: Honest Yorkshireman.
       30: Devil to Pay.

Though the American Company gave New York an opportunity to listen to not less than sixty-four tragedies, comedies, farces and operas—a record absolutely beyond the conception of a modern manager—this season brought David Douglass almost to the brink of bankruptcy, as the undercurrent against theatricals, frequently visible in the newspapers, was so strong that his exertions to gain public favor availed nothing. In fact, in his despair, Douglass offered to pledge in advance "some part of the receipts of the next season" to any public-spirited men who would step forward and prevent the dissolution of the company. It is not surprising that under the circumstances the vocalists of the company sought to make an extra and safe penny by giving concerts. This grew into a custom, and from now on the history of our early concert-life became closely affiliated with the history of opera.

If Mr. Douglass ran short of funds, the historian now runs short of data that would moisten a necessarily more or less dry record, unless refuge is taken to such glimpses into bygone times as, *e. g.*, the custom of sending the servants in the afternoon to guard the seats in the boxes against usurpers until the "Gentleman and his Lady" should arrive, or the custom of the managers

and actors to "wait" in person on fashionable theatre-
going folk to solicit their patronage, and their profuse
apologies, if involuntarily they had forgotten to pay their
respects to some influential person; or again the per-
plexities that would arise if towards the close of the
season, when the benefits began, the actor to be bene-
fited lost the tickets on his wearisome rounds of visits
to the patrons of the theatre and the poor devil would
not know what to do lest the lucky finder should fill
the house with himself and his friends as deadheads.

After his New York failure, Douglass returned to his
Southwark Theatre at Philadelphia, and as business
was unexpectedly good he extended the season beyond
the three weeks originally proposed. Musically the performances contained nothing new, as the dates will
prove. In fact, not more than two operas seem to have
been played during the two months:

        1768, Oct. 21: Honest Yorkshireman.
              Dec. 9: Contrivances.
        1769, Jan. 6: Contrivances.

Less than a fortnight afterwards, the American Company was back again in New York and occupied the
John Street house until the end of June. The repertory
at last received an addition by the introduction of
Dibdin's 'The Padlock' and Samuel Arnold's 'Maid of
the Mill.' How fast even in those days the news of
hits travelled may be seen from the fact that 'The
Padlock' was brought out at Drury Lane in October, 1768,
with a run of fifty-three nights. In New York the opera
was first presented in May, 1769! Durang says that
Hallam, who played Mungo, brought to the personification
of this part a special study of the negro character, and
that he remained unrivalled in the part until 1807, one
year before his death. Seilhamer even claims that he surpassed Dibdin himself. The few opera-nights of the

season were the following, as far as I could ascertain them from the newspapers:

1769, Feb. 24: Contrivances.
       Mar. 3: Beggar's Opera.
            —: Witches.
             6: Honest Yorkshireman.
            29: Love in a Village.
       Apr. 10: Flora.
            27: Thomas and Sally.
       May   1: Devil to Pay.
             4: *Maid of the Mill.*
             8: Thomas and Sally. ("The House for that night will be illuminated with wax.")
            11: Harlequin Skeleton. (In the *N. Y. Journal*, however, announced as "Pantomime entertainment of Orpheus and Euridice, call'd the 'Death of Harlequin.' ")
       May 15: Honest Yorkshireman.
            22: Maid of the Mill.
            29: *Padlock.*
      June 1, 15: Padlock.
          17, 19: Padlock.
            12: Damon and Phillida.

The fact that the performance of the 'Padlock' on June 1 was announced as the sixth shows that even the most careful study of the old newspapers does not always help us to establish first performances, and if we look for the original casts of the two operas first performed in 1769 we look in vain. What Douglass's reasons were for deviating from his custom of announcing full casts at New York we do not know, but the absence of such during the season of 1769-1770 at the Southwark Theatre in Philadelphia is easily explained. Douglass now advertised there in the three weekly papers printed, and as this must have entailed considerable expense, he evidently preferred to leave out the casts—really unnecessary, as play-bills were distributed—and in their stead attract public attention by all sorts of sensational news, *e. g.*, when Mr. Hallam in one of the Harlequinades was to

"run up a perpendicular scene twenty feet high," or
Mr. Wall was to recite an epilogue riding on an ass,
or when Mr. Douglass announced that he would be
obliged to any lady or gentleman who would "lend him
the burlesque opera of the 'Dragon of Wantley.'" In
this respect, too, David Douglass was the prototype of
the American manager!

However, this season, which began the middle of
September (not in November, as Mr. Seilhamer believed), was to be the most interesting the American
theatre had yet seen, also in matters operatic. The public
was acquainted, on September 29, with a "pantomime
entertainment, never performed in America, called
'The *Dwarfs*, or, the Cascade Assignation,' . . .
with entire new machinery, songs, etc." Then followed, on

1769, Nov. 8: Padlock.
           14, 17: Padlock.
             24: *Midas.* (Ballad-burletta by O'Hara, "never acted
                     in America.")
      Dec. 1: Midas.
             5: Love in a Village.
             8: Midas.
           12: Padlock.
           15: Beggar's Opera.
           19: Harlequin Collector.
           22: Midas.
           29: Harlequin Collector.
1770, Jan. 2: Padlock.
             5: Maid of the Mill.
           —: Harlequin Restored.
             6: Padlock.
             9: Flora.
           12: Maid of the Mill.
           —: Harlequin Restored. ("With alterations.")
16, 19, 23, 29: *Neptune and Amphitrite.* ("Grand masque."
                     London, 1746. Music by Arne.)
      Feb. 2: Neptune and Amphitrite.
           —: Padlock.
             9: Damon and Phillida.
      Mar. 6: Neptune and Amphitrite.
           —: Padlock.

1770, Mar. 9: *Comus.* (Presumably Dalton-Arne's version of
                    Milton's masque.)
          16: Harlequin Restored.
          19: Neptune and Amphitrite.
          —: Devil to Pay.
     Apr. 2: Harlequin Collector.
          16: Thomas and Sally.
          20: Padlock. ("The tenth time.")
          27: Devil to Pay.

Considering that usually two performances only were
given weekly, and that, of course, drama was the backbone of the enterprise, surely a remarkable showing!

After this the American Company invaded Virginia
and Maryland, where, in the meantime, independent
organizations, partly recruited from the malcontents in
Douglass's forces, had entertained the people, and preferably during the racing season. First we notice the
"Virginia Company," which "by permission of the
Worshipful the Mayor of Williamsburg at the old Theatre,
near the Capitol," began operations on April 4, 1768,
with the tragedy of 'Douglas,' and 'The Honest
Yorkshireman' in this cast:

Sir Penurious Muckworm	. .	By Mr. Bromadge
Gaylove	. . . . . .	Mr. Verling
Sapscull .	. . . . .	Mr. Parker
Slango	. . . . . .	Mr. Godwin
Blunder .	. . . . .	Mr. Walker
Arabella .	. . . . .	Mrs. Osborne
Combrush	. . . . .	Mrs. Parker

This first night was followed by a few more ventures into
the realm of ballad-opera and pantomime. Those of
which the dilapidated files of the *Virginia Gazette* make
mention are:

April — : Damon and Phillida.
     15: Harlequin Skeleton.
June 3: Beggar's Opera.

when "the musick of the opera [was] to be conducted
by Mr. Pelham *and others*."

Partly reorganized, probably with Mr. Godwin as manager, who in 1766 had been a member of the American Company and had drawn others after him, this Virginia Company, but now styling itself the New American Company, proceeded to Annapolis, Md., where they had a remarkably active season from February to June 1769. This company must have been of some merit, otherwise it could hardly have borne the burden of the following repertory:

1769, Feb. 18: Virgin Unmasked.
    22: Honest Yorkshireman.
    25: Beggar's Opera.
  Mar. 11: Honest Yorkshireman.
    15: Mock Doctor.
    16: Devil to Pay.
    18: Damon and Phillida.
  Apr. 1: Devil to Pay.
    22: The *Genii;* or, The Birth of Harlequin. (Possibly a simpler, Americanized version of Henry Woodward's spectacular pantomime first acted in 1752 at Drury Lane.)
    29: Honest Yorkshireman.
  May 4: Damon and Phillida.
    18: Beggar's Opera.
    20: Harlequin Skeleton.
    23: Mock Doctor.
    27: Chaplet.
  June 10: Love in a Village.
    13: Devil to Pay.

The next year Douglass boldly invaded Godwin's territory and soon made this gentleman's merits that "were not of the transcendent kind" fade from the memory of the theatre-goers. At least this was the opinion of one Y. Z., who, during the American Company's brief season at Annapolis, 1770-71, expressed his opinion thus in the *Maryland Gazette:*

The merit of Mr. Douglass's company is notoriously, in the opinion of every man of sense in America whose opportunities give him a title to judge—take them all in all—superior to that of any

company in England, except those of the metropolis. The dresses
are remarkably elegant; the dispatch of the business of the theatre
uncommonly quick; and the stillness and good order preserved
behind the scenes are proofs of the greatest attention and respect
paid to the audience.

Especially Miss Hallam created a sensation as *Imogen*,
and it was about this time that her admirers called on
Charles Wilson Peale to paint her in this part.

Few data only concerning this Annapolis season have
come down to us, but it is known that on August 26,
1770, 'Thomas and Sally' was played, and on September 1 'Love in a Village.'   Still more meagre are references to the Williamsburg season during the following
winter.   Mr. Seilhamer, for instance, merely mentions
the performance of 'The Honest Yorkshireman' on
April 22, 1771, and even Paul Leicester Ford could add
nothing to the entries in George Washington's ledger
which prove him to have visited the theatre very much
more frequently than Presidents are nowadays in the
habit of doing. From Williamsburg Douglass turned to
Fredericksburg, and theperformances given in the fall
of 1771 at Williamsburg, including 'Damon and Phillida' and 'The Padlock' on November 23 and December 21, were due to the efforts of an anonymous company. By this time Douglass had received the necessary
financial backing to erect at Annapolis what Durang
claims to have been the first theatre in America made of
brick. It was built on ground leased from St. Anne's
Parish in West Street and had the modest seating capacity of about six hundred persons. It was opened with
a frightfully long and tedious prologue on September
9, 1771, and the few performances recorded included, on
September 20, 'The Maid of the Mill.'   About the
beginning of February the company hurried back to
Williamsburg, where they remained until "the end of
the April Court," presenting on April 21 'Thomas and
Sally.'

Engagements then called Douglass to the northward, and after stopping at Annapolis in September he gave a fourth and prolonged season at his Southwark Theatre in Philadelphia with a repertory of more than fifty-three different pieces. They included these operas, with Dibdin's pasticcio 'Lionel and Clarissa' (London, 1768) as novelty:

1772,	Oct.	28:	Padlock.
	Nov.	2:	Midas.
		4:	Love in a Village.
		23:	Honest Yorkshireman.
		25:	Maid of the Mill.
	Dec.	9:	Devil to Pay.
		14:	*Lionel and Clarissa.*
		23:	Thomas and Sally.
		30:	Padlock.
1773,	Jan.	4:	Lionel and Clarissa.
		11:	Devil to Pay.
		27:	Midas.
	Feb.	1:	Neptune and Amphitrite.
		8:	Beggar's Opera.
		10:	Honest Yorkshireman.
		15:	Lionel and Clarissa.
	Mar.	10:	Flora.
		15:	Padlock.
		31:	Neptune and Amphitrite.

The cast of 'Lionel and Clarissa,' presented at Philadelphia under the title of 'The School for Fathers, or, Lionel and Clarissa,' was this:

Col. Oldboy	By Mr. Goodman
Lionel	Mr. Woolls
Sir John Flowerdale	Mr. Douglass
Mr. Jessamy	Mr. Wall
Harman	Mr. Henry
Jenkens	Mr. Parker
Clarissa	Miss Storer
Lady Mary Oldboy	Mrs. Harman
Jenny	Mrs. Henry
Diana Oldboy	Miss Hallam

The Orchestra to be conducted by Mr. Hallam.
**The Songs of this Opera are sold at the Coffee-House.

During this season actors and audience alike were exposed to practical jokes of the unruly elements in the gallery, and the protests of the injured and insulted in the newspapers made matters only worse. Just as bad and foreshadowing turbulent times was the behavior of the gallery at New York, where the American Company performed from the middle of April to August, 1773, at the John Street Theatre. On May 3, Mr. Douglass saw himself obliged to insert this card in the *New York Mercury:*

> The repeated insults which some mischievous persons in the gallery have given, not only to the stage and orchestra, but to the other parts of the house, call loudly for reprehension.

And he threatened to point the culprits out to the constables, and unless the nuisance stopped "the gallery for the future will be shut up."

The list of performances includes:

1773,	Apr. 19:	Padlock.
	May 3:	Midas.
	7:	Love in a Village.
	10:	Padlock.
	14:	Midas.
	17:	Maid of the Mill.
	21:	Beggar's Opera.
	June 3:	Neptune and Amphitrite.
	4:	Damon and Phillida.
	14:	Midas.
	21:	Comus.
	July 1:	Harlequin Collector.
	12:	Flora.
	Aug. 5:	Padlock.

This was the last theatrical season at New York until the officers in the beleaguered British army set up their amateur theatricals, recruiting the orchestra from the several military bands, and it is interesting to note how this procedure was anticipated even before the war, as on June 21, 1773, "between the masque [Milton's

'Comus'] and between the acts, some pieces of Musick by the Band belonging to his Majesty's Regiment of Royal Welsh Fusileer's" were to be played.

After having contributed to the gaieties of the racing season at Annapolis, the American Company once more, but only for a fortnight, made its way to Philadelphia, presenting, on November 1, 1773, 'Lionel and Clarissa,' and on the tenth 'The Padlock.' Even if Mr. Douglass had not announced beforehand his intention to set sail for Charleston, S. C., it may be doubted that he would have cared to stay at Philadelphia any length of time, for the attacks on the theatre now became very insulting. Over the signature of *Philadelphus*, for instance, a card was addressed to the *Pennsylvania Gazette*, on November 10, in which these extraordinary lines appear:

> It is a matter of real sorrow and distress to many sober inhabitants of different denominations to hear of the return of those strolling Comedians, who are travelling thro' America, propagating vice and immorality. And it is much to the disreputation of this City that more encouragement should be given them here than in any other place on the Continent.

After quoting all kinds of authorities from Hawkins's Pleas of the Crown to the Select Works of William Penn, Mr. Philadelphus sums up by claiming:

> From what has been said, I think it appears: 1st, That common Players, etc., are vagrants and sturdy beggars. 2d, That the Play-House in this city is a common nuisance.

This gentleman should have married *Cleopatra*, who on November 1, 1773, in the *South Carolina Gazette*, amiably dubbed the theatre the Devil's Synagogue. It would have been a perfect match and Charlestonians would have become rid of the indignant lady who evidently had not the slightest idea of what her pen-name stands for in the history of morals, and who sought to interfere with the pleasures of her fellow-citizens for which they were craving. If *Cleopatra* resolved never

to set foot in the Devil's Synagogue, she did not make
many proselytes, as the American Company played at the
New Theatre from December, 1773, to May, 1774, before
the largest and most brilliant audiences in its career.
The repertory of this season, on the other hand, is almost
staggering: Fifty-nine nights with seventy-seven distinct
plays, farces and operas! Of the latter, Charleston had
occasion to enjoy on

        1774, Jan. 3: Love in a Village.
                   24: Honest Yorkshireman.
                   25: Beggar's Opera.
                   29: Devil to Pay.
               Feb. 4: Love in a Village.
                    7: Midas.
                   17: Thomas and Sally.
                   24: Damon and Phillida.
               Mar. 4: Lionel and Clarissa.
                    7: Padlock.
                   10: Maid of the Mill.
                   14: Padlock.
                   21: Devil to Pay.
                   26: Flora.
               Apr. 4: Lionel and Clarissa.
                 6, 13: Contrivances.
                   18: Witches.
                   25: Midas.
               May 16: Devil to Pay.

Considering the fact that Charleston was one of the
four musical centres of America in those days, owing
to the stimulus the St. Cœcilia [*sic!*] Society had given
to musical affairs, it is perhaps surprising that Douglass
presented only thirteen operas. Still, even that is a
good showing, and that his efforts were appreciated
appears from the fact that the news of his success travelled as far north as to the *New York Mercury*, where
we read on February 21, 1774, under date of Charlestown,
December 24:

On Wednesday last the new theatre in this Town was opened.
. . . The scenes, which are new and well designed, the dresses,

the musick, and what had a very pleasing effect, the disposition of the lights, all contributed to the satisfaction of the audience, who expressed the highest approbation of this entertainment.

Another contemporary may be quoted here for a glimpse into olden times, as his words indirectly bear on the subject here treated. Josiah Quincy's "Journal of a Voyage to South Carolina, etc.," in 1772, has been preserved, and while he does not mention having gone to the opera, he devotes several entries to music (interesting, as they throw light on the St. Cœcilia Society, its orchestra, the audience, etc.) which, by an oversight, I unfortunately omitted in my book on "Early Concert Life in America." Says Josiah, *e. g.*, under March 17:

Dined with the Sons of St. Patrick. While at dinner six violins, two hautboys, etc. After dinner, six French horns in concert:— most surpassing music. Two solos on the French horn, by one who is said to blow the finest horn in the world. He has fifty guineas for the season from the St. Cecilia Society.

This might stand in a modern diary, but the delightful entry of March 3 bears the unmistakable stamp of the eighteenth century:

The concert-house is a large, inelegant building, situated down a yard, at the entrance of which I was met by a constable, with his staff. I offered him my ticket, which was subscribed by the name of the person giving it, and directing admission of me by name. The officer told me to proceed. I did, and was next met by a white waiter, who directed me to a third, to whom I delivered my ticket, and was conducted in. The music was good—the two base viols and French horns were grand. One Abercrombie, a Frenchman just arrived, played the first violin, and a solo incomparably better than any one I ever heard. He cannot speak a word of English, and has a salary of five hundred guineas a year from the St. Cecilia Society. There were upwards of two hundred and fifty ladies present, and it was called no great number. In loftiness of headdress, these ladies stoop to the daughters of the north,—in richness of dress, surpass them,—in health and floridity of countenance, vail to them. In taciturnity during the performances, greatly before our ladies; in noise and flirtation after the music is over, pretty much on a par. If our ladies have any advantage, it is in white and red, vivacity and spirit. The gentlemen, many of them dressed with richness and elegance, uncommon with us: many with swords on. We had two macaronis present, just arrived from London.

The success of the Charleston season had been so encouraging that Douglass confided to the press his very elaborate plans for the future, culminating in the promise of revisiting Charleston with "a theatrical force hitherto unknown in America." However, on October 4, 1774, Congress, less from puritanical feeling than from the necessity of meeting the exigencies of the coming national struggle, passed the resolution:

> That we will discourage every species of extravagance and dissipation, especially horse-racing, and all kinds of gaming, cock-fighting, exhibition of shows, plays and other expensive diversions and entertainments.

Douglass was notified of this resolution in a letter from Peyton Randolph, the President of Congress, He took the hint, embarked with most members of his company at New York on February 2, 1775, for Jamaica, and therewith ended the pre-revolutionary career of the American Company.

During the war, of course, our people had little inclination or time to listen to plays or operas, and when in the autumn of 1778, after the British had evacuated Philadelphia, some actors attempted to lure the members of the American Congress into the Southwark Theatre, these attempts were quickly discouraged by another resolution. Yet these resolutions had not the desired effect everywhere, and it is a fact that in 1781, two years before the close of the war, a theatre was built at Baltimore, opened under the management of Messrs. Wall and Lindsay, and kept open until the end of the war, and after. However, as these Baltimore performances properly belong to post-revolutionary times, they do not concern us here. It is different with Burgoyne's Thespians, Howe's Thespians and Clinton's Thespians, as

Mr. Seilhamer tersely names the theatrical companies made up of British officers and their "ladies" at Boston, Philadelphia and New York. Any allusion to them after they had evacuated the United States would manifestly be out of place, and consequently they call for some attention here.

Burgoyne's Thespians may be disregarded in this interlude in the history of opera in America. Howe's Thespians occupied the stage first at New York and then at Philadelphia during the memorable winter of 1777 to 1778. As far as I can see, the only opera given in both cities by the officers in Howe's army, who then still considered the war a farce, was the "Mock Doctor." They became ambitious after Clinton had led them safely back to New York, and from 1778 to 1783 without many interruptions New York was at the mercy of these military players—in more ways than one. But while these performances, at least as far as the gentler sex is concerned, stood under the influence of unwritten laws of conduct, it must be said for the honor of the "Society of Gentlemen of the Army and Navy" that they combined throughout their efforts to make garrison life in the beleaguered city as gay as possible with

The laudable purpose of raising a supply for the widows and orphans of those who have lost their lives in His Majesty's service, as well as for such other generous charities as their funds may enable them to perform.

And it is hardly necessary to add that Major André played a prominent part in these affairs as manager, actor and scene-painter. Naturally, opera was pushed somewhat to the background and comparatively few opera nights are on record.

1778,	Feb. 22:	Mock Doctor.
	May 5:	Devil to Pay.
1779,	Jan. 28:	Mock Doctor.
	Mar. 3:	Mock Doctor.
	Dec. 29:	Mock Doctor.
1780,	Feb. 7:	Mock Doctor.

```
1780,  Feb. 27:  Mock Doctor.
       Apr. 19:  Flora.
       May  1:   Flora.
       Oct. 30:  Flitch of Bacon. (London, 1778.
                 Music compiled and com-
                 posed by Shield.)
1781,  Jan. 15:  Mock Doctor.
1782,  Jan. 28:  Mock Doctor.
```

Up to this time the casts, at any rate the male parts, were entrusted entirely to officers, but in the fall of 1782 Mr. Wall, manager of the Baltimore theatre—a most extraordinary proof that actors were considered a neutral power on both sides—found his way to New York and brought with him a company of professionals. Theatrical affairs, however, were not turned over to them entirely, for on September 30 "some of the characters [were taken] by Gentlemen of the Army and Navy," and (see *Royal Gazette*, October 15) on October 16 'Love in a Village' was entirely performed by these gentlemen "for their amusement." This arrangement prevailed to some extent even in 1783, but, as most of the performances were given "by permission," as, for instance, on July 12 'The Witches,' when the "band will be led by Signior Gætano Franceschini," it is clear that the "Royal Theatre" had become more or less a professional affair.

The operatic repertory of Clinton's Thespians certainly was meagre and seems to indicate that, while the officers possessed courage enough to conquer the dramatic classics, they did not feel quite so sure of their bearings when it came to operas. Indeed, it might be taken for granted that the music was rendered less satisfactorily on the stage than in the orchestra, where the best musicians in the several regimental bands were pressed into service. At any rate, Dunlap claims that the orchestra employed by the Society of the Gentlemen of the Army and Navy in the Royal Theatre "was better filled than in the times of the real players. They had fourteen performers at a dollar the night."

PART II
POST-REVOLUTIONARY OPERA

PART II

POST-REVOLUTIONARY OPERA

1. *A Survey from* 1781 *to* 1792

The first period in the history of opera in America clearly ended with Robert Upton's failure to establish himself at New York. The second began with the advent of Hallam's London Company of Comedians, and closed with their forced withdrawal from America in 1774 after having become known as the Old American Company. The third period was inaugurated by the return of this company shortly after the War for Independence and embraced about a decade. Then a fourth began with the rivalry between the Old American Company and Wignell and Reinagle's New Company founded at Philadelphia in 1793, with the conquest of new fields of activity, with the gradual formation of Southern companies, and with the tentative introduction of French and even Italian operas by political refugees, as characteristic features. Between the second and third periods the military Thespians enacted a kind of operatic intermezzo, and attention was drawn to the somewhat ludicrous episode towards the end of this intermezzo when professional player-folk plied their trade between Baltimore and New York without breach of neutrality and without interference from either belligerent.

Though this Baltimore company did not exercise any far-reaching influence on the history of opera in our country, its existence and the fact that it formed a chronological link between the old and the new era call for a brief description of its career.

Possibly, pleasant memories of a performance which the Old American Company had given in 1772 at

Baltimore, in a stable fitted up for the purpose, prompted Mr. Wall, for many years a member of this company, to try his luck as manager and leading man at Baltimore, then a city of about ten thousand inhabitants. He associated himself with Mr. Adam Lindsay, proprietor of the Coffee House on Fell's Point, and these two gentlemen combined their brains and money to erect a "well regulated" theatre in East Baltimore Street in 1781, which was to house what they termed the Maryland Company of Comedians. From the *Maryland Journal* of December 25 it would appear that neither house nor company was complete at that time because the managers were still "resolved to give suitable encouragement to any person . . . possessed of proper talents for the stage," provided his character stood the test of inquiry. With a motley combination of amateurs and professional talent they opened the *New* Theatre on Jan. 15, 1782. They could have opened it sooner but for one difficulty, namely, to obtain "good musicians"— that is, an orchestra; and as if to head off all criticism, the managers on Jan. 8 notified the public that it would not be their fault if good music could not be procured. This obstacle partly removed, the Maryland Company embarked on a career ambitious enough to have taxed the abilities of a professional company of merit, and— what is interesting in view of the Congressional resolutions of 1778 against costly amusements of all kinds— "by permission." The first season lasted until summer, 1782, and included performances of the following operas:

1782, Feb. 15, 26: Contrivances.
          March 1;
          April 23: Padlock.
April 30; May 3, 7: Thomas and Sally ("Children in laps will not be admitted!").

The cast of the 'Contrivances' was this:

Argus .   .   .   . Mr. Heard
Hearty .   .   .   . Mr. Street

Rovewell	. . . . . .	Mr. Wall
Robin	. . . . . .	Mr. Shakespeare
First mob	. . . . . .	Mr. Kilgour
Second mob	. . . . . .	Mr. Tillyard
Boy	. . . .	Miss Wall
Arethusa	. . . . . .	Mrs. Wall
Betty	. . . . . .	Mrs. Elm

Mr. Heard was the poet-laureate of the company, and from a prologue which he concocted it would appear that also the 'Honest Yorkshireman' was given. On August 6 notice was served on "the performers belonging to the Baltimore theatre . . . to repair to Baltimore" by the end of the month; and thus summoned for rehearsal, it would seem, from less artistic professions, they began their second season under Wall and Lindsay's management on Sept. 13, and closed it, with a brief excursion to Annapolis during the races, Oct. 25 to Nov. 6, in February, 1783. It is hardly necessary to give more than a record of performances, and that necessarily incomplete:

1782,   Sept. 27:   Padlock.
           Nov. 29:   *Harlequin Landlord* (pantomime).
           Dec. 20:   Hob in the Well (better known as 'Flora').
1783, Jan. 7, 14, 17:   Witches (pant.).
           Jan. 24:   Beggar's Opera.
   Jan. 28, Feb. 7:   Mock Doctor.

With this last performance Messrs. Wall and Lindsay yielded the managerial scepter to Dennis Ryan, who had joined the company with his wife. Under his auspices the theatre reopened on February 11 and remained open for four months. The operas and pantomimes performed were the following, and it will be seen that one novelty had something of an American flavor, if it was not an American production altogether:

1783,   Feb. 14; Mar. 4; April 11: Witches (pant.).
    Feb. 21, 25:   Trick upon Trick; or, Harlequin Skeleton ("a new [?] pantomime entertainment" by Yarrow).

Mar. 21: *Columbus;* or, the Discovery of America, with
          Harlequin's Revels ("a new pantomime enter-
          tainment, being the *second* time of perform-
          ance").
April 4; May 13: Mock Doctor.

Dennis Ryan took his company the end of April for
a few weeks to Annapolis and after the close of the
Baltimore season to New York, when it was already found
in more or less harmonious coöperation with the gentlemen of the British army and navy. He evacuated New
York simultaneously with them and returned to Baltimore,
where he boldly christened his company the American
Company, though both Mr. Hallam and Mr. Henry
by that time had arrived in our country. The season
lasted from Dec. 2 to Feb. 14, 1784. After adding
theatrical amusement to the races at Annapolis, immediately afterwards, Dennis Ryan and his company
disappeared temporarily from Maryland. As Ryan's
company had been strengthened perceptibly, it is not
surprising that he gave opera a freer sway than previously. The list of performances will prove this:

    1783, Dec. 6, 27: Love in a Village.
               23: Beggar's Opera.
    1784, Jan. 3: Beggar's Opera.
                7: Love in a Village.
                9: Thomas and Sally.
               16: *Harlequin in Hell* ("a new pantomime").
               24: Mock Doctor.
               31: Witches.
      Feb. 3, 11: Virgin Unmasked.
               14: Chaplet.

Before leaving Baltimore, it may not be amiss, in
order to keep track of the heroes and heroines that
adorned the American stage in those years with more
or less success, to print here at least one cast. I select
that of
                    Love in a Village
    Young Meadows .   .   .   .   By Mr. Wall
    Eustace   .   .   .   .   .   Mr. Smith

Hodge	Mr. Davids
Hawthorne	Mr. Lewis
Sir William Meadows . . .	Mr. Keating
Justice Woodcock	Mr. Heard
Deborah	Mr. Davids
Lucinda	Mrs. Ryan
Rosetta	Mrs. Hyde

Mr. Seilhamer claims that Ryan dropped the pirated name of American Company after a few weeks, probably in consequence of objections from either Hallam or Henry. This is quite incorrect, as newspaper advertisements prove that he continued to use the designation during the remainder of his career as manager. Mr. Seilhamer may be correct in surmising that Ryan boldly invaded Quebec during the fall of 1784, but he is again in error when he calls the season of 1783-84 Ryan's last season in Maryland and when he tells us that Ryan made his home in Baltimore, where he died in January, 1786. Only the last part of the statement is true, as his widow soon afterwards solicited public patronage for a benefit performance by a house to house canvass. As a matter of fact, Dennis Ryan on August 26, 1785, protested in the *Maryland Journal* against certain "illiberal" and "scandalous" interpretations of his absence from Baltimore, explained it with ill-health and his "connections in Virginia," assured the public that the property of the Baltimore Theatre, which had cost him two thousand pounds, was now entirely in his possession, and added that his American Company, "now in Bath," would soon be back in town. The theatre was indeed opened on Sept. 7, 1785, and did not close its doors until June, 1786; after Ryan's death in January presumably under the management of his widow or possibly again of Mr. Wall, who was still a member of the company. The repertory of this, Ryan's last earthly season, included such favorites as 'The Padlock' (Sept. 7), 'Thomas and Sally' (Sept. 17),

'Beggar's Opera' (Sept. 13), 'Contrivances' (April, 1786), and on May 9, 1786, 'The Honest Yorkshireman.'

But where was Ryan with the American Company during the first half of the year 1785? At Charleston, S. C.! Mr. Seilhamer dates the revival of the American Theatre at Charleston under the Stars and Stripes, 1786. It was his misfortune to overlook not only a notice in the *Maryland Journal*, Baltimore, of April 12, 1785, in which it is distinctly stated that Dennis Ryan, having obtained the necessary permission from the magistrate of Charleston, was performing there "before crowded audiences, with great applause" and would return to Baltimore "in the course of next month," but he overlooked also the announcement in the *State Gazette* of South Carolina of March 28, 1785, which proves that Ryan's brief season at Charleston began on that day. The only real item of importance, in connection with this season, is the fact, also unknown to Seilhamer, that the very talented Maria Storer, later an American favorite as Mrs. Henry, belonged to Ryan's troupe; in other words, that she returned to America in 1785 and not in 1786.

Until then the Southern cities seem not to have assumed the hypocritical attitude of permitting theatrical performances under all kinds of disguises, some specimens of which will soon amuse the reader. This wave of hypocrisy struck Charleston in 1786. Mr. Godwin, dancing and fencing master by trade but actor by ambition—as such he had belonged to Douglass' company before the war—came to Savannah, Ga., from Jamaica in 1786 and forthwith proceeded to try his luck as manager. Not meeting with much success he went to Charleston, found a backer in a "principal merchant" of that city and erected "Harmony Hall, at Louisburgh, without the city." The fame of this suburban retreat traveled as far as New York, where the *Independent Journal* on August 5, 1786, stated that it had cost more than £500 sterling, that it contained "22 boxes with a key to each box," that it was devoted to "music meetings, dancing and theatrical amusements," and that it had been opened with a grand concert of music *gratis* for the satisfaction of the principal inhabitants who wished to see it previous to the first night's exhibition. The theatrical amusements began the end of September and continued until spring, 1787, when the enterprise came to grief partly because Godwin was not making enough money "to pay up the salaries," partly because, as Mr. Godwin himself stated in the Charleston *Morning Post*, May 31, 1787, he had "in consequence of a late act of the Legislature relinquished theatrical representations." As lectures, interspersed with songs, etc., were "tolerated throughout the States with universal approbation," Harmony Hall was converted into a lecture-hall and served also as fencing-school where, it seems, "sharp trials" were held which Godwin instigated by some highly ludicrous public challenges. The decision of the legislature must have been in the air, because Godwin's theatrical amusements, while they lasted, were usually presented as "concerts of music," with comedies, farces, tragedies, operas "between the acts." They were performed by a company picked up from everywhere, including Mr. Shakespeare and several other members of Ryan's defunct American Company. The ill-fated company does not yield much for a history of opera. 'Flora' was performed on March 14 and 23, 1787; the 'Elopement,' a pantomime brought out at Drury Lane in 1767, was introduced to Charleston on Jan. 5, and popular pantomimes like 'The Witches' figured conspicuously on the repertory. One other pantomime deserves attention, as it possibly was a real novelty: 'The *Animation and Death of Harlequin*,' performed on Nov. 24, 1786, with "dresses, music, scenes and decorations entirely new."

In the meantime, the Old American Company was finding its bearings. Leaving aside the confusing activity of several more or less anonymous, mysterious and obscure companies that frequented the South in those years, but which contributed exceedingly little to the development of opera in our country, it now becomes necessary to return to the years immediately following the war, when the real American Company showed signs of tiring of its half voluntary, half compulsory expulsion to Jamaica.

Early in 1782, John Henry embarked from Jamaica on a scouting visit to the United States, to look after the several properties of the Old American Company and also to survey chances for a permanent return. The Maryland Assembly without much hesitation confirmed the company's title to the theatre erected at Annapolis in 1771; but at Philadelphia Henry's troubles began. In vain he pleaded in a letter to William Moore, the President of the Supreme Executive Council of Pennsylvania, that he found the theatre entirely out of repair and a debt for ground rent and taxes incurred to the amount of £174 7/ 6d. Nor did it avail him much to point out that a wire dancer by the name of Templeton had been granted permission to use the theatre belonging to the Old American Company for his performances. Henry's modest and reasonable request for the use of his own theatre for Stevens' famous, popular and certainly harmless 'Lecture on Heads' was turned down and the anti-theatre law of 1778 was not repealed officially until 1789. All Henry could do was to save the property of the company from encroachment and destruction. He then went to New York, gave a series of lecture-entertainments, and presumably returned to Jamaica.

But Henry's trip to Philadelphia had borne some fruit, because when Lewis Hallam in January, 1784, laid a petition before the General Assembly to repeal the act of 1778, it was endorsed by influential citizens who, in fact, on January 14, had called a meeting for that effect, and the committee in charge actually reported in its favor, but it was voted down. Thereupon Hallam on Feb. 21 publicly gave thanks in a card "To the Friends of the Drama" who had supported him, and had at least succeeded in not being molested when he repeatedly in April and May, 1784, delivered at the theatre "A Lecture upon heads and strictures upon the most eminent dramatic authors, serious, comic and satiric." The whole was "properly diversified with music, scenery and other decorations." Equally popular, and naturally so, became "A Monody to the Memory of the Chiefs who have fallen in the cause of *American Liberty*, accompanied with vocal incantations (the music of which is entirely new) adapted to the distinct periods of the recital." This was printed by Bradford, but seems to have perished like so many other early American publications.

In December, 1784, Hallam reopened his theatre, now surrounded by the nucleus of a company. It comprised Mr. Allen, with whom Hallam soon was to enter into partnership, and the dancer John Durang, a native of Lancaster, Pennsylvania, to whose entertaining theatrical reminiscences, as edited and published by his son in the *Sunday Dispatch*, 1855, we have to look as one of the best sources for the history of the American stage.

With Hallam's second season the beating about the bush began in earnest. The entertainments now assumed the title of "Lecture, being an entertainment of representation and harmony," or more appeasing still, "Lecture *Moral* and Entertaining." As a kind of feeler, as if to see if the law-makers objected to all theatrical entertainments or merely to plays proper, an imitation of Garrick's pantomimical 'Shakespeare's Jubilee' was first exhibited under the harmless title of "Garrick's Ode on dedicating a building to Shakespeare, with the original music, vocal and instrumental, scenery, machinery and decorations entirely new." As the people willingly took the bait, "pantomimical action" and "pantomimical fêtes" with all the accessories mentioned, flourished at Philadelphia until August. The nearest Hallam dared approach to opera was on July 27, 1785 with

A Grand *Serenata*, called Peace and Liberty: Consisting of Recitation, Recitative, Airs and Choruses. The parts recited are selected from the works of Thompson, Sterne, etc., etc. The music, vocal and instrumental, composed by Handel, Arne, Tenducci, Fisher and Valentino, etc., etc. There are a number of additional voices engaged, and every endeavour exerted upon this occasion to render the Serenata as complete and pleasing as any Piece that has ever been exhibited at this theatre.

Shortly afterwards the company made its way to New York, and reopened the John Street theatre on August 11, 1785. From the beginning, of course, they met with opposition, especially from the clergy. To make things worse, Hallam and Henry did not consider it necessary to request official permission to exhibit plays, and when they offered the proceeds of a charitable performance to the authorities for distribution amongst the poor, the gift was refused with the remark that the managers' behavior was "a thing unprecedented and offensive." However, the desire for theatrical representations was too strong. The players were not seriously molested, and before long they could drop the mask of 'Lectures' and call a play a play. In November Mr. Allen and a few others withdrew from the company and tried their luck independently at Albany during the winter of 1785-86. In the meantime, John Henry had returned to the United States with a company of his own, comprising Mr. Woolls, Mr. and Mrs. Morris, the pre-revolutionary favorites, and some new members imported from the West Indies. This combination he called, and not incorrectly, the Old American Company. He seemed at first bent upon competing with the other twin-half of the time-honored organization, but he bethought himself of something better and suggested a partnership. This Hallam accepted and from Nov., 1785, on for seven years, as Mr. Seilhamer correctly puts it, the Old American Company controlled the amusement field from New York to Annapolis.

Perhaps it will be best to give first a chronological record of the performances, adhering to the rule of italicizing novelties:

1785, Aug. 20: *Genii of the Rock* (pant.; music by John Bentley).

Aug. 26: ⎱ *Cave of Enchantment;* or, the Stockwell Wonder
      29: ⎰ (pant.; music by John Bentley).

Sept. 1: ⎱ *Touchstone;* or, Harlequin Traveller (pant.; music
Oct. 7: ⎰ by John Bentley).

Sept. 23: Witches.

Sept. 27: ⎱
      30: ⎰ Flitch of Bacon (Shield).

Sept. 30: ⎱
Oct. 4: ⎰ *Elopement;* or, the Triumph of Genius (pant.).

Oct. 4: ⎱
      7: ⎬ Thomas and Sally.
1786, June 23: ⎰

1785, Oct. 11: Damon and Phillida.

Oct. 14: ⎱
Nov. 1: ⎬ Mock Doctor.
1786, Feb. 10: ⎰

1785, Dec. 2: ⎱
      7: ⎮
      26: ⎮
1786, Jan. 18: ⎮
      23: ⎮ *Poor Soldier.* (Shield; Dublin and London, 1783,
Feb. 27: ⎮ and originally called 'The Shamrock.' Perform-
Mar. 3: ⎮ ances advertised on Jan. 2, 3, 4 as "Fifth time,"
      8: ⎬ were apparently postponed; performance of
      13: ⎮ Feb. 27 "for the eighth time"; March 8, "the
      22: ⎮ tenth"; June 26, "sixteenth"; July 21, "eigh-
April 17: ⎮ teenth.")
May 24: ⎮
      31: ⎮
June 26: ⎮
July 21: ⎰

1785, Dec. 5: ⎱
1786, June 4: ⎬ Padlock.
      14: ⎰

Jan. 6: Devil to Pay.

Jan. 11: ⎱
      13: ⎮
      25: ⎬ Robinson Crusoe (pant.; music by Linley, 1781).
Mar. 6: ⎰

Mar. 24:
  31:
April 24: } Midas.
June 2:

April 19:
  21:
May 5: } *Rosina* (Shield, London, December 31, 1782).
  10:

May 3:
June 19: } Love in a Village.
July 7:

May 29: Maid of the Mill.

May 29: } *Daphne and Amintor;* or, the Fairies (altered from
July 10:   Mrs. Cibber's 'Oracle.' Pasticcio, London,
     1765).

June 5:
  12: } Harlequin's Invasion (pant., London, 1759).

June 19: Comus (masque, music by Arne).

July 10: *Duenna* (Linley, London, 1775; in New York
    "with the permission of the patentee of Convent
    Garden Theatre, the original overture and ac-
    companiments").

July 14: Flora.

July 17: *Two Misers;* or, Mufti's Ghost (Dibdin, London,
    1775).

Evidently a new era was beginning. The old favorites remained in the repertory, but the managers sailed under fresh winds and henceforth nothing could check the speedy and steady importation of novelties. Not only this, but American productions received a reasonable share of publicity and the press began to show more critical interest in the stage. The importation of the masterpieces by Shield and his rivals demanded that the generally creditable interpretation by the actor-singers be seconded by a reasonably adequate orchestra. Perhaps the most striking instance that we are now approaching modern times is the fact that Shield's 'Poor Soldier,' for years the favorite of the American public from George Washington down to the humblest gallery god, enjoyed a regular *run* of eighteen nights, something unprecedented in the annals of our stage. This success was due, of course, in the first place to the charms of the opera, but its effectiveness was enhanced

Darbys Return.

page 13. after the 9.th line from the top read.
There, Lads and little Lasses sweet as honey,
Marry for Love, and never think of money;

W.m Dunlap del. et Sc.

M.r Wignell in the Character of Darby.
There, Father Luke! one sheep's as good as two,
Nor need I count my turkeys when I row.—

THOMAS WIGNELL (d. 1803)

by the universally applauded personification of *Darby* by Thomas Wignell. Therewith the *star* régime which had commenced with the younger Hallam's *Mungo* received its second impetus in our company. The original American cast of the 'Poor Soldier' has been preserved, and though it does not disclose the full strength of the company it may follow here as a kind of historical document:

Patrick	Mr. Henry
Captain Fitzroy	Mr. Harper
Dermot	Mr. Woolls ·
Darby	Mr. Wignell
Norah	Miss Tuke
Kathleen	Mrs. Morris

That everybody would enjoy and appreciate the new school of English opera could not be expected. As always, what suited the younger generation did not suit the taste of the older, and the conservative (or rather retrospective) element, while forgetting that much nonsense stood in the real ballad-operas of olden times, were quick in showering their contempt on the poetic nonsense and nonsensical poetry in the librettos of O'Keefe and others. In fact, even in the silliest *hits* of our own time, things like this in one of his songs would be difficult to duplicate:

> Ditherum doodle adgety
> Nagity, tragedy, rum,
> Goostnerum foodle nidgety,
> Nigety, nagety mum.

or again, part of a song in the 'Castle of Andalusia':

> A master I have, and I am his man,
>   Galloping dreary dun,
> And he will get married, as fast as he can
> With my haily, gaily, gamboraily,
> Giggling, niggling, galoping, galloway,
>   Draggletail, dreary dun.

Rank nonsense like this filled the opponents of the stage with fear lest the intellect and morals of our nation be further corrupted, and it was actually brought forward by the politicians of Philadelphia as an argument against repealing the anti-theatre act of 1778, as a lengthy correspondence from there to the *New York Packet* of Dec. 5, 1785, may prove. It would be a mistake to suppose that this attitude was shared by the people at large. It was not only essentially English music which appealed to them, but, strange to say, the librettos as well, for otherwise there would have been no commercial reason for attempting to supplant the imported English editions of these librettos by numerous American reprints.

On the other hand, it is true that the people objected to the temporary predominance of the "superb" speaking pantomimes in grotesque characters. Perhaps it was the intention of the managers to test the attitude of their patrons and see their way clear towards a more legitimate opera, that the first three novelties on the list were pantomimes with "the music selected and compiled" by John Bentley, one of our prominent musicians in those days. Hallam and Henry did not have to wait long for an expression of public opinion. In the *New York Packet*, Oct. 10, 1785, a lay-critic admitted that "a theatre might and ought to be a school for virtue, elegance and politeness in general," but he regretted "that the theatre in this city is not such a school," and then went on to say:

Instead of those energetic tragedies, abounding in excellent morals, with which our language abounds, and comedies replete with justest satire, where vice and folly meet perhaps the severest castigation, and the last of ridicule, we have the Genii of the Rock, the Witches, Harlequin in the Moon, with a thousand other pantomimical mummeries at which common sense stands aghast, and idiots wonder.

The managers after this had no reason for not remedying the evil, though the speaking pantomimes continued to be attractive to many people until the end of the century. The criticism following the performance of 'The Maid of the Mill' on May 29 sounded quite different. It was the "theatrical intelligence" conveyed from New York to the *Pennsylvania Journal*, June 7, 1786. As an early and characteristic specimen of musical criticism in those days it follows in full:

New York, May 31.
Theatrical Intelligence.

On Monday evening, for the benefit of Mr. Henry, notwithstanding the inclemency of the weather, there was as numerous and respectable an audience as ever we remember to have seen in this city, above two hundred persons went away finding it impossible to gain admission. The performance of the *Maid of the Mill* gave general satisfaction . . . . all the performers exerted themselves in a particular manner, but we should do great injustice to the ambitions of Miss Maria Storer, if we did not remark that her singing is truly masterly, infinitely beyond any thing ever heard on this side of the Atlantic. Her voice is harmony itself; to be equalled only by her refined ear and great taste; her performance was both chaste and judicious; she seems not only to have made singing, but speaking her particular study. Her adoption of different dresses were elegantly characteristic of approved judgment and fancy. The afterpiece showed her knowledge of the *vis comica*, and was received with unbounded applause.

It will be noticed that not a word is said about the orchestra. Nor was it often considered necessary in later years to bestow some credit for the success of the operas on the men who labored in the orchestra. It would be an error to trace this indifference to a charitable application of the maxim "the less said, the better." As a matter of fact, the musicians in our orchestras were fairly capable men. If they were skillful enough to give pleasure on the concert-stage in symphonies, overtures, concertos, as my book on our 'Early Concert-Life' has proved abundantly, they certainly possessed the necessary qualifications to play the overtures, accompaniments, etc., in the old English operas. These accompaniments generally were not written out. They had to be supplied from the

figured bass by the official composer or arranger of the
company and consequently could and would be so ar-
ranged as to fit local conditions, that is to say, the size
of the orchestra.   It will be well to keep this point in
mind, as otherwise the frequent remark in the old announcements, "accompaniments by——," might be construed (and it has been so construed) to mean that the
musician mentioned was an accompanist in our modern
sense.   The orchestra's share in the pantomimes given
at the beginning of the season is not quite clear, for,
strange to say, John Bentley, harpichordist, composer,
arranger, also figures in the casts as pantomimist.
Probably in such cases he had a substitute, but when
Hallam and Henry joined forces, the orchestra evidently
had assumed the usual provincial size and one characteristic feature of it has lasted to this day.   John Durang
says:

> The orchestra was composed of the following musicians.   Mr.
> Philo [*recte* Phile] leader; Mr. Bentley, harpsichord; Mr. Woolf,
> principal clarinet; Trimmer, Hecker and son, violoncello, violins, etc.
> Some six or seven other names, now not remembered, constituting
> the musical force. *The latter were all Germans.*

From New York the Old American Company went to
Baltimore.   Though the old theatre, built in 1781, was
still standing, Hallam and Henry, for some reason, gave
their exhibitions in a new theatre erected on Philpot's
Hill.   It was opened on Aug. 17, 1786, and excited the
admiration of the *Maryland Gazette*, which called it com-
modiously built and bestowed praise on the "truly elegant" scenery and decorations.   The appreciative audiences were treated on Aug. 22 (not on Aug. 23, as Mr.
Seilhamer says), Aug. 29 and Sept. 8 to 'The Poor Soldier,' and on Sept. 19, during the "last week," to Shield's
'Rosina; or, the Reapers.'   From Baltimore the company
hastened to Annapolis in time for the October races.
Then, it seems, they proceeded by agreement with
Alexander Quesnay, erstwhile dancing-master, but now

the proprietor of an ambitious Academy, to Richmond, Va., where Quesnay, as a kind of esthetic *dépendance* of his academy, had erected a theatre to hold about sixteen hundred people. Again the 'Poor Soldier' proved the best drawing card.

By this time Hallam and Henry had accumulated sufficient courage to again defy the watch-dogs of Philadelphia's morals. The expedition from Richmond overland to Philadelphia in those days of slow coaches and slow-moving vans was very much more of an undertaking than in our days of rapid transit by rail. Sure enough, the opening of the Southwark Theatre had to be postponed from Jan. 5 to Jan. 15, 1787, because, from the badness of the roads — eighteenth-century Virginia roads at that!—part of the scenery had not arrived in time. When finally the theatre did open, the managers were again obliged to assume the character of veiled prophets. The fact had been established that the authorities frowned more on real tragedies and comedies than on operas or pantomimes, or rather on music and anything connected with music. Hence, Hallam and Henry chose as vehicle for their performances the term "Concert of music," between the acts of which would be delivered "Lectures, moral and entertaining," to conclude with "pantomimical finales." How legitimate opera was smuggled in, the program for Jan. 19, 1787, may illustrate:

A *Concert of Music*, Vocal and Instrumental. Between the several parts of the Concert will be delivered *Lectures*, Moral and Entertaining.

FIRST ACT

Overture   . . . . .   Kammel

PROLOGUE AND LECTURE

Song . . . .   Mr. Wools

SECOND ACT

Simphonia   . . . . . .   Schwindl

LECTURE

Song . . . .   Mr. Harper

CLARINET CONCERTO

(By Desire)

The Overture to Rosina, to which will be added, a Pantomime called 'Harlequin's Frolic,' in which will be introduced a Musical Entertainment, called 'The Reapers,' with the original music.

In this manner Hallam and Henry succeeded in fooling the official legal minds of Philadelphia, who, as legal minds sometimes will do, interpreted the letter of the law rather than its spirit, until the middle of February.

To what absurdities the half-hearted opposition to theatrical exhibitions on the one hand and the diplomatic evasion of the law on the other hand led is fittingly recorded by Durang, who says that independently of the Southwark ruse:

The first representation of the 'Poor Soldier' in Philadelphia was made through the medium of puppets at a house in Second Street . . . . The puppets were made by John Durang. The dialogue and songs of the opera were conducted by some of the actors and actresses formerly belonging to the Southwark company. The puppet theatre was located in the third story and it was crowded every night at fifty cents a ticket.

The Federal Convention, soon to frame our Constitution, was in session when Hallam and Henry again ventured to Philadelphia and on June 25, 1787, very diplomatically opened the Southwark with a benefit for the American captives in Algiers. Indeed, conditions induced them to actually call their theatre in August an Opera-House, probably the first time that any building in our country had been thus honored. While, during the previous season, the performances were headed 'Concerts,' the managers now adopted the more learned '*Spectaculum Vitæ*' as main heading for their so peculiarly mixed entertainments. This designation was deemed sufficient protection when operas were performed, but for plays something still more baffling to legal minds was invented. Not only were the titles of the plays so disguised as sometimes to be beyond recognition, but they were garnished with strictly moral and educational motives, for instance, Hamlet as "a moral and instructive tale" as "exemplified in the history of the Prince of Denmark." Thus prepared, they were offered—how sly and ingenuous this is—*gratis* between the 'acts' of the so-called concert. The climax of the mummery was reached when, on Sept. 26, 1788, the *Independent Gazetteer* announced:

Private Audience.

The *Philadelphian in Jamaica;* or, Zuleff and Zelinda will be performed to a select audience, this evening the 26th instant. Several gentlemen who have been so extremely kind as to distribute tickets on this occasion having declined receiving money renders this advertisement necessary, to inform such gentlemen as shall please to accept tickets, that the money will be received at the door. Every effort will be used to render the entertainment as agreeable as possible. Proper paintings are prepared and a *Band of Music* with Singing to which alone the purchasing of tickets are necessary, the lectures on the Slave Trade being delivered gratis, as on Thursday last they were with the approbation of several gentlemen of reputation and taste.

But even the *Faschingsschwank* of Philadelphia could not last for ever. It came to an end primarily through the efforts of the Dramatic Association, formed in January, 1789. Many of the best and most influential people of Philadelphia belonged to the association; and they presented a really remarkable memorial to the Grand Assembly on Feb. 16. It was preceded by a public petition signed by two thousand persons who were described as "men of science, friends of virtue and approved guardians of their country"; and though a counter-petition followed with more than three thousand names, including, it was charged, schoolboys and even negroes, the Dramatic Association clearly had the upper hand in the ensuing battle of arguments. They were backed in the debates by such men as Robert Morris, General Wayne, and George Clymer, and—indirectly—George Washington's avowed fondness for the theatre and the fact that he frequented it just then influenced the vote of the majority, who, generally speaking, will follow an

energetic and clear-minded minority, if it only be persistent enough.   After ten years of. skirmishing a bill
to repeal the anti-theatre act of 1778 was made a law on
March 2, 1789, and a week later the Southwark theatre
was opened "by authority" as a theatre.   It matters
little that now troubles of a different kind began, that
the friends of Hallam and Henry commenced to find
fault with them, that they were censured for allowing
smoking in their theatre, that the price of tickets—
box 7/ 6*d.*, gallery 3/ 9*d.*—was considered too high, that
the performances were unfairly criticized as not being
equal to the very latest in London.   The main object
had been accomplished, the battle for tolerance of art
for art's sake had been won at last.

The history of opera in America during those years is
so clearly a part of the history of the Old American
Company that a local treatment of the subject may
conveniently be disregarded.   By this time the regular
circuit Philadelphia-New York-Baltimore, and, as a
more negligible quantity, Annapolis, had been established.
Suffice it to say that the Company, after leaving Philadelphia, performed from the middle of February until the
middle of June, 1787, at New York, then returned to
Philadelphia, began a summer season at Baltimore the
end of August, went to Annapolis for the races in October,
appeared at Baltimore in November, and then made its
way to New York.   There the winter season began in
December and lasted until the end of May, 1788.   It
was followed until November by the ludicrous 'Spectaculum Vitæ' mummery at the Southwark Theatre
in Philadelphia, interrupted by a journey to Baltimore
in August and September.   On March 9, 1789, the Old
Americans began their first season under the wings of
law at Philadelphia.   These performances "by authority"
lasted three weeks, and then the John Street Theatre in
New York was reopened from April until Dec. 15, 1789,
and was made the scene of many a brilliant gathering,

Table A

TITLE OF OPERA	PHILADELPHIA						NEW YORK					
	1787	1788	1789	1790	1791	1792	1787	1788	1789	1790	1791	1792
Aesop in the Shades (farce, turned into an "entertainment of music")	Feb. 1											
Agreeable Surprise (Arnold, 1781)	Jan. 27, 30			July 7					Oct. 8			
Banditti (Arnold, 1781; became in 1782 'Castle of Andalusia')		Nov. 5, 10		June 28 / July 1								
Belle Dorothée (pant.)								April 21				Feb. 17
Bird Catcher (pant.)												March 9
Birth of Harlequin (pant.)					July 7, 11	May 28						April 27
Columbine Invisible (pant.)						June 9, 13						Feb. 24
Cymon and Sylvia; or, Love and Magic (M. Arne's 'Cymon,' 1767)				May 20 / June 7				Nov. 27	Nov. 27, 30			Feb. 14
Darby and Patrick (=Poor Soldier)												
Darby's Return				June 14	June 6				Nov. 24 / Dec. 15			
Dead Alive (Arnold, 1781)				Feb. 19 / March 13	Jan. 26 / May 9						Nov. 23	
Deserter (Dibdin, 1773)	July 11			July 19	May 9 / June 27, 30		June 8, 9	Jan. 16, 21 / Feb. 1			Oct. 26	
Detection; or, Servants' Hall in an Uproar	July 10											
Devil to Pay				May 10							Oct. 28	
Duenna (Linley, 1775)	July 3, 7			June 10, 17			June 1	March 3 / June 26 / Dec. 4	June 26 / Dec. 2		Nov. 7	
Dutchman; or, The Merry Girl (ballet)												
Elopement (pant.)						June 7	May 31					
Fairies; or, Daphne and Amyntor (J. Chr. Smith?)							May 16					
Flitch of Bacon (Shield, 1778)	Feb. 3						Feb. 16					
Flora				Dec. 29	Jan. 7, 29						Oct. 14 / Dec. 25, 26	
Fourth of July; or, The Sailor's Festival (pant.)		July 4, 21										
Harlequin Balloonist (pant.)												
Harlequin protected by Cupid; or, The Enchanted Nosegay (pant.)												May 3
Inkle and Yarico (Arnold, 1787)				May 17	April 27 / June 23	June 5			July 6 / Sept. 14			
King of Genii (pant.)												
Lionel and Clarissa (see Modern Love)												
Lord of the Manor (Jackson, 1780)												Feb. 29
Love in a Camp; or, Patrick in Prussia (Shield, 1786)	July 5, 10		March 25		Feb. 24 / April 6		April 9, 13 / May 9				Oct. 19	Jan. 2 / April 16
Love in a Village	Jan. 31 / Feb. 1 / June 27, 29				(date ?) / Feb. 10	June 25		May 12	Oct. 30			
Madcap		July 2	April 2					Feb. 6				
Magician of the Cave; or Harlequin's Frolic (pant.)							April 20, 23 / April 27	Feb. 11, 18, 27				
Maid of the Mill		July 21		May 20 / June 7		June 18	May 16	Jan. 18 / May 31				
May-day in Town; or, New York in an Uproar (based on Arne's 'May Day,' 1775)							May 18		Nov. 9			
Midas	Jan. 29 / Feb. 2						March 6 / April 16					
Mock Doctor	July 28	June 25									Nov. 14 / Dec. 16	
Modern Love; or, Generosity Rewarded (altered from Dibdin's 'Lionel and Clarissa')				June 1		June 18						
Neptune and Amphitrite (masque)	July 14			April 24	Feb. 2			Feb. 15				
Old Soldier ("hist. pant.")											Nov. 21 / Dec. 7	Feb. 15
Orpheus and Eurydice (pant.) (based on pasticcio from Gluck, etc., 1785?)		Nov. 1										
Padlock	Jan. 26 / Feb. 3 / Aug. 4	July 7	Mar. 13 / April 3	May 13	Feb. 4 / Feb. 9 / June 17	June 28	Mar. 14, 30 / April 30	Jan. 28 / April 11				Jan. 28 / Feb. 6 / March 12
Patie and Roger; or, The Gentle Shepherd												
Peep Behind the Curtain (with burletta 'Orpheus and Eurydice,' Barthélemon, 1767)												
Poor Soldier	Jan. 23 / Feb. 2 / June 25 / July 11	June 20 / Nov. 12		Jan. 4 / Mar. 1 / April 14 / May 5 / Dec. 13	Jan. 5 / Feb. 27 / April 5 / May 12	June 28	Feb. 14, 19, 21, 28 / Mar. 13, 16, 21, 28 / Apr. 18 / May 4, 14 / June 4 / Dec. 24, 31	May 5	May 6, 18 / May 30 / Sept. 28			Mar. 2, 5 / April 21, 30
Restoration of Harlequin (pant.)												Feb. 13
Return of the Laborers (pant.)						June 28						
Rival Candidates (Carter, 1775)					June 13, 16				June 4, 22			
Rosina (Shield)	Jan. 19, 24 / Jan. 29			Apr. 16	Jan. 17, 19 / June 6		Mar. 1	April 24				Mar. 19 / May 6
Selima and Azor; or, The Power of Enchantment (Grétry-Linley, 1776)	July 28			March 26	May 16, 19							
Thomas and Sally					June 2			Mar. 10				Mar. 5
True Blue (based on Carey's 'Nancy' of 1739)								Apr. 24, 28 / May 5, 31				
Two Misers					Apr. 9, 12 / Apr. 15 / May 5							Feb. 3 / Mar. 14 / May 14
Two Philosophers (ballet)												
Wood Cutters (ballet, based on Philidor's 'Le Bûcheron,' 1763)												Feb. 10

as New York was now the seat of government with our first, and theatre-going, President in her midst.

From January, 1790, until the middle of July, 1791, with an interruption during the summer of 1790, Philadelphia monopolized the Old Americans. They again played at the John Street Theatre in New York from October, 1791, to May, 1792. When the company reappeared at Philadelphia in September, 1792, its personnel differed considerably. This reorganization, together with the signs of birth of Wignell and Reinagle's rival company, properly inaugurates a new chapter in the history of opera in America.

During the six years preceding the reorganization the following works received a hearing by the Old Americans. [See *Table A*.]

Fifty different operas, musical farces, pantomimes and ballads performed "with the original overture and accompaniments" (as the term went), and the list does not pretend to be absolutely complete! By tracing more carefully pantomimes like Sheridan's 'Robinson Crusoe' and the inexhaustible supply of harlequinades, the list could easily be swelled to sixty different works. This minuteness of detail may properly be left to local historians. They will also have a not very fascinating opportunity for giving the absolutely correct dates of performance, if they are able to do so. It should not be forgotten that usually only three performances a week took place, sometimes less, and that postponements and changes of the bill were frequent. For these reasons no two historians will ever give exactly the same dates or numbers of performances, and those they give will sometimes conflict, as may be proved by a comparison of my statistics with those in Seilhamer. But, after all, these statistics are of minor importance. Allowing for unavoidable inaccuracy and omissions, for which in part the state of preservation of the contemporary sources is to be held responsible, one very important and interesting historical fact stands out in bold relief, the fact that the Old American Company had in its repertory, besides an equal number of tragedies, comedies and farces, between fifty and sixty musical entertainments, and these mostly novelties! This amazing activity opens a wide field for suggestion and comparison. In the first place, it proves that together with our early concert enterprises, which in many respects depended on the vocalists and instrumentalists in the theatrical companies, opera, metaphorically speaking, filled our principal cities with music and to an extent which cities of similar size do not possess to-day. If we turn to New York with her five million inhabitants, it is true enough that the quality of the repertory has improved immensely. In quantity, even New York has not fulfilled the promises of the eighteenth century, and in character her operatic life with its polyglot tendency is very much more of a hot-house product than in olden times. The excellence of the performances must not obstruct the historical view of the problem—and it is a vital problem for the future of our musical life. Why, then, this contrast in conditions, in the fundamental attitude towards opera, why this change of front in the current of evolution? For the historian, I believe, the answer is simple enough, and anybody with an open mind, not biassed by local pride, will perceive where the evils common to our nation's musical life in general have their root, but, be it hoped, an artificial and destructible root.

I can hardly be expected to go into details covering all the works enumerated. Nor would this be an easy task, as the attempt would be handicapped by the lamentable lack of anything like an adequate and comprehensive history of English opera. For instance, I confess my inability to trace, without a loss of time quite out of proportion to the results possibly to be obtained, several of the operas enumerated. In part this may be due to the fact that our American managers, as in the case of 'Darby and Patrick,' sometimes rechristened their English importations. 'The Banditti' is another case in point. Nobody would suspect, without seeing the cast, that this was "taken" from Samuel Arnold's 'Castle of Andalusia,' first performed at London in 1781, or that 'Modern Love' was identical with 'Lionel and Clarissa,' or that 'True Blue' was a ballad-farce based on Carey's 'Nancy.' In this skit the Americanization was carried so far as to treat the audience to a scene of the Battery in New York. On the other hand, if the music to Royall Tyler's libretto 'May Day in Town; or, New York in an Uproar,' was "compiled from the most eminent masters with an overture and accompaniments," it must not be supposed that this procedure was characteristic of primitive conditions in America. Such pasticcios were quite the rage and the proper thing in England. Not that the English composers lacked sufficient ideas—it must be insisted that they were men of considerable talent, and an English historian will not find it very difficult to do his countrymen full justice in this respect in a comprehensive work, which does not yet exist—but the powerful influence of the Beggar's Opera, the classic among English pasticcios, was still at work. It was part of the *form* of most of such popular operas as Arne's 'Love in a Village,' Arnold's 'Maid of the Mill,' Dibdin's 'Lionel and Clarissa,' that the composers borrowed, not surreptitiously stole like Händel and other master-cleptomaniacs, airs from Italian and even English operas. Indeed, it is very interesting to read in Hogarth how carefully, even in this part of the work, Sheridan laid his plans when he wrote the libretto of 'The Duenna,' the most successful English opera since the 'Beggar's Opera.' That the procedure could be exaggerated to the point where there was madness in the method, and assume the proportions of a veritable pot-pourri, is illustrated by Linley's 'Selima and Azor.' While Grétry's 'Zémire and Azor' formed the basis of this adaptation, the music was plainly announced as "compiled from the Italian, German, French and English operas." To this species of pasticcio 'Orpheus and Eurydice' did not belong. Distinctly called a "burletta," it was a forerunner of Offenbach's 'Orphée aux enfers,' and possibly had been derived from the pantomime of 1740, written by Henry Sommer and composed by J. F. Lampe. There are also indications that the work was identical with the "humorous entertainment" by David Garrick called 'A Peep Behind the Curtain,' as the "burletta" wound up with "a grand dance of shepherds, cows, sheep, goats, trees, etc." At any rate, in the second act of Garrick's play of 1767 there appears 'The burletta of Orpheus,' composed by Barthélemon. Also William Dunlap's 'Darby's Return,' written to order for Thomas Wignell, was intended to raise the loud laugh; and how dangerously near hurting the feelings of George Washington the author came, readers of my article on the musical side of our first President will perhaps remember. In fact, it must be said that the species of comic opera which inundates our modern stage and is turned into a hybrid between legitimate comic opera or operette and legitimate vaudeville—on one occasion this term was actually used—was about to be born. For instance, on Oct. 8, 1789, at New York 'The Agreeable Surprise' was followed by a pantomime finale called 'The Shipwreck,' in which "a real *Air Balloon*" was exhibited. And again on May 12, 1788, at New York, between the play and 'Love in a Camp,' "a grand Fête with a variety of picturesque scenes and decorations" and numerous popular ballads was squeezed in. The whole concluded "with an attack upon a Spanish fort by the Algerian fleet, the arrival of the fleet of Spain, and a general engagement in which the Algerines are totally defeated by fire ships, bombs from the fort, and blowing up their vessels."

These spectacular features, together with the dancing feats of Mr. and Mrs. John Durang and others in the pantomimes, were still harmless as compared with the card Mr. Hallam played when, owing to the absence of his partner Mr. Henry in Europe, the withdrawal from the company of such favorites as Thomas Wignell and Mr. and Mrs. Morris, the death of Mrs. Harper (Oct. 3, 1791), and other setbacks, he found himself in January, 1792, in somewhat desperate circumstances. It was then that he engaged "Monsieur Placide, first rope dancer to the King of France, and his troop." The arrival of Alexandre Placide at Charleston, S. C., a few weeks previous and his ready acceptance of Hallam's offer must have relieved the latter greatly, because Alexandre Placide, whatever his right to the title of His Most Christian Majesty's first rope dancer might have been, was indeed a European celebrity, having, so the story goes, proved as great an attraction at Sadler's Wells in 1781 as the Vestris were at the Opera House. Hallam had promised this European sensation "for a few nights only," but Placide remained with him for more than a year, and reading the old papers one really gains the impression that Placide was featured as the main attraction of the company. At any rate, the list of performances proves that the repertory was swelled with Placide's grotesque and acrobatic pantomimes to a degree warranted only by circumstances. Yet Placide must have been quite up to his reputation if he could, as announced, "dance with two boys tied to his feet, and after that with two men in the same manner." That Mr. Hallam, who certainly treated his audiences to an otherwise excellent dramatic repertory, believed in thus catering to the vaudeville instinct of the masses, may sincerely be doubted, but the box-office was a power in olden times, too, and furthermore this was still the age of benefit performances for the individual actors. They naturally sought to make their benefits, which began towards the end of the season, as attractive to their admirers and their own pockets as possible. This tendency cannot be more fittingly illustrated than by an announcement of the veteran actor Woolls on July 19, 1791, that "the Indian kings with their chief lately arrived [at Philadelphia] on their way to Congress intend honoring the theatre with their presence this evening," selected for Woolls' benefit.

It is not for the purpose of tying these actors and actresses to the historical whipping-post, but for the sake of personal record and comparison, that the full cast of the Old Americans in Linley's 'Duenna' is given here:

Don Ferdinand	Mr. Harper
Don Antonio	Mr. Woolls
Jerome	Mr. Biddle
Carlos	Mr. Hallam
Isaac Mendoza	Mr. Wignell
Lopez	Mr. Morris
Donna Louisa	Mrs. Morris
Duenna	Mrs. Harper
Donna Clara	Mrs. Henry

Though a cast like this must have filled the *connoisseurs* of days by-gone with thrills of expectation, it means nothing to a later generation, unless we revive the voice of some dead critic whose private opinion coincided with that of the public. Fortunately, reviews of the principal theatrical events were becoming more frequent, and while the art of criticism was then perhaps still in its infancy in our country, the advance notice of a performance of 'The Duenna,' printed in *The Federal Gazette*, Philadelphia, June 16, 1790, possesses at least some historical interest:

On Thursday evening, Mr. Woolls has proposed an entertainment to the public which happily unites all the powers of music with poetry and machinery. The opera of 'The Duenna,' if it is less perfect than 'The School for Scandal,' is, perhaps, more pleasing, as an amiable woman is more agreeable than a mere beauty. The wit of 'The Duenna' is of that pure kind which excites mirth without offending delicacy, or torturing sensibility, and its moral, if not striking, is at least innocent. In this piece, indeed, Mr. Sheridan has shewn the superiority of his genius; for, if it were performed without a song, the language, sentiment, incidents and humour, would still entitle it to the praise of an excellent comedy. But, in adding to these the force of harmony, the author has rescued that species of the drama called opera, from the imputation of insipidity, to which, even in its native Italy, it has hitherto been subject. The combination of wit, poetry and music, the introduction of probable circumstances, and the display of interesting characters are the merits of the author; but those, who have heard Mrs. Henry in the gentle *Clara*, will naturally be led to consider some part of the evening's entertainment as depending on her performance, in which the taste of the actress, is only surpassed by the talents of the singer. In other operas that lady has shown her power in raising the admiration of the judgment, by her skill and execution. The music of the *Duenna* (consisting principally in a fortunate adoption of the best Scotch airs) will afford her an opportunity of captivating the heart, by that melody, which is indeed "the food of love," or, with a more melancholy cadence, chaunts the lamentable tale of 'Old Robin Gray.'

While the curtain is falling on this chapter of opera in America, a few passing remarks may be made on Peter Markoe's ill-fated 'The Reconciliation; or, The Triumph of Nature. A comic opera in two acts,' Philadelphia, 1790. Strictly speaking, this was a libretto for a ballad-opera founded on Gessner's 'Erastus.' Ill-fated it was because, like Andrew Barton's 'The Disappointment,' it was accepted by the Old American Company but not performed. I have given the history of Markoe's case, a description of his work and a quotation from the "impartial review" in the *Universal Asylum* in my study on 'Early American Operas' (Sammelbände der I. M. G.), and content myself here with the opinion that the fate of Peter Markoe's 'Reconciliation' was at least a trifle more enviable than that of ambitious American operas of our own time which are not even accepted for performance.

2. *The End of the Century* : 1793-1800

In the preceding chapter it was stated that the troubles of the Old American Company were only beginning when the Thespians won their decisive victory over the Philistines, for now the friends of the drama could turn, as it were, from foreign to domestic politics. Nothing that the managers did, seemed to satisfy them. As a matter of fact, their forces really had been crippled, the Southwark Theatre was accessible only through unpaved streets, it was unbearably hot during the summer season, so much so that after all kinds of ventilating experiments in 1791, "the public was respectfully informed that in order to render the House as cool as possible, in addition to the wind sail: fire engines will, during the afternoon, be kept constantly playing on the roof and walls of the theatre"—these and the well-known fact that negotiations were pending for the erection of a new theatre in Chestnut Street which would outclass the Southwark theatre, made improvements, at least in the personnel of the Old Americans, obviously imperative. Accordingly, John Henry set sail for Europe. When he returned in 1792, after a half-year's absence, he brought with him a company which was far above mediocrity. The career of his recruits has been so carefully traced by several historians that the briefest possible remarks will be sufficient to introduce the principal new members to the reader. Before doing so, one general observation is necessary. English operas were then still practically plays interspersed with music. The dialogue was spoken. Consequently, these operas called for good actors, perhaps more than the grand operas with their recitative in which superior musical abilities might cover

84

No song no Supper.

W. Barr Del.   C. Tiebout Sculp.

Mr. HODGKINSON as ROBIN

We sing a little and laugh a little
And work a little and swear a little
And fiddle a little and foot it a little
And swig the flowing Can

JOHN HODGKINSON (1767-1805)
(From the collections of Mr. Robert Gould Shaw, Boston)

histrionic shortcomings. This has led to the fallacy
that the interpreters of English opera were merely good
actors with tolerable but untrained voices. In individual
cases this may have been true, but it does not apply,
I think, to the majority of the stars in English opera.
Contemporary accounts do not permit of the fallacy just
alluded to, and the burden of proof rests with those who
do not concede the well-balanced combination of histrionic
and musical training in the English actor-singers of
those days.

The brightest star in the new firmament was un-
questionably John Hodgkinson. Though only twenty-
six years of age when engaged by Mr. Henry, Hodgkinson
—whose real name was Meadowcraft—had lived a busy,
successful and, to put it mildly, romantic life. He was
playing an engagement at Bath and was about to invade
London when Henry captured him for America. All
accounts agree that Hodgkinson possessed a phenomenal
memory and an equally phenomenal versatility as
tragedian, comedian and vocalist. With these character-
istics he combined exceptional powers of interpretation,
and probably his biographer Carpenter did not exaggerate
much when he dubbed him the provincial Garrick.
But Hodgkinson was also incurably vain and, as Dunlap
put it, "his ambition for play-house applause was in-
ordinate, and he was as rapacious for characters as
Bonaparte has since been for kingdoms." Owing to this
Napoleonic tendency, the history of the Old American
Company soon became one of grumbling, discontent,
strife, and worse things. First, Hodgkinson succeeded
in 1794, with the connivance of Lewis Hallam, whose
maxim was to "divide and govern," in driving John
Henry from the active management of the company,
putting himself in his place; but the firm of Hallam and
Hodgkinson, with such a *par nobile fratrum* at the head,
could not possibly live long. Napoleon Hodgkinson and
Odysseus Hallam immediately began to quarrel, with

the result that in 1796 Hallam resigned as manager and
continued with the company as a mere salaried actor.
Fortunately, in the same year, William Dunlap, the
dramatist and historian, had been admitted into the
partnership, and he endeavored with more or less success
to counteract the results of Hodgkinson's pranks and
frolics as a manager. This partnership lasted exactly
two years. Then Hodgkinson, whatever his reasons
were, followed the example set by Lewis Hallam and
returned, with occasional relapses into his hobby of mis-
managing companies, to the ranks of the players.
Neither his failure as a manager, nor his utter lack of
tact, seriously interfered with his popularity as an actor.
He was idolized in almost every part in drama and opera
which he essayed. His career came to an untimely end
when he died at Washington of yellow fever in 1805. "No
succeeding performer," says Mr. Ireland, "has ever enjoyed an equal reputation for versatility and general
merit, and in many characters of comedy, both high
and low, he excelled every contemporary."

Next in consequence among Henry's recruits was
Miss Brett, whom Hodgkinson described as second only
to Mrs. Billington as a singer, reason enough to marry
her after some unsavory preliminaries after their arrival
in America. Mrs. Hodgkinson's "forte was opera,"
and "her voice, both in speaking and singing, was powerful and sweet," says Dunlap. Until her death—she died
at New York of consumption in 1803—she remained the
favorite *soubrette*. Had she not been the young, beautiful
and exemplary wife of John, who pushed her systematically to the front, undoubtedly Mrs. Pownall would have
reigned supreme as the operatic star of the Old Americans,
for she was none other than the celebrated Mrs. Wrighten
of Drury Lane. Though she had passed her prime when
she reached our shores, our people had never before
come into contact with a vocalist of finer artistic fibre,
who at the same time was a really great actress. To

Mrs HODGKINSON

in the Character of

CORA.

Publish'd for the German Theatre
by Wm Dunlap.

MRS. JOHN HODGKINSON (Miss Arabella Brett)
(d. 1803)

this must be added a generous and sympathetic character; and it is not at all surprising that the elopement of one of her daughters with Alexandre Placide, the pantomimist, proved so great a shock to her pride that she died of a broken heart at Charleston, S. C., in 1796.

Instead of repeating the twice-told tales of the other members of the company, less important, of course, but all capable, I give a typical cast to show the strength and distribution of the company in opera. It is the one of 'The Maid of the Mill' as performed at New York in the first season after the reorganization:

Lord Ainsworth	Mr. Hodgkinson
Sir Harry Sycamore	Mr. Prigmore
Mervyn	Mr. West
Fairfield	Mr. Ashton
Giles	Mr. Woolls
Ralph	Mr. Hallam
Lady Sycamore	Mrs. Hamilton
Fanny	Mrs. Kenna
Theodosia	Mrs. Hallam
Patty	Mrs. Pownall

The changes in the personnel of the orchestra were due, naturally, less to recruiting trips to Europe than to an adaptation to local conditions. As New York became the main battlefield of the Old Americans after their reorganization, logically the orchestral forces were principally selected from resident musicians. By the way of inference we may argue that the "principal performers" who appeared on the local concert-stage, also formed the backbone of the theatre orchestra. That it had not increased materially in numbers since John Bentley's time is almost certain. I should have to content myself with the rather vague statement that it was just like other provincial orchestras of the time, perhaps better, had not Mr. Ireland mentioned its members by name when speaking of the opening of the Park theatre in 1798. He says: "Mr. Hewitt, leader of the orchestra, which consisted of Messrs. Pellesier, Gilfert, Everdell, Nicolai, Samo, Ulschoeffer, Henri, Lilrecheki [*recte* Libeschesky], Dupuy, Nicolai, jr., Adet, Hoffman and Dangle."

In all, fourteen musicians, who cost the management $140 a week, or approximately ten per cent. of the entire expenses. Occasionally a few performers might have been added, but it is questionable if the orchestra ever contained more than twenty musicians. At any rate, as late as about 1822, fewer than this number appear in a picture of the interior of the Park Theatre, preserved by the New York Historical Society, when the veteran George Gillingham was leader. The musicians mentioned by Mr. Ireland, however, are exactly those whom one would expect to find in a good theatre orchestra if confronted with those frequently mentioned in old concert programs. At least two may with safety be recorded as men of real merit, measured by any standard: James Hewitt and (as I prefer to give the name spelled in many different ways) Victor Pelissier, horn virtuoso and, together with Hewitt, the accredited composer and arranger of the Old American Company.

This indulgence in personalities has a pertinent historical reason. Quite apart from the desire to perpetuate their memory it is the necessity, in the face of previous historical impressions, to insist by all possible means on the fact that not only a great number of operas were made familiar to American audiences, but also that they were well given and that the performances, from the very nature and career of the performers, could bear comparison with those in England, with the possible exception of London. This will become all the more clear, with very obvious inferences, when the company formed by Wignell and Reinagle in competition with the Old Americans passes review.

After its reorganization the Old American Company first proceeded to Philadelphia, and did not present itself at the John Street Theatre in New York until Jan. 28,

Mrs. WRIGHTEN as Fatima in CYMON.

Tax my Tongue, it is a Shame?

Song 1029

Published by J Bew Dec 1 1778

MRS. A. M. POWNALL (Mrs. Wrighten) (d. 1796)
(From "The Vocal Magazine," 1778)

1793. The season lasted into June. The theatre was reopened in November, and closed the end of June, 1794. The players returned in the middle of December for a similar period. The yellow-fever epidemic at New York during the fall of 1795 caused the company to flee to Boston; they did not return to their New York home until February, 1796, when they again played until the end of June. After a recess of about three months the John Street Theatre was occupied by Hallam, Hodgkinson and Dunlap from the end of September, 1796, for the usual season. During the summer and fall of 1797 the company visited Newport and Boston, awaiting with anxiety the completion of their new center of activities, the Park Theatre at New York; but on their return it was not quite ready for occupancy, and the John Street Theatre was therefore reopened from December 11, 1797, until January 13, 1798. This was to be the last performance on the boards of the good old John Street temple of dramatic art, then looking back on a more or less glorious career of thirty years.

Wignell and Reinagle, not satisfied with building their Chestnut Street Theatre in Philadelphia, entertained plans of boldly invading the sphere of interest of their New York rivals. They must have succeeded in interesting some monied persons in this scheme, as the *Daily Advertiser* of Jan. 14, 1793, contains the announcement of a meeting of the subscribers to Wignell and Reinagle's "New Theatre in this City." For some reason the Philadelphians dropped their plan. Yet the mere suggestion of a possible rival must have put Hallam and Henry on their guard, and actually in the following year advertisements appeared in the papers showing that Hallam and Henry hurried to take the wind out of the sails of their opponents by also proposing a new theatre. Committees were appointed, and they reported that no place was found "so eligible as where the present theatre stands." In other words, a stock company was to be formed to tear the John Street Theatre down and build a new one on the same spot. This plan, too, failed, and gradually a proposition to erect a theatre in Park Row assumed tangible shape. This, the Park Theatre, was thus first projected in 1795 and the plans for its construction were originally furnished by Marc Isambard Brunel, the celebrated French engineer; but as carried out they lost much of their intended splendor, and were revised beyond recognition in 1806 by Mr. Holland. Well adapted for its purpose, substantial but plain and barn-like of exterior, the Park Theatre was erected at an estimated cost of $42,375, but the actual cost, Mr. Ireland claims, amounted to more than $130,000. It should have been ready for occupancy in October, 1797, but could not be opened—and then in an unfinished state—until Jan. 29, 1798. The Park Theatre enjoyed a theatrical career of exactly fifty years. It was destroyed in by fire 1848.[1]

From 1793 until the season of 1799–1800 closed, the following operas, pantomimes and kindred works were performed by the Old Americans, first at the John Street and then at the Park Theatre. [See *Table B*.]

In eight years, more than one hundred and twenty musical dramas, operas, musical entertainments, musical farces, ballad-operas, speaking pantomimes, ballets, or whatever other names was bestowed upon the dramatic music of the age! And besides hearing the operas that had runs of upwards of one hundred nights at London and sometimes, as it were, by return mail, New Yorkers were deluged with the favorite songs from these and other operas at the concerts where the opera-stars reigned supreme as vocalists. In order not to become tiresome with my theories on early music in America, I ask the

[1]But *see* "Chapters of Opera" (1908) by Mr. Krehbiel, who says: "At the close of the season of 1820, the Park Theatre was destroyed by fire . . . . On its site was erected the new Park Theatre, which was the original [New York] home of Italian opera, performed in its original tongue, and in the Italian manner. . ." Of this *old* new Park Theatre destroyed by fire in 1848, Mr. Krehbiel has a façade view in his book.

reader to draw his or her own inferences from this chronological record which, though carefully extracted from a voluminous mass of notes, does not pretend to be infallible or beyond the possibility of additional works and dates of performance.

The repertory quoted is full of suggestions in several ways. In the first place it will be noticed that some French works had crept in, but I prefer to draw attention to this new branch on our tree of operatic knowledge in the finale of my monograph. Then, we moderns are somewhat puzzled by the great importance attached to the pantomimes. Strictly speaking, many of them were not real pantomimes but, to use the hybrid term of the age, "speaking" pantomimes. How far the English pantomime writers and composers learned their lesson from the French this is hardly the place to discuss. Exaggerating a trifle, it might be said that the genuinely French opera grew out of such "speaking pantomimes" and—now exaggerating still more—it might even be said that the *grand* opera à la Meyerbeer was merely the degenerate historical descendant of the old French speaking pantomimes and ballets. Lully and Rameau proved the artistic possibilities of the genre in practice and men like Noverre in theory, and the nineteenth century witnessed a nation's pride centered in the beautiful dramatic ballets of a master, namely the sadly neglected grand old man of Denmark, Johann Peter Emil Hartmann. In fact, the speaking pantomimes or ballets with their mixture of *all* the arts came, in theory at least, very near being a *Gesamtkunstwerk* in the sense of Wagner and his predecessors. Indeed, the English speaking pantomimes, leaving aside the harlequinades, a by-product the world over in those days, not infrequently impress us as deserving the name of opera more than the works which created a furore on the English stage under the name of musical dramas, operas, and what not. In our country, the dramatic features of the pantomimes soon seem to have been driven to the background for the display of what had become their strong and at the same time their weak points, "dancing, machinery, scenery and dresses." This tendency does not appear to have been exposed in the earlier importations. The juxtaposition of the announcements of two grand pantomimes will make this clear. Taking Gluck's 'Don Juan' ballet as the musical starting-point, Mr. Delphini had "composed" (that is, written) a tragic pantomimical entertainment in two acts, and William Reeve had weeded out some of Gluck's music and planted "songs, duets and choruses" of his own composition in the score, which was thus brought out with Mr. Dixon's scenery at London in 1787. As 'Don Juan; or, the Libertine Destroyed,' we know how popular the pasticcio became in our country after 1793; and here is an announcement of 'Don Juan' in the American Minerva, Feb. 27, 1796:

> On Saturday evening the 27th . . . the grand pantomime of *Don Juan;* or, the Libertine destroyed, with all the music, songs, dances, etc., etc.
>
> | | |
> |---|---|
> | Don Juan . . . . . | Mr. Hodgkinson |
> | Don Guzman (the Commandant) . . . . | Mr. Hallam |
> | Don Ferdinand . . . | Mr. Tyler |
> | Pedro . . . . . | Mr. Durang |
> | Villagers . . . . | Messrs. King, Munto, Cleveland, Hallam, jr., etc. |
> | Alguazales . . . . | Messrs. Woolls, Johnson, Roberts, etc. |
> | Sailors . . . . | Messrs. Lee, Durang, Des Moulins, etc. |
> | Furies . . . . | Messrs. Leonard, M'Knight, etc. |
> | Scaramouch . . . . | Mr. Jefferson |
> | Confidante . . . . | Mrs. Brett |
> | Banqueting ladies . . | Mrs. Hodgkinson, Mrs. Munto, Mrs. Tyler, Mrs. King, Mrs. Tompkins, etc. |
> | Village lasses . . . | Mrs. Hallam, Mrs. Durang, Mrs. Cleveland, etc. |

FIRST PARK THEATRE

Facsimilie of an etching in the New York Historical Society Library

Cottagers . . . . Miss Brett and Miss Broadhurst

Donna Anna . . . Mrs. Gardie

How carefully the dramatis personæ are enumerated in this earlier pantomime! Now the announcement in in the same paper, June 8, 1796:

Never performed here, a splendid National, Historical, Pantomime in 2 acts, called *The Independence of America;* or, the ever memorable 4th of July, 1776.

America . . . . . . Mde. Gardie
Britannia . . . . . Mrs. Cleveland
Goddess of Liberty . . . . Mrs. Hallam
Senator . . . . Mr. Cleveland
1st British Officer . . . . Mr. Munto
2d British Officer . . . . Mr. Lee

Characters in the Pantomime

The General . . . Mr. Tyler
Officer . . . . . Mr. Jefferson
1st Citizen . . . . Mr. Durang
2d Citizen . . . . Mr. Woolls
Messenger from Boston . Mr. Lee
President . . . . Mr. Hallam, jr.
Citizens . . . . Messrs. Roberts, M'Kenzie, etc.
Citizen Soldiers . . . Messrs. Leonard, M'Knight, Jenkins, etc.
Old Woman . . . . Mr. Francesquy.

IN ACT 1st
The principal event that happened on that day.

IN ACT 2d
The Destruction of Despotism. A pastoral dance and verses, sacred to Liberty.
The whole to conclude with *The Declaration of Independence.* And the Rights and Privileges of America; with a Country Dance by the characters. Previous to the Pantomime an Allegorial Prologue. *Vivat Respublica!*

In this American pot-boiler there is already a suspicion of weakening. Still, the center of attraction had not been shifted, but compare the 'Independence of America' with the ludicrously Americanized—I quote the announcement in the New York *Daily Advertiser*, May 19, 1800—show-piece:

The celebrated Dramatic Masque of *Arthur and Emmeline; or, the Prospect of Columbia's Future Glory.* Written originally by Dryden, and from him first altered by Garrick.

The public are respectfully informed that owing to multiplicity of business, the scenery of this Masque was not sufficiently prepared for exhibition on the night the piece was represented; it is now compleat, and consists of the following new and splendid decorations:

ACT 1st

A Gothic temple, being a place of Heathen worship; the three Saxon Gods placed on pedestals, Woden, Thor, and Friga.

2d. A camp by moonlight, and an elegant pavillion.

ACT 2d

1st. The descent in a cloud of the Spirit of Light.

2d. The *Enchanted Wood*, in which a tree being struck by Arthur spouts blood. The Golden Bridge.

To conclude with an

Allegorical procession of figures. By which Merlin, the British enchanter, displays to King Arthur the progress of the American nation, from its infancy to its present power and a prophetic view of Future Glory.

INDIAN MUSIC

1. American wilderness
2. Indians in canoes

SPANISH MUSIC

3. Columbus and Spanish ships

BRITISH MARCH

4. European settlement
5. Commercial settlements
6. A City
7. British soldiers
8. A storm expressive of disunion

WASHINGTON'S MARCH

9. Figure of Washington
10. American soldiers
11. Figure of Liberty

JAMES HEWITT (1770-1827)
(From a portrait in possession of the family)

PRESIDENT'S MARCH
12. Federal Constitution
13. American Navy
To conclude with a song and chorus.

This certainly was a bona fide pantomime of the Hippodrome brand, and both Dryden and Garrick would have shuddered at the atrocious taste displayed in this *masque*, which was merely a more learned and dignified title for pantomime.

Evidently, anti-esthetic tendencies were here at work in the name of a public daily craving more and more for sensational *frissons*, and how viciously the managers would confuse the already muddled terminology of the different genres of dramatic music may fittingly be illustrated by an announcement in the *New York Gazette*, June 1, 1799:

. . . . never performed here, a play in three acts, interspersed with music, written by Harriet Lee, called *"The Mysterious Marriage; or, the Heirship of Roselva."*
Scene 1. The Entrance and distant view of the castle of Roselva. In act 1. A grand chorus of hunters, returning from the chase. End of act 1. A procession of the domestics of the Count, a grand march, with an accompaniment of Cymbals, Drums, etc., by Turkish slaves—they are met by the retinue of Lord Albert, and the procession enters the castle. In act 3. Distant chorus of peasants over the grave of Constantia. Scene, the chapel of the castle, a view of the altar, and the tomb of Constantia hung with garlands of flowers. Chorus of peasants in honor of their victory over the Turks.—Procession of soldiers, peasants and Turkish captives in chains.—Scene the last. Glee and Full chorus by peasants and soldiers over the body of the Count. They drop their banners and invert their spears, while the curtain falls to slow music.
The music and accompaniments composed by Mr. Hewitt.

The Biographia Dramatica, this vast storehouse of entertaining information, claims that the 'Mysterious

Marriage' was never acted; this may be true as far as England is concerned, but the play certainly was performed in America, though in a manner to destroy the dividing lines between play, opera and pantomime. But the climax of the esthetic confusion is reached with the announcement in the *New York Daily Advertiser*, July 4, 1799, of

> . . . . a splendid, allegorical, musical drama, never exhibited, called "*The Fourth of July;* or, Temple of American Independence." In which will be displayed (among other scenery, professedly intended to exceed any exhibition yet presented by the theatre) a view of the lower part of Broadway, Battery, harbor and shipping, taken on the spot.
>
> After the Shipping shall have saluted, a military procession in perspective will take place, consisting of all the uniform companies of the city, horse, artillery and infantry in their respective places, according to the order of the march. The whole to conclude with an inside view of 'The Temple of Independence' as exhibited on the birthday of Gen. Washington. Scenery and machinery by Mr. Ciceri.—Music by Mr. Pelesier.

This patriotic speaking pantomime was called "a splendid, allegorical musical drama"! However, all this happened at the end of the century, when suddenly a temporary anticlimax in musical taste generally appears to have set in. Until then, and on the whole, such aberrations were sporadic, and in their more serious efforts American authors strove to continue in the vein of O'Keefe, Colman, Prince Hoare, Sheridan, and their musical *Dioscuri* Dibdin, Linley, Arnold, Arne, Reeve, Shield, Storace, and others. If they further diluted the blood in this vein, that is but natural, and the clever, attractive works of the Englishmen were Americanized only in so far as Victor Pelissier, Alexander Reinagle, James Hewitt and Benjamin Carr found it necessary to write new orchestral accompaniments or new music for the changes in the librettos adopted for the American stage. I have given a fairly complete list of such rearrangements in my study on 'Early American

Operas' and, to repeat it, have there described with sufficient minuteness the more serious, original American operas by these and other Americanized composers.

To these serious efforts 'Needs must; or, the Ballad Singers' did not belong. It merely served for the reappearance of Mrs. Pownall, who had broken a leg and was still on crutches when the skit was made public. Apparently the plot had been so concocted by Mrs. Anne Julia Hatton as to allow Mrs. Pownall to sing favorite ballads without moving about the stage. Nor was John Hodgkinson's 'The Launch; or, Huzza for the Constitution' of much account. It was a patriotic trifle in honor of "the Frigate Constitution breasting the curled surge," and in an advance notice on Sept. 13, 1797, in the *Columbian Centinel* of Boston, when the piece was first performed there, it is said to contain a great diversity of national character, and incidental song. "The idea is novel, the occasion happy." Hodgkinson also appeared in his rôle as author, for which Dunlap concedes him extremely little talent, in 'The Purse; or, American Tar.' His reasons for bestowing "alterations and additions" on Cross's 'The Purse; or, Benevolent Tar,' set to music by William Reeve, do not appear.

One of Hodgkinson's first contributions to literature was his prologue to Mrs. Anne Julia Hatton's "serious opera," 'Tammany; or, the Indian chief,' with music by James Hewitt. Only the lyrics of the libretto seem to have been preserved, and if the whole book revelled in equally impossible flights of poetic imagination the loss is not to be regretted. This serious opera was taken seriously only by the Anti-Federalists, and one critic insisted that Hallam and Henry had put it on the stage only because the powerful Tammany Society so decreed, being of the opinion that it was "one of the finest things of its kind ever seen. " The *New York Magazine*, on the other hand, called it "that wretched thing," and William

Dunlap, a Federalist, dubbed it "literally a melange of bombast." He was not quite so severely outspoken on the merits of his own productions. For instance, of his opera 'Sterne's Maria; or, the Vintage,' for which Victor Pelissier composed the music, he remarks in his History of the American Theatre: "The piece pleased and was pleasing, but not sufficiently attractive or popular to keep the stage after the original performers in it were removed by those fluctuations common in theatrical establishments." In his operatic version of Kotzebue's "Der Wildfang," under the misleading title of "The Wild-goose Chase," he seems to have taken greater pride, for he made desperate efforts to save it from speedy oblivion. First brought out in four acts, Dunlap cut it down in Feb., 1800, to three; and when this amputation did not prove satisfactory he compressed it in December, 1800, into only two acts. How James Hewitt, his musical collaborator, liked these surgical operations, which, of course, must have affected his share in the work, we are not told, nor am I even in a position to criticize his music, as the "favorite songs" published in February, 1800, in Joseph Carr's *Musical Journal* have not yet come to my notice.

Without doubt Dunlap's most ambitious contribution to opera-lore was his 'Archers; or, the Mountaineers of Switzerland,' received at New York "with unbounded applause," of which Benjamin Carr, the composer, received his full share. It is one of the blemishes in Seil-hamer's History that his antagonism to Dunlap led him to treat this work with superficiality and contempt. 'The Archers' deserves neither. In the essay on "Early American Operas" I have summed up my impression of the libretto as follows:

. . . Dunlap was not a master-poet, but merely a dramatically gifted stage manager. However, it would be unjust to deny 'The Archers' some forcible monologues and skilfully contrasted scenes in which the mongrel form of English opera is well kept in mind.

SONG IN BENJAMIN CARR'S OPERA "THE ARCHERS," 1796

It would also be unjust to condemn Dunlap where his version differs from Schiller's later masterwork merely because it differs . .
For instance, no esthetic objection can be raised against Dunlap's endeavors to picture Tell as an active 'politician,' or to keep Tell's wife more in the foreground than Schiller did.

Dunlap falls short less in such details than in his arid lyrics and in the general aspect of the play. The Tell story is bound to be the theme for a serious drama, and no theme is less appropriate for a comic opera, as the story contains no comic elements whatsoever. If therefore an author stoops to make of it a comic opera, he will be forced to use violence. This Dunlap has done, and this combination of heterogenous elements has been futile; the more so, as the comic scenes decidedly smack of low comedy.

Of Benjamin Carr, as the predecessor of Rossini, very little can be said, because the music seems to be lost except the dainty Rondo from the overture published in No. 7 of Joseph Carr's *Musical Miscellany* in 1813 and the song "Why, huntress, why," published by B. Carr about 1800 in his "Musical Journal." The original cast of 'The Archers'—a comparison with Schiller's dramatis personæ will prove instructive—was this:

William Tell, Burger of Altdorf, Canton of Uri	Mr. Hodgkinson
Walter Furst, of Uri . .	Mr. Johnson
Werner Staffach, of Schweitz .	Mr. Hallam, jun.
Arnold Melchthal, of Unter-walden	Mr. Tyler
Gesler, Austrian Governor of Uri	Mr. Cleveland
Lieutenant to Gesler . . .	Mr. Jefferson
Burgomaster of Altdorf . .	Mr. Prigmore
Conrad, a seller of wooden ware, in Altdorf	Mr. Hallam
Leopold, Duke of Austria .	Mr. King
Bowmen	Messrs. Lee, Durang, etc.
Pikemen	Messrs. Munto, Tomkins, etc.
Burghers	Messrs. Des Moulins, Woolls, etc.
Portia, Tell's wife . . .	Mrs. Melmoth
Rhodolpha, Walter Furst's daughter	Miss Broadhurst

Cecily, a basket woman . . Mrs. Hodgkinson
Boy, Tell's . . . . . Miss Harding
Maidens of Uri . . . . Madame Gardie, Madame
Val, Miss Brett, etc.

Whatever may be the defects of Dunlap's 'Archers,' they were not so self-evident as those of Elihu Hubbard Smith's 'Edwin and Angelina,' accepted in 1794, re-modelled into an opera, and as such performed in 1796 with Victor Pelissier's music for the first and last time. For the lyrics, Mr. Smith availed himself liberally of Goldsmith's own words, but for the rest certainly not of Goldsmith's spirit. The plot, though simple, is full of improbabilities and complicated developments. The language is disagreeably *exalted* and *sublime*, as in so many productions of the Storm and Stress era, and the characters show an impossible mixture of sentimentality and stage-villainy. As for the "opera" 'Edwin and Angelina,' suffice it to remark that the heroes and heroines all come in for their share of the dozen lyrics which protract the dramatic agony, and that the whole winds up with an elaborate but commonplace finale.

These American operas clearly took the English operas for models and therefore contained, if not their virtues, their esthetics defects; though it is perhaps worth noticing that they refrained from the double-entendres to which our people frequently objected in their English favorites. If their dramatic value was not very great, we must not forget that their English models called for similar strictures. The plots in these were often little more than hastily though cleverly constructed vehicles for charming, catchy music set to more or less witty, sentimental and easily remembered Arcadian and Bacchanalian verses. Perhaps it would be unjust to expect light operas and operettas—for such most of these English operas were, after all is said—to comply with all the dramaturgic laws as expounded since Aristotle. On the other hand, it is curious to note that the American

critics of the time were not blind to these defects. Indeed, possessing as one admitted "unscientific ears" for
music, they usually directed really critically attention
towards the literary merits or demerits of the operas
which often sailed under the flag of musical *dramas* and
therefore logically invited criticism as dramas. In the
newspapers of the time no sustained effort was made to
comment critically on the several theatres and their
repertory, dramatic or operatic. This was considered
the province of the magazines, but they, too, only slowly
and tentatively embraced the opportunity to be public
mentors in matters artistic. The most notable step in
this direction was taken by the *New York Magazine*
in the years 1794 and 1795, and a careful perusal of its
Theatrical Register "of every piece played" is indispensable for anybody who wishes to understand the
attitude taken by American audiences, or, at least, by our
literary men towards the dramatic productions of the
time. Incidentally, this Theatrical Register reflects the
impression made by the several members of the Old
American Company; in short, it is a kind of dramatic
mirror for these years. Throughout this book, stray
criticisms are interspersed to keep the reader in touch
not only with the operas and actors but with the public.
Consequently, it is not necessary here to follow step by
step the arguments advanced by the contributors to the
New York Magazine. One quotation will suffice to prove
that our early professional critics had their matter well
in hand and that they did not accept anything and everything in the spirit of ignorant and unprogressive gratitude. I select for my purpose the criticism of Arne's
'Love in a Village' as it appeared in the December
number (1794) of the *New York Magazine:*

The merit of *Love in a Village*, though superior to many of those
heterogenous performances which pass under the indefinite title of
operas, is not of a very distinguished nature. The plots are too numerous, the higher characters destitute of any striking discrimination,

and the piece passes off without leaving upon the mind any distinct and useful impression. We recollect generally, that we have been pleased; but we find a difficulty in determining with what in particular: for these faults we are, however, compensated, in part, by a lively and pleasing dialogue and, occasionally, by just and useful sentiments. This praise cannot be extended to all parts of the play. The two best drawn characters (Hodge and Madge) are a disgustful exhibition of folly and vice; and what adds to their impropriety is the imperfect conclusion of this plot, which might have been rendered eminently moral and important. The character of Hodge is a representation of the detestable villainy which is not restrained to persons of more polished education and which the low and ignorant fail not to imitate and practise. Considered in this view, the character is moral, but the effect is weakened, nay, almost destroyed, by the slight mortification which the wretch receives, while the unfortunate victim of his wickedness is left to shame, misery and the town. We hope the managers will not esteem us too officious if we take this opportunity of recommending to them several omissions in these parts, should this piece be again exhibited. This would be the more agreeable, as the performance is much too long; and the inattention of the audience during the third act, is a strong hint for the suppression of those songs which may be omitted without injury to the opera. Justice Woodcock's song, we are sure, will, on reflection, appear to the managers incompatible with the professions made by one of them to the house last night. This song might be altered very easily, still keeping its characteristic excellence, and expunging its reprehensible expressions. Indeed the whole scene between the justice and Rosetta in the garden, is indelicate in the highest degree, and would be omitted with great advantage to the piece, both in respect to decency and interest. The opera was thus cast:

Young Meadows	Mr. Carr
Hodge	Mr. Hallam
Eustace	Mr. Munto
Justice Woodcock . . .	Mr. Prigmore
Sir W. Meadows . . .	Mr. Richards
Hawthorn	Mr. Hodgkinson
Madge	Mrs. Pownall
Lucinda	Mrs. Solomons
Deborah	Mrs. Hamilton
Rosetta	Mrs. Hodgkinson

Mr. Carr made on this occasion his first appearance on our stage; and we confess, to us a very prepossessing first appearance. Good sense and modesty, united to a perfect knowledge of his profession

BENJAMIN CARR (1769-1831)
(Portrait by J. C. Darley, as in Simpson's "Eminent Philadelphians," 1859)

as a musician, and a pleasing and comprehensive voice are not the only qualifications which this young gentleman possesses for the stage; he speaks with propriety, and we doubt not but practice will make him a good actor, in addition to his being an excellent singer.

Mr. Hallam's Hodge is too well known, and his excellence in this line of acting too generally acknowledged to require our commendation.

Mr. Munto is new to our stage. His person is manly and pleasing. He spoke low, but appeared to us to have a good voice. Eustace is not a character in which we could judge thoroughly of his abilities; not but that superior qualities will make every part, founded on truth, respectable.

We compliment Mr. Prigmore upon his improvement in his old men. Justice Woodcock was a well supported character. Sir William Meadows was a *very well* supported character.

Mr. Hodgkinson's Hawthorn was justly conceived and inimitably executed. The song of "My Molly was the fairest thing" ranks him as a musical performer almost as high as he stands in the higher lines of his profession.

To say that Madge was very well played would not be saying enough, it was extremely well played. As indiscriminate praise is no praise at all, Mrs. Pownall will pardon us if we think that she made use of the word "lingo" to the injury of the author and the effect of a very comic, and otherwise very well delivered speech. The song of "How happy were my days" was exquisitely sung.

We were pleased with Mrs. Solomon's appearance (another candidate)—we were pleased with her speaking generally; but we were very much pleased with her speaking these words, "I was frightened out of my wits lest you should not take the hint," and pronounce her a valuable acquisition to our stage.

Deborah was supported by Mrs. Hamilton in her usual manner, which is always respectable in parts of this cast.

Though last, not least is the charming Rosetta; with voice and power of expression equal to her taste, she never fails to fascinate both eye and ear. Mrs. Hodgkinson adds a propriety of speaking and playing, both serious and comic, with her delightful singing, so as to render her undoubtedly the most generally useful performer on the stage .   .   .   .

Until 1796 the Old American Company practically controlled the amusement field at New York, but in this year Ricketts' Amphitheatre in Broadway "in addition to the great variety of Equestrian exercises and stage performances" added to its attractions such pantomimes as 'The Power of Magic; or, Harlequin everywhere,' and 'Triumph of Virtue; or, Harlequin in New York,' evidently forerunners of the amusing globe-trotting nonsense of the Rogers brothers. Mr. Ricketts soon enriched his entertainments with concert music. His successes emboldened him to open a New Circus in 1797 in Greenwich Street, where he continued with his pantomimic entertainments, among them as novelty 'The Old Soldier.' But his successes also proved to a Mr. Lailson that the circus business was profitable, and this gentleman forthwith erected in the very same street another New Circus, run on still more ambitious lines. He presented, for instance, on Oct. 26, 1797, the heroic pantomime in three acts 'Peter of Provence, and La Belle Maguelone,' on Nov. 2 "a grand tragic-comic pantomime ballet, in 3 acts, never performed here, called 'The New Deserter; or, the Supposed Marriage' . . . . the music and the original overture by the celebrated Grétry," and on Nov. 14 "a first representation of 'Richard Cœur de Lion,' an historical pantomime, in three acts, with military evolutions, dresses, scenery and decorations, as performed in Paris with the greatest applause." Mr. Lailson, of course, forgot to tell New York that Grétry had not intended his master-opera as a vehicle for pantomimic pageantry. Though properly these performances should be relegated to the promised French finale of my book, mention was made of them here because they interfered with the business prospects of certain gentlemen.

The Old Americans had gone to Boston after the close of their New York season and Mr. John Sollee, the French proprietor of the City Theatre, Charleston, considered the time opportune for occupying their John Street Theatre with his Southerners and the principal performers of the Boston Theatre. Originally he intended to stay two nights only, beginning with Aug.

18, 1797, and it would have strengthened his financial status had he adhered to this plan. Instead, he protracted his sojourn until Oct. 17, and left New York a sorely disappointed man who had found out that at least a slight knowledge of the English language and literature was necessary to manage theatricals successfully in New York. During his unprosperous expedition to New York, he presented to lovers of opera, etc.:

Oct. 7:	Adopted Child
Oct. 10:	Deserter of Naples (pant.)
Sept. 5:	Highland Reel
Aug. 21; Oct. 5, 23:	Mountaineers
Oct. 3:	Poor Soldier
Aug. 24:	Romp
Sept. 21; Oct. 17:	Sultan; or, Peep into the Seraglio
Sept. 1:	Waterman

What could the ill-advised Mr. Sollee expect, if simultaneously the most formidable rivals possible were competing for public favor and occasionally with the same pieces on the same night as announced by him? These rivals were none other than Wignell and Reinagle, who had at last ventured to New York, had taken possession of Ricketts' circus in Greenwich Street and fitted it up as the "New Theatre." At least, Mr. Sollee had the satisfaction that they, too, were made to feel very uncomfortable by Mr. Lailson towards the end of their season, which lasted from Aug. 23 (postponed from Aug. 21) until Nov. 25. However, posterity is less interested in Wignell and Reinagle's financial affairs than in their artistic efforts. It will be seen from the following record that they lived up to their reputation by devoting themselves strongly to opera:

Nov. 10:	*Abroad and at Home* (Shield, 1796)
Sept. 8:	Adopted Child
Nov. 22:	Agreeable Surprise
Oct. 9, 13:	*Animated Statue* ("anacreontic ballet")
Oct. 30:	Castle of Andalusia

Oct. 20:	Columbus; or, a World Discovered (music by Reinagle)
Sept. 30; Oct. 4:	Death of Captain Cook (pantomime-ballet)
Aug. 23:	Dermot and Kathleen (pant. based on Shield's 'Poor Soldier,' "composed" by Mr. Byrne, the company's pantomimist. A pantomime of the same title was performed at London in 1793)
Sept. 25:	Deserter (Dibdin)
Aug. 25:	*Drunken Provençal* (pant.-ballet, "composed" by Byrne)
Oct. 20:	Farmer
Nov. 20:	Harlequin's Invasion (pant.)
Nov. 8:	Highland Reel
Nov. 4, 6:	Inkle and Yarico
Oct. 11:	Iron Chest
Sept. 27; Nov. 1:	Lock and Key
Oct. 23:	Mountaineers
Sept. 5:	Peeping Tom of Coventry
Sept. 1; Oct. 18:	Poor Soldier
Aug. 25:	Prize
Sept. 13; Nov. 17:	Purse
Oct. 9, 16:	Robin Hood
Sept. 29:	Romp
Sept. 22:	Rosina
Sept. 11:	Waterman

A peculiar feature of these performances was this, that the operas were repeatedly advertised as "composed into an after-piece." This was the first and last visit of the Philadelphians to New York. To remain longer would have been incompatible with hygienic principles. Ricketts' circus must have been detrimental to the health of the audiences and the actors alike, for the managers found it necessary to announce on November 22 that "large fires will be kept in the theatre, the remainder of the season."

Leaving aside the few stray performances in the New Circus, Greenwich Street, of 'Rosina' (Aug. 6, 1798) and "positively, absolutely and categorically" of 'Inkle and Yarico' on Aug. 8 by Mr. Prigmore, who had been an unruly element in Hallam and Henry's company, I hasten to the first Summer Theatre established at New York. It was Joseph Corré, the famous caterer, who conceived the happy idea of engaging the principal performers of the Park Theatre for the theatre opened in his Mount Vernon Garden in July, 1800, and Dunlap willingly admits that Corré was a more successful manager than he. The public were respectfully informed that "there will not only be a select dramatic piece of two, and sometimes three acts, each night, but a regular Grand Concert, leader of the band, Mr. Hewitt." Indeed, Corré carried the plan to a successful end on September 19, and part of his success was due to his well-known desire to please his patrons whenever he could. For instance, though the season was drawing to a close, he informed the public that "it having been reported to him the inconvenience of an audience, seeing on a level surface, he has raised and elevated seats sufficiently for between 4 and 500 persons in such a manner as they can see the whole performance without being in the least incommodated."

To this Summer Theatre New York flocked to enjoy the following operas and pantomimes:

Aug. 18:	Adopted Child
Sept. 15:	Children in the Wood
Aug. 22; Sept. 5:	Highland Reel.
July 11:	*Love and Magic* (pant.)
Sept. 17:	Medea and Jason (pant.)
July 14, 16:	Old Soldier (pant.)
Sept. 19:	Poor Soldier
Aug. 11:	Purse
Aug. 15:	Romp
Sept. 3:	Shipwreck
Sept. 12:	Wildgoose Chase

To give an idea of the nature of these mixed entertainments, which began at nine o'clock (weather permitting), cost four shillings admission and were enhanced

by the allurements of Corré's culinary genius, I append
the announcement for Aug. 18:

Summer Theatre, Mount Vernon Garden . . . this Evening . . . . the much admired musical drama of the *Adopted
Child;* or, Milford Castle.

Michael	Mr. Hodgkinson
Sir Bertrand	Mr. Hallam, jr.
Le Sage	Mr. Fox
Spruce	Mr. M'Donald
Flint	Mr. Lee
The Adopted Child . . .	Miss Harding
Nell	Miss Brett
Lucy	Miss Westray
Jeannette	Mrs. Hogg
Clara	Mrs. Hodgkinson

After the drama there will be a *Grand Concert* . . . .
Leader of the band, Mr. Hewitt.

Sinfonie	Haydn
Song, 'Bonny Bet' . . .	Mr. Fox
Recitation, 'The Pilgrims and the Peas'	Mr. Jefferson
Song, 'What can a lassy do' .	Miss Brett
Recitation, The Pictures of the audience, taken by . .	Mrs. Hodgkinson
Song, 'John Bull was a bumpkin'	Mr. Jefferson
Recitation and Song of True Glory	Mr. Hodgkinson

The record of opera at Philadelphia was carried down to the season of 1791-92. It will presently be seen that the Old Americans did not immediately drop the Quaker City from their sphere of interest, in fact did not do so even after Wignell and Reinagle had established headquarters at Philadelphia.

But more significant for the fact that managers could count on a sufficient interest in theatrical performances to compete with each other in the same city, is the pressure of another company at Philadelphia whilst the Old Americans still occupied their Southwark Theatre.

This other company consisted of the Kenna family and some minor comedians who belonged to and probably were the best of the several strolling companies that may be traced during these and subsequent years in all directions throughout our country. The Kennas had slowly moved northward until they reached Philadelphia in 1791. Under the ambitious name of the "New American Company" they turned the Concert Hall in the Haymarket, Northern Liberties, into a theatre and from April 1791 to May 1792 defied the Old American Company to oust them from the city, though Durang doubts that they were very successful financially.

During this year they also contributed in a modest way to the city's knowledge of opera. As my own notes yield but meagre information I have to rely almost entirely on Mr. Seilhamer for a record of their activity:

TITLE OF OPERA	1791	1792
Agreeable Surprise	....	Jan. 17; Mar. 3 May 16
Devil to Pay...................................	Sept. 14, Nov. 26	....
Duenna	....	May 11
Harlequin Barber (pant.)...........................	Nov. 29	....
Harlequin Dead and Alive (pant.)..............	Dec. 3, 6	....
Harlequin Magician (pant.).......................	Dec. 1	....
Harlequin Turned Doctor (pant.)................	Dec. 13	....
Padlock	Dec. 10	....
Poor Soldier...................................	Aug. 22, 27 Sept. 21; Nov. 5 Nov. 14	Feb. 10
Tempest of Harlequin (pant.)......................	....	Jan. 23
Thomas and Sally.......................	Oct. 5; Nov. 5	Jan. 27
Virgin Unmasked...........................	Oct. 1	....
Waterman (Dibdin, 1775)........................	Apr. 8, 11	....

The Harlequinades in this short list gave some French dancers, connected with the Kennas, an opportunity to show their dexterity; indeed, the Kennas on more than one evening relied upon them to fill the bill. This "New American Company" did not risk another season at Philadelphia, but the Kennas allowed themselves to be absorbed temporarily by the Old Americans. Even had this not happened, it would have been folly to continue independently, for Mr. Henry, as we know, was just then in Europe engaging the best foreign talent available for the next year's campaign.

With the Hodgkinsons and their other stars, Hallam and Henry reopened the Southwark Theatre the end of September, 1792, and remained there until the middle of January, 1793. In the meantime the New Theatre in Chestnut Street was nearing completion, but this did not deter the Old Americans in the least. Bent on reaping harvests as long as they could, they certainly were not disgruntled because of Wignell and Reinagle's preparedness to begin operations at their new theatre. Accordingly, Hallam and Henry hastened from New York to Philadelphia for a summer season covering the months of July and August, 1793. Then the famous yellow-fever epidemic, one of the worst in our country's history, set in at Philadelphia, and neither company could have opposed this dreadful foe. After the city had shaken off the signs of the pestilence, Wignell and Reinagle at last saw their way clear to start operations. Hallam and Henry were wise enough not to compete with an organization in no way inferior to their own, and which had the additional advantage of novelty; but when in the fall of 1794 Wignell and Reinagle betook themselves to Baltimore, the Old American Company, under Hallam and Hodgkinson, once more and now for the last time opened the doors of their Southwark Theatre, as if to make sure that they were no longer wanted or needed at Philadelphia. This, their last season in the city of Brotherly Love, lasted from the end of September 1794 until early in December. Without further comment, I submit the operatic record for these three intermittent and asthmatic efforts of the Old Americans to endear themselves to Philadelphia:

TITLES OF OPERA	1792	1793	1794
Agreeable Surprise..................................	Dec. 14, 28	Jan. 2 Aug. 9	....
America Discovered (=Tammany)......			
Battle of Hexham..................................			Nov. 7
Beggar's Opera.....................................			Oct. 17, 20
Bird Catcher (pant.).............................			Nov. 31
Birth of Harlequin (pant.)...................			Nov. 19
Children in the Woods			Nov. 24 Dec. 4
Danaides (pant., Pelissier)...................			Oct. 10, 13
Deserter	Oct 3, 8	July 31	....
Devil to Pay..	Oct. 19 Dec. 31	July 5	

TITLE OF OPERA	1792	1793	1794
Don Juan (pant.-ballet, Gluck-Reeve, 1787)	Dec. 19	....	Oct. 27
Farmer	....	Jan. 4 Aug. 16	....
Flitch of Bacon	Oct. 1, 5 Nov. 26	....	....
Harlequin Pastry-cook (pant., Pelissier)	....	....	Nov. 21
Haunted Tower	....	....	Dec. 2
Highland Reel	....	....	Oct. 3 Nov. 5
Hunt the Slipper	....	....	Nov. 26
Lionel and Clarissa	....	July 27 Aug. 5, 12	....
Love in a Village	Oct. 10 Nov. 9	....	Sept. 24
Maid of the Mill	Oct. 15, 17 Nov. 14	July 3	....
Midas	Nov. 23	....	....
No Song, no Supper (Storace, 1790)	Nov. 30 Dec. 5, 7, 17 Dec. 31	July 18 Aug. 23	Sept. 29 Oct. 24
Padlock	Sept. 28 Nov. 5	July 20	Oct. 1
Poor Soldier	Dec. 3	....	....
Quaker	....	....	Oct. 6
Rival Candidates	....	....	Oct. 15
Robin Hood	....	Aug. 2	Oct. 10
Romp	Oct. 22, 26 Oct. 29 Nov. 7, 14 Nov. 17 Dec. 10, 12	Jan. 9 July 22, 29	Sept. 22 Nov. 28
Rosina	Oct. 24 Nov. 2, 24	Jan. 11 July 25	Oct. 29
Sophia of Brabant (pant., Pelissier)	....	....	Nov. 1
Tammany	....	....	Oct. 18 Nov. 10
Two Philosophers (pant.)	....	....	Oct. 24 Dec. 4
Wedding Ring	....	....	Nov. 12

When Thomas Wignell, whose personification of such parts as Darby were so excellent that for years even his best rivals did not summon courage to compete with him, broke away from the Old American company, he

Inside View of the New Theatre, Philadelphia.

WIGNELL AND REINAGLE'S CHESTNUT ST. THEATRE, PHILADELPHIA, 1784
(From "The New York Magazine," 1794)

experienced little difficulty in convincing some financiers of Philadelphia that the erection of a new theatre garrisoned with a company to defy comparison would pay. The project soon assumed tangible shape; a stock company was formed and Wignell and Alexander Reinagle, the gifted musician, were appointed managers, each for his respective department. Then Wignell went abroad to recruit a company, while Reinagle superintended the erection of the New Theatre in Chestnut Street. The plans for the building were entrusted to Mr. Richards, Reinagle's brother-in-law, who had furnished the designs for remodelling Covent Garden theatre. The interior of the Philadelphia establishment was a perfect copy of the Theatre Royal at Bath and though the façade, measuring ninety feet on Chestnut Street, was not finished until 1805, the theatre was ready for occupancy long before Wignell arrived with his company. Indeed, so energetically had the erection of the theatre been pushed, that the *Federal Gazette* on Jan. 29, 1793, could offer its readers a description, stating that the theatre could hold "2000 people, or, about 600 pounds." The building soon came to be considered one of the seven wonders of America, and Henry Wansey in his "Excursion in the United States of North America in the Summer of 1794" admits that it was "an elegant and convenient theatre, as large as that of Covent Garden." In its April number, 1794, the *New York Magazine* had a plate illustrating the "Inside view of the New Theatre in Philadelphia." This was accompanied by a good description, with comments on the "pencil and genius of Mr. Milbourne," the scene painter; but I prefer to quote the description contained in a letter by Ezekiel Forman to his friend John C. Rockhill, dated March 25th, 1793, [error for 1794] and reprinted in the *Pa. Mag. of Hist.* in W. J. Potts' article on "Amusements, and Politics in Philadelphia, 1794":

. . . When I had the pleasure of seeing you last in town, the New Theatre was then expected to be opened in a short time, which was done on Monday evening the 17th of February last with one of the most brilliant and numerous audiences I ever beheld on a similar occasion.—The stated days or rather evenings of performance are Monday, Wednesday & Friday Nights in every Week & sometimes occasionally on Saturday evenings.—The doors open at five—The curtain draws up at six, [the] exhibition commonly finishes at about twelve o'clock.—I will however attempt to give you a short description of the House & Performers as well as my poor abilities are capable of.

The Boxes run in the form of a semi-circle by which construction you have a full view from any part of them without having it obstructed by those near to the stage which was too generally the case in all the old theatres.—There are three rows of Boxes, two of which extend from the stage quite round the House & that part of them fronting the Stage is immediately underneath the Gallery, while the third & upper row extends only half way on each side till it meets the Gallery which is separated from it by a partition & iron banister with sharp pointed spikes, & the front part of course forms the Gallery in the front of which & over the board wall is an iron railing of two bars so that a person is in very little risque of falling into the Pit.—The ascent from the front to the back parts of both Pit and Gallery (but more particularly the latter) is very steep, which tho' it may appear a little inconvenient at the first entering of them still proves a great advantage to the persons in the hinder parts, as it renders their view of the Stage, unobstructed by those sitting in front of them.—The Stage is large and commodious— the lights numerous & good & the Scenery & decorations may be justly said to partake of both the *beautiful* and *sublime*, especially those used for some particular plays almost surpass description— of which those used in a new Opera lately introduced here, called 'Robin Hood; or, Sherwood Forest,' very much partakes. The Orchestra may justly boast of having a band of Music & Musicians superior to what any other theatre in America ever did or does now possess.—

Over the stage & in full view of the whole House two beautiful & descriptive figures are painted, one representing the Genius of Tragedy who sits in a mourning mellancholly [!] attitude, & the other that of the Genius of Comedy, who stands a little to the left of where the other *sits* and in her hand she holds a scarf on which these words are inscribed in large legible characters: 'The Eagle suffers little Birds to sing,' & over the heads of these two figures the American Eagle with extended wings is displayed.

As the stockholders showed considerable impatience, Reinagle soothed their ruffled spirits by first throwing the doors open for public inspection of the house and then by arranging three popular concerts in February, 1793. After this the house was again closed for exactly one year. The reasons for this strange procedure were simple enough. In the first place, Wignell exercised such deliberation in the selection of his company that he did not reach America until September, 1793, and when he arrived the first news from Philadelphia conveyed to him was that of the terrible yellow-fever epidemic. Under the circumstances, the company could not very well proceed to the stricken city. It had to be quartered in the villages of New Jersey until Wignell saw his way clear to counteract the bad effects of idleness by a theatrical trip to Annapolis in December, 1793, and January, 1794. As by the terms of the contracts, so the actor-manager William B. Wood informs us in his "Personal Recollections of the Stage," the actors were to receive pay from the moment of their arrival in America, and as they had to be boarded and fed, Wignell incurred debts to the amount of $20,000 before he could open the Chestnut Street Theatre on February 17, 1794, with Arnold's 'Castle of Andulasia'!

The best-known vocalist in Wignell and Reinagle's troupe was Miss George of the Haymarket Theatre and Drury Lane, who was equally famous as an oratorio singer. She is said to have had a voice of astonishing compass and sweetness and her taste and execution were pronounced equal to that of any singer on the English stage. She seems to have resembled Mrs. Eames of our own time in this that, as one critic put it, "she had been taught apparently rather to astonish the ear than to please the heart." Just previous to her American engagement she married Sir John Oldmixon, a noted beau of the day, and as Mrs. Oldmixon she won the enthusiastic applause of American audiences for many years.

Only a little less resplendent as a star was Miss Broadhurst, whom Wignell captured at Covent Garden when she was barely out of her teens. In fact, she had not reached the age of twenty when she made her first bow to an American audience. Here and abroad, considering her age, as Mr. Seilhamer says, her musical accomplishments were considered truly wonderful and they shone with equal brilliancy on the concert-stage. On the other hand, Dunlap claims that Miss Broadhurst never developed much skill as an actress. Verdicts like these of old-timers—they might be duplicated by the score—should set those thinking who still entertain the notion that during the eighteenth century the acting abilities of the great operatic stars counted for little or nothing.

These two ladies were seconded, besides by Wignell himself, by such experienced artists as Mr. and Mrs. Marshall (the latter subsequently known as Mrs. Wilmoth), the Warrell family, and the Darleys, who all enjoyed a good reputation in England. Of Mr. Marshall, Durang had this to say: he "was a vocalist of very fine powers, sustaining the principal tenor in opera, and being excellent in fops and Frenchmen . . . He returned to England in 1801"; and of his wife: "Her operatic powers were of a very fine order. She possessed a melodious, powerful and extensive soprano voice which she used with skill and musical precision."

These personal remarks may be concluded with a reference to Mr. and Mrs. William Francis. Wignell must have congratulated himself in after years on his selection of these popular and clever dancers and pantomimists, particularly as Mr. Francis' skill in arranging and superintending pantomimes and ballets, many the "compositions" of his own fertile brain, was of no mean order. This worthy couple combined talent with thrift, and old Francis died in fairly comfortable circumstances in 1827, aged 64 years.

The cast of 'The Castle of Andalusia' will give a good idea of the team-work of the company:

Don Scipio	Mr. Finch
Don Cæsar	Mr. Darley
Don Fernando	Mr. Marshall
Don Juan	Mr. Morris
Don Alfonso	Mr. Moreton
Perdrillo	Mr. Bates
Spado	Mr. Wignell
Sanguino	Mr. Green
Philippo	Mr. Darley, jr.
Victoria	Mrs. Warrell
Lorenza	Mrs. Marshall
Isabella	Mrs. Bates
Catalina	Miss Broadhurst

The company—and this was quite in keeping with the ambitious policies of the managers—was supported by a good orchestra, probably the best yet united in this country. Durang corroborates Ezekiel Forman's statement above quoted, thus:

The orchestra department was under the direction of manager Reinagle and the musicians were deemed equal in general ability with the stage artists—the celebrated violinist from London, George Gillingham [being] the leader. In truth, the orchestra contained about twenty accomplished musicians, many of them of great notoriety as concert players on their respective instruments.

As a characteristic feature of this orchestra, and historically important because the predominance of the Germans was temporarily destroyed, must be mentioned the fact that it was largely composed of Frenchmen, musicians either by choice or by necessity, as almost without exception they were political refugees. Indeed, tradition has it that pseudo-marquises and counts back of the footlights were accompanied by real marquises and counts in the orchestra. Dunlap devotes considerable space to the romantic, or, more justly, tragic fate of some of these ill-starred persons whose troubles by no means came to an end when they reached our shores. A cloud of mystery seemed to hover over many of them and quite an effective libretto of the realistic neo-Italian brand might be constructed, for instance, on the career of Monsieur Gardie, a French nobleman who, with his wife, a beautiful and deservedly admired balleteuse, barely escaped the guillotine, first joined Wignall and Reinagle, shortly afterwards the Old Americans, and in a fit of despondency in 1798 murdered his wife and then committed suicide.

But back from such gruesome tales to Alexander Reinagle, the distinguished general of the musical forces, whom C. Ph. Em. Bach esteemed enough to request his silhouette for his *cabinet* of friends and celebrities. Data on the life of Reinagle, who made this country his home in 1786, are now so easily accessible that they may be dispensed with here. Suffice it to say that Reinagle, together with Raynor Taylor and Benjamin Carr, who about this time was singing minor operatic parts with the Old Americans, formed a trio of accomplished virtuosos and composers of whom Philadelphia was and remained justly proud. Instead of biographical data I prefer the pen-picture of Reinagle as conductor in Durang's reminiscences, a pen-picture singularly fitted to allow a curious glimpse into music and manners of by-gone times:

Who that only once saw old[1] manager Reinagle in his official capacity, could ever forget his dignified *personne*. He presided at his pianoforte looking the very personification of the patriarch of music—investing the science of harmonious sounds, as well as the dramatic school, with a moral influence reflecting and adorning its salutary uses with high respectability and polished manners. His appearance was of the reverend and impressive kind, which at once inspired the universal respect of the audience. Such was Reinagle's imposing appearance that it awed the disorderly of the galleries, or the fop of annoying propensities and impertinent criticism of the box lobby, into decorum. No vulgar, noisy emanations, were heard from the pit of that day; that portion of the theatre was then the resort of the well informed critic. The intellectual taste and analytical judgment of our city congregated there to listen, to follow

[1] This is an afterthought. Reinagle was not yet forty when the new theatre opened, and he died at the premature age of fifty-three!

ALEXANDER REINAGLE (1756-1809)
(From a miniature in possession of the family)

the track of the actor's readings . . . . It was truly inspiring
to behold the polished Reinagle saluting from his seat (before the
grand square pianoforte in the orchestra) the highest respectability
of the city, as it entered into the boxes to take seats. It was a scene
before the curtain that suggested a picture of the master of private
ceremonies receiving his invited guests at the fashionable drawing-
room. Mr. Reinagle was a gentleman and a musician. His compositions evinced decided cleverness and originality and some of his
accompaniments to the old operas were much admired by good judges.

The observation that Reinagle's imposing appearance
awed the disorderly of the galleries, is not only interesting
but fortunate, as it leads with ease to another pen-picture
by Durang. Though in its first part it refers to the Southwark Theatre, the scene described may be considered
typical of the decorum surrounding our President's ap-
pearances at the theatre in those days:

The east stage box in the South Street Theatre, was fitted up
expressly for the reception of Gen. Washington. Over the front
of the box was the United States coat of arms; red drapery was
gracefully festooned in the interior and about the exterior, the seats
and front were cushioned. Mr. Wignell, in a full dress of black,
hair powdered and adjusted to the formal fashion of the day, with
two silver candlesticks and wax candles, would thus await the general's arrival at the box door entrance, and, with great refinement of
address and courtly manners, conduct this best of public men and
suite to his box. A guard of the military attended. A soldier was
generally posted at each stage door; four were posted in the gallery,
assisted by the high constable of the city and other police officers,
to preserve something like decorum amongst the sons of social
liberty . . . .

A few lines from Wansey's Excursion may supplement
this delightful glimpse into aristocratic democracy. Says
he, when describing Wignell and Reinagle's New Theatre:

. . . . to judge from the dress and appearance of the company
around me, and the actors and scenery, I should have thought I
had still been in England. The ladies wore the small bonnets of
the same fashion as those I saw when I left England; some of
chequered straw, etc., some with their hair full dressed, without
caps, as with us, and very few in the French style. The younger
ladies with their hair flowing in ringlets on their shoulders. The

gentlemen with rounded hats, their coats with high collars, and cut
quite in the English fashion and many in silk striped coats. The
scenery of the stage excellent, particularly a view on the Skuylkill,
about two miles from the city. The greatest part of the scenes,
however, belonged once to Lord Barrymore's theatre at Wargrave.

But pen-pictures of a nature not quite so idyllic have
also been preserved. For instance, Durang wrote:

With all [the] array of civil and military power and preventive
police regulations it was sometimes a matter of difficulty to keep the
house in reasonable order. As soon as the curtain was down, the
gods in the galleries would throw apples, nuts, bottles and glasses
on the stage and into the orchestra. That part of the house being
always crowded it was hard to discover the real perpetrators . . .
Vociferating with Stentorian lungs 'Carlisle's march,' 'Cherry Char-
lotte's Jig,' 'Mother Brown's Retreat.' These were the names of
notorious characters, with their slang and flash appellations, as
given by the rowdies of that day.

Possibly the severest rebuke of our early manners was
administered by Monsieur Perrin Du Lac in his "Voyage
dans les Deux Louisianes . . . en 1801, 1802 et 1803,"
when he narrates his experiences at the theatre in Philadelphia:

Il ne règne dans l'intérieur de la salle ni ordre ni décense. Le
bruit des allans et venans trouble continuellement l'attention du
spectateur qui, malgré les défenses portés sur les affiches, a souvent
encore beaucoup à souffrir de la mauvaise odeur des cigarres qui
l'on y fume continuellement. Les hommes gardent le chapeau sur
la tête et restent aussi placés devant les dames; il s'en trouve
rarement d'assez galans pour leur offrir leur place. Tout y prouve
que la politesse et la liberté marchent difficilement de compagnie. . ."

Be it said in fairness to Philadelphia that the "mauvaise odeur des cigarres" was not confined to her limits,
for Weld and other travellers have commented on this
same then national and "shocking custom" of ours. How
things have changed, by the way! No American gentleman still "guards" his chapeau *sur la tête*, whereas this
shocking custom has in the meantime taken possession of
such "polite" countries as France and Italy!

Worse scenes than described by Durang would occasionally be enacted. For instance, on Nov. 2, 1796, at New York, two sea-captains—I am quoting Dunlap—doubtless intoxicated, being in one of the stage boxes, called during an overture for 'Yankee Doodle.' The audience hissed them, they threw missiles into the orchestra and defied the audience, some of whom pressed on the stage and attacked the rioters in conjunction with the peace officers; one of the latter was injured by a blow from a club. The rioters were dragged from their box, one turned into the street and the other carried into a dressing-room. These madmen afterwards returned with a number of sailors, attacked the door of the theatre, and were only secured by the city watch.

On such incidents of rowdyism Ritter worked up his theory that Americans were not prepared to enjoy classical music! He could have found still worse things in Dunlap's book, worst of all the disgusting fashion of the day to suffer professional beauties and beautiful professionals to use the best boxes in the house as a kind of stock exchange. This custom became so unbearable that the managers, when called upon to regulate some other abuses, informed the public on Jan. 21, 1795 that henceforth "no persons of notorious ill fame will be suffered to occupy any seat in a box where places are already taken." The managers wished their theatre to be "esteemed a moral, rational and instructive amusement free from the least riot and disorder"; and with this view in mind they attacked another time-honored custom (corroborated by Weld) when they announced in Nov., 1796:

Much confusion having arisen from the introduction of liquor into the house during the performance, the managers respectfully hope that Gentlemen will not call for any till the conclusion of the first piece, as the door keepers are, in the strictest manner, ordered to prevent its admission.

It would be utterly absurd to attribute such things to the unpreparedness of the American public for good music, or even to consider such behavior an indigenous American characteristic. The truth of it is that our audiences were just as well or ill behaved as those of Europe, and that in our country, too, the theatre was used occasionally for other purposes than the enjoyment of dramas and operas. Here the latest gossip was passed from box to box and here politics were discussed and political sentiments publicly and noisily aired whenever the lines of the actors seemed to have any bearing on political issues. Just then the French Revolution was raging, and though the Frenchman of the Jacobin type certainly was not the best-mannered man in public, yet, being a Frenchman, he was the *arbiter elegantiarum* both in Europe and America. Add to this the fact that the two opposed political parties in our country were, in substance, savagely either pro-French or anti-French, and it is clear that occasionally scenes were enacted at our theatres which compared in quality with those enacted at the theatres in Paris. The climax would be reached when the managers and actors themselves wilfully stimulated the political feuds. Says Dunlap:

It was customary (and very naturally so) for the actors, who were all emigrants from the English stage, to interpolate jests and witticisms at the expense of the French, who were then at war with England; and these often gave great offence, excited disapprobation and sometimes created great uproar in the house. The anti-Federal (or as it was then called, the Jacobin) party, were so exceedingly sensitive that they took great offence at the representation of 'The Poor Soldier,' pretending that the character of Bagatelle was a libel on the whole French nation. They were encouraged in this by the French consul, then residing in Boston. A pretty smart quarrel was excited between him and the editor of the *Boston Gazette;* and the controversy at last became so bitter, that a mob on one occasion attempted to stop the performance of this farce, and did considerable damage to the benches, doors and windows of the offending house.

Such outbursts of passion were, of course, childish, but occasions occured when the public exhibitions of patriotism

or politics at the theatres really must have been impressive or at least picturesque. For instance, Dunlap remembered this scene preceding a performance of the 'Gre-
cian Daughter,' put on the bill to celebrate the evacua-
tion of New York by the British.

One of the side boxes was filled by French officers from the ships
of war in the harbor. The opposite box was filled with American
officers. All were in their uniforms as dressed for the rejoicing day.
French officers and soldier-sailors (we find the expression in a note
made at the time) and many of the New York militia, artillery, in-
fantry, and dragoons mingled with the crowd in the pit. The house
was early filled. As soon as the musicians appeared in the orchestra,
there was a general call for *ça ira*. The band struck up. The French
in the pit joined first and then the whole audience. Next followed
the Marseillois Hymn. The audience stood up. The French took
off their hats and sung in a full and solemn chorus. The Americans
applauded by gestures and clapping of hands. We can yet recall
the figure and voice of one Frenchman, who, standing on a bench
in the pit, sung this patriotic song with a clear loud voice, which his
fine manly frame seemed to swell with the enthusiasm of the moment.
The hymn ended, shouts of 'Vivent les François,' 'Vivent les Améri-
cains', were reiterated until the curtain drew up, and all was silent.

As stated, Wignell and Reinagle opened their New
Theatre in Chestnut Street on Feb. 17, 1794, with
Arnold's 'Castle of Andalusia' and did not close it until
the middle of July. The fall was spent at Baltimore, as
that city had been decided upon as a permanent sub-
station. The first days in December, 1794, saw them
back at the Chestnut Street Theatre, where they did not
close until early in July, 1795. This same schedule was
repeated in 1795-96. After this until the end of the century the company was obliged by the trips south and
north of Philadelphia, including the expedition to New
York, to close in May, but Wignell and Reinagle only
once deviated from the rule of opening in December, when
they did not begin the season at Philadelphia until February 5, 1799. Of course, when the century drew to its
end, the company did not show the same faces as on the
memorable February 17. Some changes had taken

place, especially after Wignell and Reinagle overhauled their troupe in 1797.   To follow these changes in detail would be futile, but to allow a comparison with the cast of 'The Castle of Andalusia' in 1794 and to show that the reorganization of the company did not materially affect the operatic department, I select from my voluminous collection of casts the one of the Beggar's Opera, as announced in a deodorized version for April 8, 1799:

Peachum	Mr. Warren
Lockit	Mr. Francis
Macheath	Mr. Marshall
Filch	Mr. Blisset
May o' Mint	Mr. Darley
Ben Budge	Mr. Fox
Nimming Nad	Mr. Warrell, jr.
Harry Paddington	Mr. Warrell
Wat Dreary	Mr. Doctor
Jenny Twitcher	Mr. Lavancy
Robin of Badshot	Mr. Woolls
Mrs. Peachum	Mrs. Morris
Polly	Mrs. Marshall
Lucy	Mrs. Warrell
Mrs. Vixen	Mrs. Lavancy
Mrs. Slamakin	Miss L'Estrange
Molly Brazen	Mrs. Doctor

From 1794 until the season of 1799-1800 the Chestnut Street company performed the following operas, pantomimes, etc. [See *Table C.*]

The fact that an opera was selected by Wignell and Reinagle to inaugurate their career as managers of the Chestnut Street Theatre, is significant, because the whole project was based on the idea of giving equality to the dramatic and the operatic departments.   Much has been made of this by the historians of this departure, so fruitful for the development of high-class opera in English, and to this departure is attributed Wignell and Reinagle's failure, that is, failure to enrich the stockholders.   To be absolutely impartial in this matter, I quote from Wood's "Personal Recollections of the Stage" (1855, pp. 92-95) a few pertinent lines. They give a contemporary actor-manager's point of view and incidentally throw suggestive side-lights on the stage-affairs of those days:

The musical part of the entertainment being now made so prominent, greatly swelled the expenditures. These included the enormous charge of a perfect orchestra of instrumental performers of undoubted abilities, carefully selected from the great theatres abroad. The musical instruments of all kinds, (then the property of the manager,) including two grand pianos and a noble organ, swelled this sum yet more. Then again the skeleton of a chorus, to be constantly kept and filled up as wanted, formed another item. The orchestra *music*, (afterwards destroyed by fire,) was obtained at an expense of nearly two thousand dollars. The Darleys, Marshall, Mrs. Oldmixon, Miss Broadhurst, Mrs. Marshall and Mrs. Worrall [Warrell], with many others, were engaged as principals from the London theatres, and at the highest salaries . . . .

It is needless to say the *discords* among the singers proved a great addition to the poor manager's cares. As most of the operas had been composed with a view to the peculiar powers and voices of some original representative, it frequently happened that these pieces were not suited to the ability of later singers, and it became necessary to omit much of the composer's music, substituting such popular and approved airs as were most certain of obtaining applause. As a natural consequence, each artist insisted on a share of this privilege until the merciless introduction of songs, encored by the admirers of the several singers, protracted the entertainment to so late an hour, as to leave the contending songsters to a show of empty benches, and a handful of tired-out hearers; the audience preferring to retire at a reasonable hour . . .

In its connection with the regular drama, it is useless to say that opera, occasionally, increases the receipt of the house. It does, undoubtedly, often increase *gross* receipts, and these are all the public judges from. But this is a matter of balance of receipts and expenditures; and our books have constantly proved that the extra expenditure for a large chorus force, additional performers, and band, added to the enormous demands of the principal singers, render a profit scarcely within probability. The great sacrifice of time necessary to produce an opera with any effect, and its limited run, is also a matter of serious disadvantage. Besides, during a musical preparation, the stage is so daily occupied as to utterly prevent any successful attempt to furnish other novelties. Late instances, since the price of singing has been so enormously advanced, give lamentable proof of the truth of the assertion, in the fact that more than one theatre has been abruptly closed in consequence of the failure of some ill-judged operatic experiment. To show how badly the union of the two entertainments affected the manager, Mr. Wignell used to refer in later times the advocates of the junction to his books of receipts, which presented such contrasts as 'Love in a Village,' 'Robin Hood,' or 'Artaxerxes,' (all musical dramas,) performed to an audience of one hundred to one hundred and fifty dollars, while the 'Revenge,' 'Romeo and Juliet,' 'Alexander,' or almost any other tragedy, seldom fell below a receipt of from five hundred to seven hundred dollars. My own management confirms his views. I myself remember listening to one of the best operas, and well sung, which yielded a receipt of only forty dollars.

Dunlap and Durang held similar views, and it cannot be denied that the system of combining in one huge and extraordinary company tragedy, comedy, opera, panto-mine and ballet was costly and complicated—a herculean task, as Durang fitly calls it. Only men of the determi-nation of Wignell and Reinagle could carry this system to its sweet or bitter end, a system which, in a country where municipal or state subvention of theatres is still a matter of constitutional doubt and a dream of the dim future, was bound to become antiquated. Viewing the problem in this light, what does a *post-mortem* examination reveal?

Of course, there must be several grains of truth in the contemporary verdict against Wignell and Reinagle's error of judgment, but my statistic tables, with all allowance for the perfidy of statistics, prove that the Old American Company cultivated opera in New York just as strenuously, and this company prospered! Nor can the equal encouragement of opera be held responsible for the yellow-fever epidemic in 1793 and its only a trifle less virulent outbreak in 1797 at Philadelphia; and a manager who starts operations with debts amounting to twenty thousand dollars on salaries alone (in those days a very considerable sum of money), is surely seriously handicapped, no matter what he does after-wards; even though Durang places the receipts for the *première* of 'Castle of Andalusia' from an overcrowded house at $850.

Mr. Wood says, and we have no reason to doubt him, that Wignell himself—he died, by the way, in 1803—later referred the advocates of the equal encouragement of drama and opera to his books of receipts, which presented such contrasts as 'Love in a Village' and 'Robin Hood' performed to an audience of one hundred to one hundred and fifty dollars, while 'Romeo and Juliet' and other dramas seldom fell below five hundred to seven hundred dollars. Indeed, Mr. Wood remembered having listened to one of the best operas, and well sung, which yielded a receipt of only forty dollars. This bait has been taken greedily by several historians, connecting it with 'Robin Hood,' but, as a matter of fact, Mr. Wood neither mentions any particular opera by name nor even makes it clear whether this happened under Wignell's management or his own. However, 'Romeo and Juliet' was worth from five to seven hundred dollars to the manager! Is it not curious then that, exactly as in New York, the full vocal and instrumental strength of the company was thrown into the performmances of 'Romeo and Juliet' with Arne's music, of 'Macbeth' with that of Locke, of the 'Tempest' with that of Purcell, and that the managers took evident pride in featuring this incidental music? Mr. Wood further forgot to tell us if these minimum receipts were taken in on nights of first performances, which would throw a different light on the subject, because, strange as it may seem, the craze for the *première* was yet a thing of the future. Here is a curiously interesting bit of evidence for what I mean. Said the Philadelphia correspondent of the New York *Daily Advertiser* on October 10, 1800, when reviewing the reopening of the New Theatre: "As the *beau monde* repudiates the idea of a first night performance, we were not surprised at meeting but few ladies there"!

The historical truth of the matter is, that with two yellow-fever epidemics against them, with a company numbering between fifty and sixty artists, with salaries ranging from $37 to $10, and only three or four (frequently fewer) performances a week and with $20,000 in debts to be paid off, the Chestnut Street Theatre could not have become a gold mine, even if opera had not been cultivated at all by the company. There are still other points which have not properly been taken into consideration.

It was the crucial period in our country's history, when Colonial tastes, standards and traditions were making place for those of an infant democracy, politically, economically, socially unsettled and with a population which was becoming kaleidoscopic in its (often undesirable) elements. The spectacular, the sensational instincts in this heterogeneous and somewhat crude new mass of humanity were bound to make their demands, and, just like their colleagues in New York, Wignell and Reinagle had to supply these demands as best they could. Hence perhaps the amazingly large numbers of pantomimes and ballets, gotten up by Mr. Francis alone or in conjunction with Mr. Byrne, formerly of Covent Garden, and Mr. Milbourne, the scene painter. By no means all of these were original with these hard-working gentlemen, and though they were frequently announced as "composed by," it would be comparatively easy to show that most of them were mere adaptations and Americanizations of pantomimes, etc., received, as the phrase went, with unbounded applause at London or Paris. Some, however really seem to have been born on American soil, as, for instance, 'The Battle of Trenton,' Byrne's 'Alonzo and Imogen,' his 'Dermot and Kathleen' (based on the 'Poor Soldier'), or his 'William Tell,' or 'Harlequin Shipwrecked, or, the Grateful Lion':

The music compiled by Mr. De Marque from Pleyel, Grétry, Giornowicki, Giordani, Shield, Reeve, Morehead, etc., etc. With new scenes designed and executed by Mr. Milbourne. The pantomime under the direction of Mr. Francis.

But, whether original or imported, these generally short-lived affairs entailed a considerable expenditure, probably more than the operas. To make matters worse, just then began the era of the American circus; and the novelty of equestrian and acrobatic feats combined with pantomimes sumptuously gotten up, like 'Bucephalus' or 'Don Juan,' presented year after year first at Rickett's circus, then at Lailson's, and finally at both, must have seriously interfered with the business of Wignell and Reinagle and therefore incidentally with the healthy development of opera at Philadelphia. Indeed, in 1796 the competition became very bitter and Rickett did not hesitate to perform his pantomimes every evening, or even to include regular comedies in his repertoire; and Mr. Lailson actually went so far as to include Grétry's 'Le Tableau parlant,' not as a pantomime, but as an opera! How hard Wignell and Reinagle must have been pressed appears from their attack on Rickett's establishment located also in Chestnut Street, in the skit 'T'Other Side of the Gutter,' in which Joseph Doctor, of Sadler's Wells, glorified in his feats of tumbling, equilibrium, dexterity and what not. Yes, in their desperation, they even stooped to put a "real" elephant into the cast of a play that happened to call for a procession. But this was the "rational" age, and I am sure that the elephant did not draw as well as the *telegraph* which—we are told—conveyed messages one hundred miles in seven minutes and which smart Mr. Rickett made the main feature of his show for a while.

Just as damaging to their prospects was the rumor, shortly after the new theatre had been opened, that the building was unsafe. Though the managers hastened to trace the rumor to the breaking of a bench and though at their request some experts, amongst them Major L'Enfant, examined the building and pronounced it absolutely secure, the doubters were not to be downed. In addition to all this, in 1798 some of the public favorites made their exit from the company without paying the slightest attention to their contracts, as stars will do. Moreover, in those years, the world over, a change in literary taste was latent. Perhaps not so much in the plots, because the psychological problems which confront the dramatist will ever remain essentially the same, but as to the manner of expression, make up, style of utterance. The managers themselves could not very well stamp a new literature out of the ground and were therefore often at a loss what to do. People began to object especially to the broad suggestiveness of the dialogues, or at least they were becoming tired of the low garb in which slippery double-entendres were presented during the eighteenth century, and the hypocritically prudish, high-collared, but just as slippery nineteenth century was not yet born. In America this propaganda for a fig-leaf from crown to sole was assisted by the peculiar attitude which our people assumed towards the theatre, illustrated by many "cards" and communications to the press and the fairly frequent editorals on the subject. In our young and somewhat crude democracy the didactic, political, ethical, and "have-a-good-time" ingredients of art were supposed to be of greater importance than the artistic essentials, and it was just then that the absurd and American custom originated of taking children to plays really intended and fit only for adults, and some only for adults of more brains and culture than the average citizen musters. That those parts of the plots in drama and opera the meaning of which was most obvious, namely, the double-entendres, would arouse the indignation of parents acting as escorts to their children, was but natural under the circumstances. Indeed, in 1798 one father, guilty of that American sin against common sense, aired his disgust vehemently after he had led his two daughters into the moral slaughter-house in Chestnut Street.

Perhaps the most outspoken protest against the theatrical literature of this time was delivered by "Spectator" in the *Columbian Centinel*, Nov. 19, 1796. He made a rather strong case of his grievances, commenting on the "corrupted morals" of British audiences and regretting that "through a deficiency of native genius or some other cause, we are obliged to import our plays from Europe," which are "not calculated, in many respects, to please a New England audience." Then, directing the missiles of his wrath against the "grossness of the double-entendres," he concluded his diatribe by challenging in a lapidary sentence the manager to make "the Boston theatre, what no theatre has ever yet been —*a place in which a modest woman need never blush to be seen.*"

I have dwelt at some length on these matters because it appears to me that the last decade of the eighteenth century was a transitional period in theatrical history. I am not prepared to span by a bridge this period and the first quarter of the nineteenth century, but however my observations may be modified by those who care to build on these foundations, it is certain that English opera was gradually being condemned to a Cinderella existence. Under the circumstances it is not surprising that the industrious activity of the talented Alexander Reinagle as opera-composer or chaperon of "accompaniments" in the imported works was doomed to speedy oblivion. Not a single score of his has turned up; and if we remember what a deep impression was made by the 'Monody' which he and Raynor Taylor composed in Dec., 1799, as a tribute to the memory of George Washington, this loss certainly is to be regretted.

The reorganized Old American Company and Wignell and Reinagle's Chestnut Street Company undoubtedly, on the whole, raised the standard of opera in our country. Of course, the original companies did not remain intact. Interchanges—intermarriages, as it were

—took place, new members were added; others seceded and joined other companies or returned to England; but the changes did not visibly affect the historical aspect. "Philadelphia and New York," says Dunlap tersely, "became from this time territories of rival monarchs, who, after annual invasions and hostile incursions, for a short time found it necessary to divide the United States between them until other potentates raised independent standards and every city, town and village had to own its own stage, and its own *king of shreds and patches*."

BOSTON AND NEW ENGLAND

At Boston the anti-theatre blue law of 1750 had put an effective check on the establishment and development of opera. It could not, however, exterminate those persons who were merely waiting for an opportunity to brush the law aside. Nor could it prevent the theatrical instincts of Boston from coming to the surface on more than one occasion. For instance, on Feb. 19, 1751, the *Boston Gazette* announced:

> Propos'd to be printed by subscription. The Suspected Daughter; or, the Jealous Father, a farce of three acts, both serious and comic, as it was acted by a number of gentlemen and ladies. Written by T. T. jun."

Though this farce might have been on the repertory of the rebuffed company of the previous year, yet some Bostonians apparently must have been known not to turn their minds with horror from things theatrical. This holds true if Rivington & Miller of the London Bookstore in 1762 saw fit to advertise their importation of the 'Musical Lady,' 'Don Quichote,' 'Love in a Village' (first performed in this very year!), and other plays.

The opera just mentioned was among those pieces which this clan of Bostonians in July and October, 1769, went to hear *read* "at a large room." In the following spring, on March 23, the 'Beggar's Opera' seems to have made its appearance in very much the same manner as the amazingly clever Leopoldo Fregoli nowadays renders *grand* opera. The "Person who has read and sung in most of the great towns in America" announced that "the songs (of which there are sixty-nine) will be sung" and further that "he personates all the characters and enters into the different humours, or passions, as they

133

change from one to another throughout the opera."
This person was Mr. Joan, whom I believe to be identical
with the American would-be Stradivari, James Juhan;
and John Rowe, the genial merchant-prince of Boston,
who was among the "upwards one hundred people,"
noted in his diary that Mr. Joan "read but indifferently,
but sung in taste." In this manner also 'Damon and
Phillida' was "performed."

Then followed by a "number of officers and ladies
having formed a society" some theatrical amusements
in 1775, the "overplus" of which was to be "appro-
priated to the relief of distress'd soldiers, their widows
and children." After the war, during the fall of 1788,
Mr. and Mrs. Smith, by permission, indulged in some
'Moral Lectures' at Concert Hall, including among
other blood-curdling but morally instructive things a
"dialogue on the horrid crime of murder, from
Shakespeare's Macbeth."

Two years later Hallam and Henry of the Old American
Company submitted a formal petition for permission
to open a real theatre at Boston. It was refused, and
now the friends of the drama would submit to the antediluvian attitude of the authorities no longer. In the
autumn of 1791 two meetings were held at Faneuil
Hall to urge the repeal of the law of 1750. The meetings
must have been stormy if even Samuel Adams could not
gain the ears of the assembly when he attempted to speak
in favor of the act. Mr. Tudor was instructed to bring
the grievance of the meeting before the legislature. This
he did on Jan. 17, 1792, and now the channels for argumen-
tative discussion pro and contra were dug wide and deep.
The most elaborate effort in favor of the repeal was that
of John Gardiner, subsequently printed as a pamphlet.
Though the committee in charge admitted that he
delivered "a learned and elaborate essay," and though
they admitted the "blaze of eloquence" displayed by
Dr. Jarvis, they succeeded in convincing the house of the

necessity of voting the petition down. This vote by no means settled the problem. Defiance of the law without getting into its grip now became the watchword, and a number of influential gentlemen forthwith proceeded to erect a building in Board-Alley which would be a theatre in everything but name. Mr. Seilhamer and Mr. Clapp have minutely described this amusing crusade against the Philistines. For my purposes it is sufficient to state that this first theatre at Boston was called the "New Exhibition Room," and that it was opened on Aug. 16, 1792, by Mr. Harper, Mr. Woolls, Mr. and Mrs. Placide (the dancers and pantomimists), with a "Gallery of Portraits," songs, feats of tumbling and the ballet-pantomime of 'The Bird Catcher.' Before the end of the month, ladies had found the courage to venture into this new abode of 'Lectures, Moral and Entertaining,' and by the end of September the company had been strengthened sufficiently to attempt the usual dramatic repertory of the day. The papers sided with the law-breakers and paid considerable attention to these performances, though, it is curious to note, they did not quite like opera. The 'Romp,' for instance, was considered by one critic "flat, stale and unprofitable." While the benefits were in progress, in December, 1792, Governor Hancock suddenly remembered the act of 1750, and as the disguise of 'Lectures, Moral and Entertaining' was a trifle too thin for his Excellency, he instructed the Attorney-General to begin legal proceedings against the players. This was done. Mr. Harper was arrested in the midst of a performance, but released later on bail and thus ended the first theatrical season of the Hub. During these few months, the musical people of Boston had occasion to relish or not to relish the following operas and pantomimes:

1792   Nov. 26: *Bear Hunters* (pant.)
        Aug. 16; Nov. 7: Bird Catcher (pant.)
          Sept. 10: Birth of Harlequin

1792	Nov. 28:	Devil to Pay
	Oct. 12:	Duenna
	Nov. 9:	Harlequin Balloonist (pant.)
Aug. 27; Sept. 18:		*Harlequin Doctor* (pant.)
	Sept. 3:	Harlequin Skeleton (pant.)
	Aug. 29:	*Harlequin Supposed Gentleman* (pant.)
	Nov. 19:	*Indian Heroine;* or, Inkle and Yarico (pant.)
	Nov. 23:	Love in a Village
	Oct. 17:	Mock Doctor
	Aug. 22:	Old Soldier (pant.)
	Nov. 12, 16:	Padlock
Sept. 26; Oct. 9; Nov. 2:		Poor Soldier
	Sept. 24:	Robinson Crusoe (pant.)
	Dec. 3:	Romp
	Oct. 15, 26:	Rosina
	Oct. 10:	Thomas and Sally
Aug. 20; Sept. 3:		Two Philosophers (pant.)
Sept. 5; Nov. 23:		*Two Woodcutters* (pant.)
	Sept. 10:	Virgin Unmasked

To give an idea of the company, I quote the cast of the "moral lecture 'Rosina' as delivered by" Messrs. Harper, Murry, Solomon, Robinson, Roberts, Mrs. Gray, Mrs. Solomon, Mrs. Morris. To these must be added, of course, Mr. and Mrs. Placide, without whose pantomimic activity the company possibly would have come to grief sooner. Mr. Seilhamer states that the orchestra was led by Mr. Reinagle. This I have not been able to verify, and am inclined to doubt it for obvious reasons. Our historian is certainly in the wrong in giving us the impression that with the Attorney-General's raid the performances at the New Exhibition Room came to a sudden end. They were merely reduced to vaudeville features, and I find in the *Columbian Centinel* that towards the end of January 1793 Mr. and Mrs. Placide again saw their way clear to fill the gaps between their feats of activity with pantomines, comedies and operas, *e. g.*, on March 1, the 'Virgin Unmasked.' More than this, at the end of March they acquainted

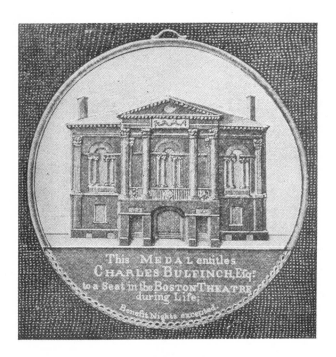

BULFINCH MEDAL
With façade of his original Federal Street Theatre, Boston
(From Winsor's "Memorial History of Boston")

Boston with French operas, but these will be considered later. That they could so defy the law was due to the fact that the friends of the drama had gained the ascendency over their opponents, and early in 1793, at least, the prohibition act of 1750 was argued to eternal slumber, though it is said not to have been really repealed by the customary two-thirds of both branches of the legislature. Immediately a fund was raised for the erection of a theatre at the corner of Federal and Franklin Streets. Charles Stuart Powell was appointed manager and was sent early in June to England to engage a suitable company. In the meantime, the New Exhibition Room continued to thrive and, besides the French, such English operas, etc., as the 'Mock Doctor' (May 1), 'Rosina' (May 13, 23; June 10), 'Padlock' (May 17), 'Poor Soldier' (May 29; June 10), were performed by substantially the same company as had, the winter previous, made the acquaintance of the sheriff.

The Federal Street Theatre, a substantial brick building 140 feet long, 61 feet wide and 40 feet in height, was ready for occupancy in January, 1794; but the first performance did not take place until February 3, when, as Judge Sumner tells us in a letter to Judge Wm. Cushing, dated Roxbury, 14 February, 1794 (N. E. Hist. & Gen. Reg., 1854), "gallery tickets were sold by speculators for more than twelve times their prime cost." The trustees went about their business with the utmost seriousness, and were bent on running a model institution which should give offence to nobody. Indeed, so great was their respect for the sentiments of the community, that when the Rev. Mr. Belknap selected a playnight for one of his lectures at the church in Federal Street, the theatre remained closed! The orderly manner in which the trustees desired the Federal Street Theatre to be managed became clear when they published on January 22 a long set of "Regulations" which went beyond anything American audiences until then had been requested to observe.

But also the actors received their share of admonition and the third paragraph read:

> If in the opinion of the trustees, there be a deficiency in the music, the manager at their request, shall be held to enlarge the band, and if any of the performers on the stage or in the orchestra, shall be guilty of gross misconduct, the manager shall dismiss the delinquent at the request of the trustees.

In order to enforce all the regulations, Col. John S. Tyler was appointed "Master of Ceremonies," and, indeed, the whole management was exceedingly ceremonious.

Col. Tyler's first pronunciamento, however, was rather unceremonious, as he publicly requested

> The ladies, as may be seated in the boxes where the seats are low, would attend without hats, bonnets, feathers or any other high head dress, *that the sight of the gentlemen, who are seated behind them, may not be obstructed!*

Our master of ceremonies further decreed that

> The music will be assigned for each evening—it is therefore requested that no particular tunes may be called for by the audience, as the compliance with such a request would destroy the arrangement and of course cannot be attended to.

This was too much for the "mobility"—not I, but Mrs. John Adams is responsible for this fearful pun—and what they proceeded to do becomes clear from the manly protest submitted through the press on Feb. 22, 1794:

> The musicians that perform in the orchestra of the Boston Theatre, assure the public that it is not more their duty than it is their wish to oblige in playing such tunes as are called for, but at the same time they wish them to consider the peculiar poignancy of insult to men not accustomed to it. Thus situated they entreat a generous people so far to compassionate their feelings as to prevent the thoughtless, or ill disposed, from throwing apples, stones, etc., into the orchestra, that while they eat the bread of industry in a free country, it may not be tinctured with the poison of humiliation.

This protest was timely, for the music assigned for each evening as curtain raiser was of such a character that no true musician and no true Bostonian could possibly submit to these insults without indignation. One assignment, the one for the opening performance of February 3, will suffice:

YANKEE DOODLE
Grand Battle Overture in Henry IVth [Martini]
General Washington's March
Between the Acts

A Grand Symphony	Sig. Charles Stamitz
Grand Overture	Sig. Vanhall
Grand Symphony	Sig. Haydn
Grand Symphony	Carlos Ditters

The ceremonious management of the Federal Street Theatre was praiseworthy in many ways, but unfortunately, as Mr. Seilhamer correctly puts it, "between newspaper suggestions and strictures and the quarrels and jealousies in his theatrical family, the manager had a lively time from the outset." Indeed, Boston's attitude towards the stage, or at least that of her leading champions of the theatre, was entirely too didactic. One need but read the "Effects of the stage on the manners of a people, and the propriety of encouraging and establishing a Virtuous Theatre. By a Bostonian [William Haliburton], Boston, 1792," to feel this. Such a curious mixture of lofty ideas, phantastic enthusiasm, pedantry, impracticability, erudition, ignorance, common sense and common nonsense has rarely left the press. His treatise was to be a panacea for all social evils, a school for virtue in which even angels would have blushed like sinners, a gold mine for Boston, Massachusetts, the whole United States—with a seating capacity of 6200 in a community of about 20,000 inhabitants! In this vast structure for esthetic discipline Haliburton provided for "a band of music, of which one to be a master of composition, two viols, three vocal performers." A few pages further on, however, the calculation concluded "six of the band, 150£ each, two viols 250£ and three vocal performers, 300£." And with this ludicrous consortium our Bostonian intended to put opera on a pedestal so high that Richard Wagner would have looked dwarfish. I cannot refrain from quoting from among the bombast woven around this proposed American Bayreuth in the clouds of Boston, the most salient and surely entertaining passages:

The theatre should be a mirror of life with its good and bad. The good to encourage the good and the bad to move the bad to leave the scene with "solemn vows of amendment" . . . .

Here music lends her aid divine, softens the savage heart, awakes the sympathetic powers of love and melting pity, lifts the rapt soul to Him who educes good from evil, who sees and shelters virtue in distress. With the animating descriptions of the Stage, music combines her soft, deep-felt, retentive sounds, her enhancing powers, and thenceforth united they return with trebled energy, dwell on the fancy and govern the man when busied on the daily concerns of life.

The burthen of the interludes should be the praise of the virtues of heroic souls, and all such personages as truly deserved the name of great; particularly the virtuous characters described in the scenes then acting, previously composed by the author of the play, in numbers well adapted to the subject, most affecting, and set to music by the greatest masters.

Banished forever, should be all unintelligible Italian airs, trills, affected squeaks and quavers, nothing but the deep-felt voice of nature, in harmonic sounds (vocal and instrumental united) can convey with fullest energy, the powers of music to the enraptured soul. Hence the stage would become to America not only the nurse of wisdom, but the school of oratory, sculpture, painting and music.

The modern music is not only faulty in such unintelligible sounds, but the variety of loud harsh notes, of bassoons, trumpets and hautboys combined (better adapted to excite the rage of war and drown the cries of battle) and the noisy organ are such that the human voice cannot be heard, and all sentiment is lost, instead of soothing or raising the soul and delighting the delicate fine ear, they only serve to rack and torture it with the violence of sounds. Therefore to the attentive, feeling mind, to the delicate, exquisite ear, the appeal is made and the following trial proposed.

Let sublime, affecting sentiment in the voice of manly or feminine harmony, be accompanied with some instrument or instruments capable of the full, deep, and well toned bass, as the viol, aided by the clear symphonie of the violin, tuned and executed in such manner, as only to give harmony to the human voice, and leave the sentiment at liberty, when the heart is thus attuned to take full possession of the soul, and lift it in ecstacy, to the loftiest heights of passion; or, move it delighted, into the profoundest depths of softened humanity, (etc.).

But back to reality! An idea of the Boston company under Powell may be gained from the cast of the first opera performed, 'The Farmer,' on Feb. 10, 1794:

Farmer Blackberry	Mr. Collins
Capt. Valentine	Mr. Nelson
Col. Dormant	Mr. S. Powell
Fairly	Mr. Kenna
Rundy	Mr. Bartlett
Counsellor Flummery . . .	Mr. Baker
Jemmy Jumps (the Stay Maker) .	Mr. Jones
Betty Blackberry	Mrs. Baker
Louisa	Miss Baker
Molly Maybush	Mrs. Abbot

That Powell's company was not without merit, even Wansey in his "Excursion" conceded. Calling "Boston the Bristol, New York the Liverpool and Philadelphia the London of America," and thinking the Old Americans of New York "altogether far inferior to the Boston company," he had this to say about the Federal Street Theatre and its occupants:

A very elegant theatre was opened at Boston about three months ago, far superior in taste, elegance and convenience to the Bath or any other country theatre that I have ever yet seen in England. I was there last night with Mr. and Mrs. Vaughan. The play and farce were Inkle and Yarico, and Bon Ton; I paid a dollar for a ticket. It held about twelve hundred persons. One of the dramatis personæ was a negro, and he filled his character with great propriety. The dress of the company being perfectly English and some of the actors (Jones and his wife) being those I had seen perform, the last winter at Salisbury, in Shatford's company, made me feel myself at home. Between the play and farce, the orchestra having played *Ça ira*, the gallery called aloud for Yankee Doodle, which after some short opposition was complied with. A Mr. Powell is the manager of the play-house. Mr. Goldfinch, the ingenious architect of this theatre . . . .

This season of 1794 closed on July 4 and Mr. Powell again hastened to England to strengthen the company. The theatre was reopened on Dec. 15, 1794, but when shut towards the end of June, 1795, Mr. Powell was practically bankrupt. Tired of the attacks upon his management, which was at least characterized by good taste, he withdrew in a frame of mind so bitter that he announced for publication by subscription "A true and perfect account of the Rise, Progress and Tragi-Comical Revolution of the Boston theatre, interspersed with curious and whimsical anecdotes, by S. C. P., late manager of said house."

The company recruited by Mr. Powell on his second trip to Europe did not contain celebrities, but the new members are said to have been well known in the provinces. Together with the old members they formed quite a respectable company. The cast of 'No Song, no Supper' on June 1, 1795, will help to form their acquaintance:

Robin	Mr. Jones
Crop	Mr. Collins
William	Mr. Hipworth
Endless (with a song in character)	Mr. Taylor
Frederick	Mr. Bartlett
Margaretta	Mrs. Hellyer
Louisa	Miss Harrison
Dorothy	Mrs. Jones
Welly	Mrs. Collins

It is curious to note that the Federal Street Company, though not the best in America (with all due respect for Mr. Wansey's contemporary judgment), was treated in Boston to more critical consideration in the press than had been customary. Nor were the critics satisfied with praising or condemning. There are signs that they, for

the first time in Boston, now considered it their duty
to instruct the artists on technical points. For instance,
Mr. Nelson was told on one occasion in the Theatrical
Department of the *Columbian Centinel* that the cold-
ness and indifference of the audience could only be ac-
counted for by "his not throwing out his voice sufficiently
to fill the house and permit the *pianos* to reach the
distant parts of the building." Mrs. Abbot, otherwise
the favorite during the first season, was told that as
Leonora in the 'Duenna' "she was much deficient in action
and seemed more like a statue than a volatile Miss."
The critic felt happy that in the same opera Mrs. Baker
"appears practically sensible of her precipitancy in some
parts of her periods." Mr. Clifford's "style of singing
is that of the most approved authors." From the performance of Mrs. Hellyer, the future Mrs. Gottlieb
Graupner, much pleasure was expected "when she can
get the better of those palpitations which have been
visible every time she has appeared," and that her "elegant voice only wants professional experience to make
it captivating—study and a little stage *degagée* will
render her highly agreeable." On the other hand, the
critic expressed his infinite regrets at the shocking
contrast between Mr. Taylor's Octavian in the 'Mountaineers', which would "sanction any eulogium," and
Mrs. Hughes' "total languor and insipidity" as Flor-
entine in the same opera. As a rule, however, the
criticisms were friendly in spirit, with discrimination, and
the old-time ammunition of such phrases as "in their
Syren notes [Mrs. Abbot and Mr. Powell] the audience
fully realized the pleasure they anticipated" was visibly
being exhausted. A change in taste and a gradual
adoption of new weights and measures!

After Mr. Powell withdrew from the management, the
Master of Ceremonies, Col. Tyler, was entrusted with
the furtherance of the Federal Street Theatre. He accepted the call and proved the wisdom of the choice by

immediately entering into arrangements with Hallam and Hodgkinson to bring on the New York company, with the result that this combination of the "House of York with the House of Boston"—Mr. Clapp's bon-mot in his Record of the Boston Stage—brought before the public a company, for the time being the strongest in America. But this feast of talent lasted only from November, 1795, to January, 1796, when the Old Americans had to hasten home and the Bostonians were again left to themselves. In April Col. Tyler voluntarily resigned. He was succeeded until the middle of May by Mr. J. B. Williamson, from the Covent Garden theatre, and a recent acquisition to the Boston company. The fourth season began exceptionally early, the middle of September, 1796, and did not end until January, 1797. The fifth began exceptionally late, in January, 1798. Early in February, just when everything betokened prosperity under Messrs. Barrett and Harper, fire broke out in one of the dressing-rooms and the whole theatre, with wardrobe and scenery, fell a prey to the conflagration. Though not protected by insurance, and consequently heavy losers, the shareholders resolved to rebuild it, and they certainly did not heed the wise and knowing who saw in the calamity the hand of God. Mr. Bulfinch, the architect, did his best to make the new building one of Boston's attractions, and it remained a landmark until 1852. The erection of the new Federal Street Theatre progressed so rapidly that John Hodgkinson, the new lessee, could open it the end of October, 1798. The season lasted only until April, 1799. Nor was his successor G. L. Barrett much luckier with the equally short season of 1799-1800. He tried to pay off debts contracted in New York by his earnings in Boston, and it was his further misfortune that the grief prevailing throughout the community at the irreparable loss of George Washington was detrimental to theatrical exhibitions everywhere.

During these ups and downs in the career of the Federal Street Theatre as far as it concerns us here, Boston was treated to the following repertory, with Monsieur Trille Labarre, later Mr. Van Hagen, as leader and purveyor of ready-made arrangements. [See *Table D.*]

At first glance this record seems to fall far below that of Philadelphia and New York, as would become a city just in her operatic teens; but it will be noticed that the difference really lies in a less extravagant display of pantomimes and ballets. This cannot but have had a beneficial effect on the taste of Boston, or rather, it was not deteriorated by artificial means. On the whole, the repertory impresses one as conservative, and certainly the several managers of the Federal Street Theatre did not cater to "American Opera," though on the other hand the custom of singing patriotic American airs between the acts, particularly during the troublesome year 1798, was carried farther in Boston than elsewhere. John Hodgkinson especially delighted in thus endearing himself to the public and incidentally reaping the "unbounded" applause for which he so craved with such patriotic airs as the "Green Mountain Farmer,' 'Adams and Washington,' or 'Hail Columbia.' The two latter, though nonpartisan, owed their birth to our diplomatic difficulties with France, and Hodgkinson or other imported English vocalists would naturally put all their heart into them. Had they been partisan songs, it is very questionable if the stockholders would have countenanced their performance night after night, as the Federal Street Theatre was owned by the Jacobin element of Boston, the political friends of France. This led to certain ludicrous neutralizations of favorite plays like the 'Poor Soldier', in which the character of *Bagatelle*, become offensive to American Frenchmen, was cut out and replaced by the makeshift character of *Domingo*, a negro valet.

This party standpoint was further made an issue when Boston was called upon to support a second play-house.

Whether it was his revenge for previous treatment at the Federal Street House, or an idiosyncrasy to manage theatres, or his opinion that Boston, though still in her theatrical teens, could support two rival companies, Mr. Charles Stuart Powell in April, 1796, advertised proposals for erecting a new theatre near the corner of Tremont and Boylston Streets, which he called the Haymarket. The sixty shares at $200 each were rapidly subscribed for, and a fourteen-year lease at an annual rental of $1200 was granted the ambitious promoter. While the new theatre, an immense wooden structure with three tiers of boxes, pit and gallery, and said to have been just as spacious as Covent Garden, was being built, Powell hastened to England, where he engaged the vocalists Williamson, Mr. and Mrs. Barrett, Mr. and Mrs. Simpson and the three Misses Westray, who were soon to turn the heads of men, young and old, in Boston. These, together with some faithful members of the old company and American favorites like Miss Broadhurst, opened the Haymarket Theatre on Dec. 26, 1796. Now a ludicrous war began between this and the Federal Street Theatre, for the supporters of the Haymarket were known to be Federals, that is, friends of John Bull and enemies of Monsieur Pantalon. Powell's company could not compare in merit with their rivals, and he therefore resorted to rather artificial and sensational methods to gain the upper hand. Not only did he produce typically American plays like John Burk's 'Bunker Hill' and William Brown's 'West Point Preserved,' which naturally would appeal to patriotic Americans of both parties and fill his house from both sides, but he soon imitated the Old Americans and Wignell and Reinagle by making pantomimes and ballets a feature. Consequently, for a while, the Haymarket Theatre played to crowded audiences. To offset this, the owners of the Federal Street Theatre, who were wealthier than their rivals, gave to every shareholder a benefit night, which

THE HAYMARKET THEATRE, BOSTON

(From a water-color at the Boston Public Library as reproduced in
"Winsor's Memorial History of Boston")

meant, in this case, that he had to pay all expenses and incidentally that he took pride in cramming the house with *deadheads*. In return, these were supposed to pledge themselves never to enter the Haymarket Theatre. Not only this, the trustees sought to kill competition by lowering the price in the pit to fifty cents and in the gallery to twenty-five. The net result of these machinations was that neither institution flourished, but the main purpose was accomplished: Mr. Powell found himself sometimes unable to pay salaries. He gave up his lease and disbanded his company in June, 1797. One month later, John Hodgkinson, whom nothing could cure of his mania to manage theatres at the greatest possible cost, opened the Haymarket for a "regular summer and fall season," recruiting his forces among the several stranded companies. At the end of July he entered into an agreement with John Sollee, the proprietor of the City Theatre, Charleston, by which they leased *both* theatres at Boston for five years—with the understanding that the Haymarket was to be reserved for summer exhibitions and the Federal Street Theatre for winter. The plan for the latter further provided that one company should play in Boston and one in Charleston, to be exchanged every season. These plans evidently miscarried, and this is perhaps the reason why the alliance has escaped the attention of all other historians. However, they were formulated and published; proof for this statement will be furnished in the chapter on Charleston.

In November of the same year a few stray benefits took place at the Haymarket. Then came the conflagration of the Federal Street Theatre and Bostonians immediately realized what a by far more dangerous fire-trap the immense wooden pile of the Haymarket Theatre was. Indeed, one of the shareholders promised to contribute three hundred and forty dollars if the authorities would only decree that the theatre be demolished and that no other be erected in Boston.   He and others were up in arms when Messrs. Barrett and Harper and their company, whom the conflagration of the Federal Street Theatre had reduced to most uncomfortable circumstances, attempted to reopen the Haymarket without proper permission.   But the differences between them, the trustees and Hodgkinson, the nominal manager, were adjusted; and, adopting the motto: "Necessitas legem non habet," Barrett and Harper occupied the Haymarket from April to June 1798.   After this, its career was very asthmatic indeed during the period covered by this monograph. In fact, only an equally short spring season in 1799 under Hodgkinson himself is worth noticing.   In the accompanying table all the performances given at the ill-fated Haymarket Theatre are tabulated regardless of the different managements.   [See *Table E.*]

A good idea of the forces assembled at the Haymarket Theatre under Powell's management may be gained from the typical announcement in the *Columbian Centinel,* Jan. 25, 1797:

This evening will be presented the Historical Tragic, Comic Opera, called the *Battle of Hexham;* or, Days of Old.   With new scenery, dresses and decorations.   Music by Dr. Arnold.   Orchestra accompaniments entirely new, composed by Mr. Van Hagen, leader of the Band.

Gondibert (Capt. of the Banditti) .	Mr. Barrett
Prince of Wales (her first appearance)	Miss E. Westry
Lavasenne	Mr. Taylor
Fool	Mr. S. Powell
Barton	Mr. Marriot
Drummer	Mr. Dickinson
Fifer	Mr. Wilson
First Robber	Mr. Williamson
Corporal	Mr. Hughes
Villagers	Miss Broadhurst, Mrs. Pick . . . .
Gregory	Mr. Simpson
Adeline	Mrs. S. Powell
Queen Margaret	Mrs. Barrett

As the disastrous competition of the two theatres at Boston, carried even to the point of presenting the same works, throws no new light on the subject of opera in America, either as to repertory, critics and criticism, formation of orchestras, behavior of audiences, and so on, we may turn our attention to other cities in New England. But before so doing, a few remarks are necessary on one enterprise at Boston, which is absolutely unique in the early annals of the American stage: *operas and pantomimes performed by children.*

This hideous spectacle was another immediate result of the conflagration of the Federal Street Theatre. Mr. Lege, the ballet master of the fire-victims, "having witnessed the great success of exhibitions performed by children" in Europe, and anxious to let the public of Boston "judge by themselves if performances done by children, perfect in their respective parts, were not worthy their attention," met "with some children whose disposition and forwardness" prompted him to thus try the experiment on the good people of Boston. Accordingly, Mr. Lege rented Mr. Dearborn's Exhibition Room, called it Mr. Dearborn's Theatre, and here the poor little "forward" creatures, in February, 1798, gave a series of "infantile exhibitions," including the opera 'The Purse' and pantomime-ballets like the 'Hunter's Reconciliation' and the 'Collier and the Miller.'

Comparatively few of the actors who found their way to America returned to England. As the number of imported Thespians was speedily increasing, as the large companies were repeatedly reorganized, strengthened or weakened, it is clear that an outlet for the surplus must be created. It was found in decentralization. Thus it happened that theatrical performances occurred in many small cities of the Union which, under ordinary circumstances, would hardly have been deemed sufficiently lucrative stations on the theatrical circuit. This point should be kept in mind, if a fair appreciation of the theatrical activity in our country at the end of the eighteenth century is desired. We should not forget that Philadelphia in 1800 was a city of only 70,000 inhabitants, New York of only 60,000 and Boston of only 25,000. Baltimore was of about the same size as New England's metropolis, whereas Charleston, S. C., contained only 20,000 inhabitants. These were the large cities in our country, but mark the contrast between them and Richmond, Va., with about 6,000, Washington, 3,000, Salem, Mass., 8,000, New Haven, Conn., 4,000, Providence, R. I., 9,000, Portsmouth, N. H., 5,000, or Hartford, Conn., with 3,000 inhabitants only. Yet all these and a good many more towns came in for one or several "seasons." That gave them an opportunity to form at least a superficial acquaintance with the English opera of the day in more or less creditable performances. This fact is significant so far as the towns of New England are concerned, for there, we have been taught, the pleasures of life were not looked upon as necessities, as down South. It cannot be denied that outside of Boston the people of New England were just a trifle shy of widening the channels of the legally authorized pleasures of life, yet it is a curious fact that while Boston was still handcuffed by the prohibitory act of 1750, a company of comedians, headed by a Mr. Watts, appeared in the summer of 1792 at Portsmouth, N. H., without being molested. The performances there took place in a warehouse, but in 1796 the Assembly Room was turned into a theatre, and there Mrs. Arnold and her daughter with the assistance of "gentlemen of Portsmouth" gave, among other works, 'Rosina' (Sept. 26) and 'The Devil to Pay' (Oct. 28; Nov. 2). When she left, Mrs. Arnold submitted through the medium of the "Oracle of the Day" a proposition for erecting a real theatre at a cost of $1,500, where "good performers" were to "play twice or oftener in every week during the summer months." I do not know what became of this fantastic plan. At any rate, when she returned as Mrs. Tubbs, in February, 1797, for a *season* of three nights, the Assembly Room was again occupied by a fairly good company, including among others Mr. Harper, Boston's first manager. The ambitions of this combination ran as high as the 'Mountaineers' (Feb. 15) and the 'Battle of Hexham' (Feb. 27), with a plentiful supply of incidental amusements.

Possibly Mrs. Tubbs was responsible for the scheme of erecting a theatre at Portsmouth, since "Mrs. Tubbs, late Mrs. Arnold of the Theatre Royal Covent Garden . . . . . and now from the Boston Theatre," in the middle of November, 1796, mentioned in a concert announcement that Mr. Tubbs intended setting up a theatre at Portland, Me. But here again they contented themselves with the Assembly Room, where on Dec. 12 'The Devil to Pay' and the pantomime 'Harlequin Skeleton' adorned the boards. This cannot have been the first night, for on the same day "a correspondent [to the *Eastern Herald*] who at first censured and afterwards praised the theatrical performances in their town, thinks it necessary to make further observations." According to these, 'The Waterman' was given on Dec. 2 and the 'Padlock' on Dec. 5. On Dec. 16, Messrs. Clapham and Partridge had their benefit with the 'Devil to Pay'; on Dec. 30, Mrs. Tubbs, with the 'Mountaineers' and 'Rosina'; and Miss Arnold on January 12, 1797, with the 'Deserter,' "translated from the French." That the company was not assisted by an orchestra is pretty certain, for "the whole of the music of 'Rosina' [was] to be accompanied on the pianoforte by Mr. Tubbs." This pianistic ability proved to be Mr. Tubbs' downfall, as our correspondent in his observations had already taken occasion to remark: "Mr. Tubbs performs well on the pianoforte, but he cannot sing. Why does he not oftener introduce that instrument? and why does he attempt to sing at all?" Poor Tubbs fared still worse when he put some amateurs on the stage. Public opinion, as represented by our critic, rebelled against this imposition, "and every one present seemed literally to sweat with relief. The exhibition and the sweat continued about one hour and a half!" It is really not surprising that Portland, Me., after this preferred the feats on wire of "Don Pedro Cloris, known in general by the name of Doneganey," or in 1798 "the exhibition of innocent amusements" by Mr. Maginnis, a ventriloquist who performed, with "real figures," John Hodgkinson's 'Launch.'

The few exhibitions of Mr. Hogg, "late of the Boston theatre," in the Hall over the School Room at Worcester, Mass., in June 1797 were probably not less primitive than Mr. Tubbs' exertions, and perhaps some local historian will be able to garnish the performances of the 'Waterman' and 'Oracle; or, Daphne and Amintor' (June 21) with curious observations à la Portland. Somewhat less primeval, to judge from the tone of the announcement, was the attempt of Mrs. Solomon, a favorite Southern actress, to introduce drama and opera at New London, Conn., between Nov. 1791 and Jan. 1792. At any rate, the newspapers prove that New London had occasion to enjoy the 'Romp' on Nov. 4, the 'Female Madcap' and the 'Padlock.' on Nov 11, the 'Mock Doctor' on Jan. 13, and the 'Virgin Unmasked' on Jan. 20.

New London was not the only town in Connecticut—village would perhaps be more appropriate—which tasted the sweets of operatic lore in those years. Hartford was another, and keeping in mind that Connecticut's capitol then counted but 3,000 souls, Mr. N. H. Allen's amazement was very natural when he was writing his noteworthy, interesting articles on "Old-time music and musicians" for the *Connecticut Quarterly*, Vols. I-IV, and saw himself confronted by Hartford's first plunge into drama. Like others, he had laid weight at first on sacred music, but as his work progressed he became "conscious of having done scant justice to the stage player who entertained and instructed the Hartford people during the summer months of several years preceding the act of May, 1800, which forbade theatrical representations." He made amends for his sins of omission, and it would be well for the history of music in our country if local historians would systematically take up the threads of history in a manner similar to that of Mr. Allen, as it is hardly the business of the general historian (and certainly not in a survey like mine) to gather all the local threads into one big Gordian knot.

The fact is, that the Old American Company made Hartford one of their main stations and performed there from July 3, 1794, until the close of the century almost every summer with a very considerable contingent of its forces, managed by John Hodgkinson. Also contingents from the Boston and even the Charleston, S. C., theatres would appear there, *e. g.*, in 1797, including the best ballet-dancers, pantomimists and prestidigitateurs America could boast, Mme. Gardie, Monsieur Lege, and others. Just why Hartford was selected is not clear, because before long everybody, except perhaps John Hodgkinson, saw that a hamlet of 3,000 souls could not properly support such a company. However, this does not concern us here, whereas the surprising fact should briefly but forcibly be pointed out, that Hartford in those years was really an operatic summer resort. Just where the performances took place at first, I do not know. Perhaps Mr. Frederick Bull's Long Room had been turned into a "theatre," as the announcements were headed. At any rate, the theatre contained "boxes" at 3/9, pit 2/3 and gallery at 1/6, "children under 12 years of age, gallery tickets 9*d*." For the convenience of the public, the box office was moved to the Post Office, where places could be taken during post hours and—what was unusual—tickets could be had until after seven on play evenings, which were to be "on Mondays, and Thursdays, without variation."

In July, 1795, however, Hallam and Hodgkinson invited Hartford to the "New Theatre," where they intended to perform, beginning with Aug. 3, three times a week; and it is, therefore, pretty certain that they must have erected or at least remodelled a suitable building for theatrical exhibitions. The detachment of the Old Americans consisted in 1794 only of minor members such as Mr. and Mrs. Martin, Mr. and Mrs. King, Hodgkinson appearing only as what Germans call a "guest"; but in the following years the company at Hartford was sometimes almost as strong as at New York! Of course, the Hartford campaigns were but skirmishes in the history of opera in America and did not turn the current in any new direction. The record of Hartford's seasons, therefore, follows here without further comment. [See *Table F.*]

Hartford was not only accorded the honor of first American performances, but was also distinguished by an almost unique deviation from theatrical custom. Usually all the actors and actresses everywhere would come in for their benefits, but it was quite contrary to the rule to accord this privilege to the members of the orchestra. It is therefore worth noticing that on Nov. 1, 1799, the benefit took place for the treasurer and Mr. William Priest, leader of the band. On the whole, though Hallam and Hodgkinson reaped no harvest, they could not complain of bad treatment at Hartford. The files of the *Connecticut Courant* leave no doubt that at Hartford audience and actors lived on terms of mutual good will. The city seemed to feel proud of her selection and was perfectly willing to endorse the boast of a correspondent in 1795, namely, that persons who had been in London and Paris agreed that the performances at Hartford did not fall far below such in the Old World and were equal to those in New York and Boston. Nevertheless, as the custom did not yet prevail to try novelties on provincial audiences before setting them before the supposedly

TITLE OF OPERA	1794	1795	1796	1797	1798	1799
Adopted Child			Aug. 31	Sept. 27		
Agreeable Surprise		Sept. 23	Aug. 8			Nov. 1
Battle of Hexham			Aug. 27			
Boiteuse (pant.-ballet)		Sept. 7		Aug. 17		
Caledonian Frolic (ballet)		Apr. 17				
Children in the Wood		Oct. 2	July 18; Aug. 29	July 6		
Columbus						
Daphne and Amintor						Sept. 16
Deserter				Sept. 29		
Double Disguise				Sept. 14, 25		Sept. 23
Elopement (pant.)		Sept. 21				
Enchanted Island (pant., Shield, 1786?)						Sept. 30
Farmer		Sept. 28	Aug. 12			
Flitch of Bacon			July 27			
Forêt Noire (pant.)		Sept. 14		Sept. 5		
Harlequin Gardener (pant.)		Oct. 2				
Harlequin in Hartford (pant.)						Nov. 11
Harlequin Restored (pant.)		Aug. 31	Aug. 22			
Harlequin's Cook (pant.)	Sept. 8					
Haunted Tower		Aug. 24				
Highland Reel		Aug. 26	Sept. 29; Oct. 6			Oct. 14, 25
Highland Wedding (pant.)		Sept. 28				
Inkle and Yarico			Aug. 29	Sept. 11		
Launch				Nov. 20		

My Grandmother			Aug. 5		Aug. 1?
No Song, no Supper	Aug. 11, 25				Aug. 5
Old Sergeant (pant.)		Sept. 28			
Padlock					Nov. 4
Poor Soldier		Sept. 7	July 27	Sept. 5	
Poor Vulcan		Oct. 9	Aug. 1		
Prisoner			Sept. 2		
Prize		Sept. 21			Sept. 2
Purse		Oct. 5	July 11		Aug. 19
Quaker		Oct. 5	July 20	Nov. 15	
Rival Candidates		Aug. 3			
Romp		Sept. 25	July 25		
Rosina	Sept. 1	Aug. 10	July 13		
Shipwreck					Nov. 11
Siege of Belgrade				July 5	
Siege of Quebec ("taking of Q.")				Oct. 6	Sept. 9; Oct. 30
Smugglers					Oct. 7, 23
Sophia (pant.)		Sept. 25			
Tom Thumb the Great				July 7	
Two Philosophers (pant.)		Sept. 23			
Virgin Unmasked				Aug. 21	
Waterman			Sept. 5	Aug. 28	
Zorinski				Sept. 27	

more critical public of New York, the managers always hastened to remark in the advance notice that the work had met with "unbounded" applause in New York, Philadelphia or Boston. They also begged the people of Hartford to drop the prejudice against the stage and to believe that "a theatre well conducted, may and ought to be considered as a National School, where the unwary are taught to guard against vice of every kind, and inspired with a love of all that is great and good." This was well put, and several friends of the drama used the columns of the *Connecticut Courant* to elaborate on this idea and to convince the unbelieving that the theatre was really a place for "rational" and moral enjoyment. It became a school for scandal, however, when the managers quite unintentionally violated the principals of truest democracy. Noticing that the ladies of Hartford still entertained the time-honored prejudice against frequenting the pit, with its *mauvaise odeur* of "segars," the managers first notified the public that a partition would be set up for their female customers. When this did not prove satisfactory they explained that everywhere else in the world merchants and their wives and persons of moderate income preferred the pit to the more expensive boxes. Immediately the hated class-distinction was scented between the lines of this explanation and the managers very apologetically protested against such a construction of their advice to the "most respectable citizens with their families"—and reduced the price of admission to the boxes to three quarters of a dollar; pit, half a dollar; gallery, one quarter of a dollar, the latter, by the way, the price of admission for colored people.

The open door policy with reference to theatricals was adopted in Rhode Island about the same time. Here Mr. Joseph Harper, after his release from prison in Boston, made the rival cities of Newport and Providence the centres of his activity. Although the law against theatrical entertainments was not repealed in Rhode Island until February, 1793, public opinion, so Mr. Willard in his History of the Providence Stage says, condemned its severity. This attitude is apparent, since Mr. Solomon and Murry's company of comedians were permitted to present themselves towards the end of February, 1792, in such works as the 'Poor Soldier.' Accordingly, Mr. Harper did not find it difficult to obtain the Court House of Providence for his exhibitions in December 1792 and January 1793 on condition that the proceeds of the sale of tickets on every fifth night be paid into the town treasury. The performances given, for safety's sake, in the traditional disguise of "Moral Lectures," proved profitable, and a movement was started to provide Providence with a real theatre. When Mr. Harper returned in Dec. 1794 to remain until the middle of April 1795, he had to content himself with a makeshift affair in the rear of the building known as the Old Coffee House; but in April 1795 subscriptions for a new theatre were so liberally promised that in August the workmen commenced raising the edifice which stood at the corner of Westminster and Mathewson Streets. Indeed, such was the enthusiasm for the enterprise, that the carpenters of the town, clubbing together, formed a "bee" and, abandoning all other employments, laboured without fee or reward upon the edifice until the opening night, Sept. 3, 1795. The company which ushered in the season, of course, was recruited among members of the Old Americans and such other players as were available, and while numerically not very strong was a creditable one. The season closed in November, when "Harper and Co." joined Hodgkinson at Boston. After this he returned regularly for the summer season, if this term may be stretched to include, as in 1797, the latter part of April and the autumn. It is also worth noticing that the long season of 1797 proved rather asthmatic, owing to an outbreak of yellow fever and

TITLE OF OPERA	1795	1796
Adopted Child		
Beggar's Opera	Apr. 13	
Children in the Wood	Oct. 12	July 28
Cooper (pant.)		
Devil to Pay	Apr. 6; Oct. 29	June 17
Farmer		June 27
Highland Reel		Aug. 1; Sep
Inkle and Yarico	Apr. 3	Aug. 22
Lock and Key		
Love in a Village	Apr. 17; Oct. 29	
Mirza and Lindor (pant.)		
Mountaineers	Oct. 19	July 11, 15; 9
No Song, no Supper		Aug. 5
Oscar and Malvina (pant.)		Sept. 10
Padlock	Mar. 5	July 1
Poor Soldier	Feb. 6, 21; Sept. 11	July 8
Prize		July 25
Purse		
Quaker	Sept. 4	June 10
Robinson Crusoe (pant.)	Nov. 2	
Romp		
Rosina	Mar. 16; Apr. 10; Sept. 3	
Son-in-law		Aug. 8
Sultan		
Thomas and Sally	Mar. 9	
Three Quakers (pant.)		
Triumph of Mirth; or, Harlequin's Vagaries	Oct. 6	
Two Philosophers (pant.)	Sept. 25	June 2
Witches (pant.)	Sept. 18, 20; Oct. 2	

1797	1798	1799
....	Sept. 3	....
....	....	....
Apr. 20	Sept. 4	....
June 5	....	....
....	....	....
July 14; Sept. 4	....	....
....	Sept. 17	July 26
July 21	....	....
....	Sept. 6	....
Apr. 24	....	Sept. 6
June 9	....	....
July 7	Sept. 20	....
....	Oct. 5	....
....	....	July 26
Sept. 8	....	....
June 19	....	....
....	....	....
....	Sept. 21	....
June 23	....	....
....	....	....
June 16	....	....
July 10	....	....
....	....	....
....	....	Sept. 6
Nov. 16	....	....
June 5	....	....
....	....	....
....	....	....
....	....	....

other causes. Not only this, Mr. Harper found himself obliged to rely very much on the rope-dancing, etc., of Mr. Spinacuta, Mr. Francisquy, Mad. Val and their allies in order to make both ends meet. The "moral lectures" of 1792-93 included the 'Poor Soldier' (Dec. 26) and the pantomime *'Birth, Death and Animation of Harlequin'* (Jan. 1), a very modest contribution indeed to the history of opera in Providence; but from 1795 on Harper & Co. became more ambitious, as the following table will show. [See *Table G.*]

It is obviously impossible to keep track of the companies as they stroll through the country shifting their personnel and their abode with lightning rapidity, until the local historians have supplied the general historian with road-houses for shelter and information. Newport, Providence's rival, is a case in point. But, by combining the data in Mr. Willard's book and that of Mr. Seilhamer with my own, extracted from the musty, dusty files of contemporary newspapers, at least a superficial account may be given of the beginnings of opera at Newport. Here Alexander Placide, the pantomimist, in 1793 obtained permission to convert the upper stories of the brick market of 1762 into a play-house, and it was also here that Joseph Harper in 1793 and 1794 kept his company busy, while he was awaiting developments at Providence. These performances were preceeded on Jan. 21, 1793, by an anonymous representation of the "comic lecture" the 'Padlock' at the Court House for the benefit of the poor. Mr. Harper's, together with Mr. Placide's, experiments at Newport included:

1794,	July 19:	Beggar's Opera
1793,	July 3:	Bird Catcher (pant.)
1794,	June 26:	Devil to Pay
1793,	Aug. 8:	Harlequin Skeleton
	Sept. 12:	Harlequin Skeleton
	Oct. 3:	Love in a Village
	Aug. 28:	No Song, no Supper
	Aug. 29:	Padlock

```
1794,   July 1:   Quaker
1793,   July 10:  Robinson Crusoe (pant.)
1794,   May 22:   Romp
        June 10:  Romp
        July 15:  Romp
1793,   Aug. 8:   Rosina
1794,   May 29:   Thomas and Sally
        Aug. 14:  Thomas and Sally
1793,   Oct. 3:   Two Philosophers (pant.)
1794,   July 31:  Witches (pant.)
```

In 1796 the pantomime and ballet contingent of the Old Americans together with some other player-folk visited Newport and treated the city to the 'Cooper,' 'Robinson Crusoe,' '*Harlequin's Ramble*,' and similar works. Their most serious efforts were bestowed on 'Inkle and Yarico', turned into a pantomime, and on the 'Poor Soldier' (July 19). From a pitiful appeal to the public it would appear that John Durang and his associates barely escaped starvation. In the following year (1797) Mr. Harper again descended on Newport from April until August, with interruptions. His repertory this time included 'Love in a Village' (April 5), 'Rosina' (April 12), 'Poor Soldier' (June 27), 'Mountaineers' (Aug. 2), 'Romp' (Aug. 23).

The vulgar fellow with a wry neck, as Dunlap dubbed Mr. Watts, the same who had given Portsmouth, N. H., a taste of drama and opera, made himself and his company agreeable at Salem, Mass., from Nov. 1793 to Jan. 1794—so agreeable, indeed, claims Mr. Seilhamer, that even the families of several of the clergy went to see the wicked players. Mr. Watts' company was not without merit, as it included Mr. and Mrs. Solomon and Mrs. Mechtler, *née* Fanny Storer, a popular soubrette. They had selected Washington Hall, Court Street, for their purposes and there they exhibited in the operatic line the 'Poor Soldier' (Nov. 19); 'Padlock' (Dec. 16, Jan. 14); 'Agreeable Surprise' (Dec. 20); 'Thomas and Sally' and the 'Romp' (Dec. 26). That the company, whose members (as was often the case on provincial tours) appeared both in comedy and opera, did not include an orchestra, appears from the announcement that music would be obtained from Boston. It is also curious to note that the 'Padlock' seems to have been considered an especially complicated and difficult opera, since "the public was respectfully informed that no disappointment will take place with respect to the performance of the Padlock on account of the music."

After his venture to Salem, Mr. Watts moved to Dorchester, then to Boston, and silence seems to have reigned at Salem in the realm of opera until 1797. By this time, it will be remembered, Mr. Powell had reached the climax of his Boston career and outlets had become necessary for the talent accumulated at Boston. One outlet was found at Washington Hall at Salem, practically a suburb of the Hub, during June and July of 1797. The company comprised such experienced actors (mostly Mr. Sollee's Southerners) as Mr. Cleveland, Mr. and Mrs. Jones, Mr. and Mrs. Hughes and Mrs. Graupner, whose husband Gottlieb, fairly famous in American musical history, very probably sat in the orchestra. At Washington Hall, "fitted up like a regular theatre," the Salemites had occasion to listen to the following works during this their second operatic experience:

July 21:	Battle of Hexham
June 21:	Inkle and Yarico
June 30, July 4:	Mountaineers
June 23:	No Song, no Supper
July 21:	Padlock
July 4:	Poor Soldier
June 29, July 7:	Purse
July 14:	Romp
July 12:	Rosina

As the whole *season* consisted of only fifteen nights, it follows that the honors were about evenly divided between drama and opera. Apparently the company did a fairly profitable business at Salem; otherwise it would not have returned, with slight differences in the personnel, to Washington Hall in 1798. This third season lasted from May to early July. Headed by a Mr. Simpson they reappeared in June 1799, but, contrary to expectation, interest in theatricals flagged, and after a fortnight the manager betook himself to other climes, brooding over his losses. The performances of 1798 and 1799 were characterized by a plentiful supply of incidental popular and patriotic songs. To judge from the advance puffs he received in the *Salem Gazette*, the "comic" Mr. Villiers must have braved storms of applause with 'Hail Columbia,' 'Death or Liberty,' and the local "Salem Patriotic song to the tune of Yankee Doodle." Other patriotic songs which here as elsewhere helped to enliven matters on several occasions were 'Washington's Council for ever' and 'Adams and Liberty.' Such songs illustrate just as well as ponderous political histories the mood of our people in the cloudy year 1798. The less patriotically and more sentimentally inclined received their dues when Mrs. Graupner, accompanied by Gottlieb's hautboy, would move their souls, with 'Sweet Echo' and 'How d' ye do,' and it is a delightful touch of the times that Gottlieb Graupner "presents his compliments to the public and informs them that to prevent a disappointment he will himself go to Boston for the instrument." The operas, etc., performed at Salem in 1798 and 1799, always allowing for irrelevant omissions, were:

1798,	May 23:	Adopted Child
	June 22:	Agreeable Surprise
	June 26:	Farmer
	June 29:	Harlequin Skeleton (pant.)
	July 3:	Harlequin Skeleton (pant.)
	June 5:	Inkle and Yarico
1799,	May 28:	Inkle and Yarico
1798,	May 25:	Mountaineers
	June 26:	No Song, no Supper

1798, May 30:   Padlock
      June 12:   Padlock
      May 28:   Poor Soldier
      May 11:   Purse
      May 16:   Romp
      June 15:   Rosina
      May 30:   Sicilian Romance
      June 8:   Sicilian Romance
1799, June 14:   Waterman

It cannot be said that outside of Boston opera was of great moment in New England, but Puritan New England did not and seemingly would not escape its fascinations and these sporadic and asthmatic *seasons* should not be underestimated. At least, the people of New England received a taste of opera, generally well performed, and if it be kept in mind that the sojourn of theatrical companies invariably led to concerts given by the vocalists and instrumentalists with more or less noteworthy programs, it is clear that these attempts at provincial and country opera helped to broaden the musical horizon of the people and to lead them out of the narrow channels of psalmody into which they had been drifting. The New Englanders could not help but notice the difference between the amateurish singing of their townsmen who figured as soloists at the Singing Societies and local musical events and that of these professional songsters, or again between the skill of a Gottlieb Graupner and that of some self-taught local and probably very irritable, melancholical, yet conceited oboist. After all, taste is merely the faculty for distinction, and once the seed of distinction has been sown, it will grow even in arid soil, though perhaps at first but slowly. For these reasons, readers with a historical retina may smile, but they certainly will not laugh at these somewhat irregular injections of opera into New England.

In a previous chapter the operatic history of Baltimore was traced down to the year 1788 in connection with the career of the Old America Company before its reorganzation. No mention, however, was made of the comparatively few operas, etc., performed during the last season of 1787 and 1788. They may be enumerated here for the completion of the record together with the two opera performances by the Old Americans between the the middle of August and October, 1790:

1788, Sept. 19:	Banditti	
1790, Sept. 22:	Dead Alive	
1787, Sept. 11:	Deserter	
Sept. 25:	Duenna	
Oct. 5:	Duenna	
Sept. 7:	Love in a Camp	
1790, Sept. 24:	Love in a Camp	
1787, Aug. 31:	Love in a Village	
Sept. 25:	Love in a Village	
Sept. 14:	Neptune and Amphitrite (masque)	
1788, Sept. 12:	Padlock	
1787, Aug. 27:	Poor Soldier	
Aug. 29:	Poor Soldier	
Sept. 23:	Robinson Crusoe (pant.)	

Just three months previous to the summer season of the Old Americans, Baltimore received her first taste of French opera by a motley company of French refugees. In Feb., 1791, Messrs. West and Bignall, "managers of the Virginia company," invaded Baltimore, but their performances at the New Assembly Room consisted only of that "elegant and fashionable pasticcio, the *Evening Brush* for rubbing off the rust of care," a curious mixture of recitations, songs and such pieces as the

162

'Battle of Prague.' One month later they were followed by the Kenna family's self-appointed "New American Company," but announcements of operas performed by them at the Old Theatre near the Middle Bridge must have escaped me, if indeed they performed any. Another set of strolling players reached Baltimore in April, 1793. They called themselves the Maryland Company and were managed by two of the most erratic actors America then knew, M'Grath and Godwin. Though joint-managers, they were not friends, and on parting both indulged in invectives of no mean order. Godwin, for instance, described his ex-partner in one of Baltimore's papers as "a spoiled priest, turned itinerant player," but he, at least, gave Christopher Charles M'Grath (who died at Reading, Pa., in 1799) credit for being "capable of doing up a smart piece either in prose or verse." Both gentlemen were jacks of all trades— singers, actors, authors, managers. In this latter capacity their combined energy gave to Baltimore shortly after their arrival a "New Theatre" situated near the Market, between Philpot's and the Lower Bridge. It was opened "by authority" at the end of April, a fact evidently unknown to Mr. Seilhamer, as he merely mentions performances by M'Grath and God-win in September. The company included Mr. and Mrs. Solomon, Mr. and Mrs. Murry, and others. The break between the two managers occurred in September, when Godwin took sudden leave for Annapolis. On the surface everything seemed to be smooth, since over the signature of both gentlemen on Oct. 2, 1793, a card ap-peared in the *Maryland Journal* to the effect that the theatre would remain closed until the arrival of rein-forcements for the Maryland Company. These did not come. At any rate, I have found only one performance announced in November, for the benefit of Mrs. Solomon, and in the cast neither M'Grath's nor Godwin's name appears! Culling the dates and titles from the *Maryland*

Journal I find that the following operas, etc., were in M'Grath and Godwin's repertory in 1793:

June 21, 25: Agreeable Surprise
    July 5:   America's Independence; or, Fourth of July
    Aug. 2:   Beggar's Opera
    July 5:   Damon and Phillida
    July 16: Devil to Pay
    June 14: Elopement ("musical farce")
    Aug. 2:   Honest Yorkshireman
    June 8:   Padlock
    June 4:   Romp
    Nov. 11: Romp
    Nov. 11: Thomas and Sally
    July 30: Waterman
    July 5:   Woodman

This repertory contained nothing very bold or new, but in one respect this Baltimore season is interesting, even important, though in another direction. It is known that Joseph Hopkinson, when he wrote the words of 'Hail Columbia' in 1798, had not forgotten certain striking lines in his father's 'Temple of Minerva'; but it is not known that the very title of his patriotic hymn did not originate with him. If proof for this somewhat startling discovery is desired, we need but turn to the announcement of the above-mentioned 'New prelude, called America's Independence; or, the Fourth of July' in the *Maryland Journal* of July 2, 1793. The performance was "to conclude with 'Hail! Columbia!' with an application to General Washington." (!!) Was this patriotic song, too, perhaps set to the tune of the 'President's March' and was Christopher Charles M'Grath, who is known to have written patriotic poetry, perhaps responsible for the words of this first and original 'Hail Columbia'?

Baltimore was now duly prepared for a more substantial theatrical diet. As previously stated, it was administered by Wignell and Reinagle, who selected

Baltimore for their professional summer and fall outings. The "New Theatre," probably the one erected or adapted by their predecessors, was to be opened by them on Sept. 24, 1794, but the first performance did not take place until Sept. 25. After two nights the theatre was closed until Oct. 13, at the request of the Committee of Health, on account of the outbreak of yellow fever. The season ended Nov. 22—not Oct. 31, as Mr. Seilhamer claims. The company returned at the end of July, 1795, and did not leave the city until early in December. The next year's season began about the same time, but closed the end of October. In the winter of this year (1796) several gentlemen contemplated building a "Private Theatre," the parts dramatic and musical to be taken by amateurs; but what became of this enterprise I do not know. When the Philadelphia company returned in the middle of May, 1797, they announced that the prices of admission "established many years ago in the infancy of the American stage" had been found impracticable. They were raised for box seats to 1 dollar 25 cents; pit, 7/8 of a dollar. It would therefore seem that M'Grath and Godwin had not provided a gallery in their theatre. We are not told how the public greeted the advance in the price of admission, but probably the fact that the season ended on June 10 was not due to the unwillingness of Baltimore to support Wignell and Reinagle on these new terms. Then came the lean years in the career of the Philadelphia company. Still, it is very likely my fault that I did not find more than two performances in Baltimore recorded for 1798, and these in May. The managers themselves gave the best clue to the extent of the season of 1799, as it was announced on May 30 to last "for eight nights only," but the theatre was reopened on Oct. 1 and did not close until Nov. 23.

That the attitude of the public towards the company had changed, is illustrated by the fact that full casts were then hardly ever printed in the papers, and indeed the whole tenor of the announcements leaves the impression of a policy of retrenchment. This must have poured joy into the soul of the critic of the *Maryland Journal*, who in 1795 treated the company to a series of curtain-lectures, unprecedented in the annals of the American stage. He would, to be sure, occasionally find a few words of praise, but not one of Wignell and Reinagle's costly imported stars escaped severe attacks, epithets like "wretched style," "a laboured piece of acting," "horribly insipid," "more ridiculous than the piece," coming from the critic's pen with delightful fluency. This treatment lasted three weeks, until the *Maryland Journal* shut down on its critic. It was the first time in our history that the liberty of the press was tampered with by the press itself in the interest of the advertising department; and the introduction of this deplorable principle into American journalism is certainly more to be regretted than the attitude of the critic, who failed to see that he was dealing with a company which could not have been duplicated outside of London. That Wignell and Reinagle and their company, including the useful pantomimist Francis, Lege and Byrne, did much during these limited seasons to develop Baltimore's musical taste, will appear from the appended record. [See *Table H.*]

Reviewing this table, we notice that during these summer seasons operas were given at Baltimore three and four times a week, sometimes two on the same evening, a practice which was slowly gaining ground everywhere if one opera was not long enough for an evening's entertainment, and in lieu of a mixed exhibition of drama and opera. Indeed, Wignell and Reinagle would seem to have laid greater stress on opera than on drama at Baltimore. Still, Baltimore was not an operatic centre, but merely an operatic suburb of Philadelphia. It was different with Charleston, S. C. Throughout the century the then Queen of the South was practically inde-

Table H

TITLE OF OPERA	1794	1795	1796	1797	1798	1799
Adopted Child				May 17		
Agreeable Surprise	Nov. 21	Sept. 25				Nov. 11
American True Blues; or, Naval Volunteers	Nov. 4					
L'Amour trouve les moyens; or, Fruitless Precaution (ballet)	Nov. 21					
Battle of Hexham		Nov. 28				
Beggar's Opera						
Blue Beard (pant.-ballet)				May 31		June 10; Oct. 5
Castle of Andalusia	Nov. 14	Aug. 5				Oct. 30
Children in the Wood		Aug. 24; Sept. 19	July 25; Oct. 5	June 9, 10		June 1
Columbus (Reinagle)	Nov. 11					Nov. 15
Comus (masque)			Oct. 2			June 3
Constellation		Sept. 9				
Dead Alive				June 2		
Death of Captain Cook (pant.)	Oct. 28	Aug. 22	Aug. 12	May 24, 27		
Death of General Wolfe (pant.-ballet)			Sept. 1			June 7; Nov. 1
Dermot and Kathleen (pant.-ballet)						
Deserter ("music by Monsigny, Philidor, Dibdin")						
Deserter of Naples (pant.)		Aug. 31		May 17		
Devil to Pay						
Deux Chasseurs (pant.-ballet)		Nov. 24		May 23, 30		
Drunken Peasant (ballet)		Oct. 23				
Duenna		Nov. 9				
Farmer		Aug. 22	Aug. 6			June 8
Flitch of Bacon	Sept. 25	Aug. 1				
Forêt Noire (pant.)	Nov. 18	Aug. 10				
Harlequin Conqueror; or, Magician of the Enchanted Island (pant.)		Aug. 26; Sept. 7				
Harlequin hurry-scurry (pant.)		Nov. 30	Sept. 7			
Harlequin Shipwrecked (pant.)		Oct. 24; Nov. 2, 13	Sept. 6			
Harlequin Skeleton (pant.)		Nov. 24	Sept. 3			
Harlequin's Invasion (pant.)			Sept. 30			
Hartford Bridge		Oct. 23				
Haunted Tower		Nov. 9				
Highland Festivity (ballet)				May 31		
Highland Reel	Oct. 29; Nov. 3	Aug. 31; Nov. 4	Aug. 27	June 6		
Inkle and Yarico	Nov. 5, 12	Aug. 15	Sept. 21	June 1		
Iron Chest (R. Taylor)				June 2		
Lionel and Clarissa	Nov. 19	Sept. 7				
Lock and Key				May 16, 22, 30		
Love in a Camp	Sept. 26	Oct. 29				
Love in a Village		Oct. 15	Sept. 26			
Lucky Escape (pant.)		Aug. 12; Nov. 7	July 29; Aug. 31			
Maid of the Mill	Oct. 22					
Midas		Nov. 17				
Miraculous Mill (pant., De Marque)		Nov. 21				
Mountaineers			Aug. 10; Oct. 19	June 3		Oct. 28
My Grandmother	Nov. 15	Aug. 29; Oct. 5	Oct. 28			
No Song, no Supper	Nov. 17		July 27			
Padlock		Sept. 30				
Patriot; or, Liberty Obtained (Carr)	Nov. 7, 13					
Peeping Tom of Coventry	Nov. 1	Aug. 14; Oct. 12	Sept. 3			
Poor Soldier		Sept. 22; Oct. 9	Sept. 5	May 27		
Prisoner			Aug. 1			
Prize	Oct. 23, 30	Aug. 8, 17	Aug. 31	June 7		
Purse; or, Benevolent Tar (Reeve, 1794)		July 29; Sept. 14; Dec. 1	Aug. 5; Oct. 12	May 23		June 5; Nov. 6
Quaker		Sept. 26	Sept. 28			
Rival Soldiers (dates?)						
Robin Hood	Nov. 6	Nov. 19	Sept. 2			
Robinson Crusoe (pant.)	Nov. 10		Oct. 5			Nov. 8
Romp		Aug. 3; Oct. 10	July 23			
Rosina	Sept. 29; Oct. 13, 25					
Sailor's Return; or, Thomas and Sally						
Saint Tammany's Festival (ballet-pasticcio)					May 18	June 6
Shipwreck					May 21	
Sicilian Romance			Sept. 9			
Son-in-law		Nov. 21				
Spanish Barber; or, Fruitless Precaution	Nov. 22	Oct. 9				
Spoiled Child (as "musical farce")	Oct. 27		Sept. 8			
Surrender of Calais	Nov. 10					
Tom Thumb the Great		Aug. 15, 21; Sept. 12				
Two Misers		Oct. 1				
Two Philosophers (pant.-ballet)		Oct. 5				
Virgin Unmasked	Oct. 15					
Waterman		Oct. 31		May 19		Nov. 20

pendent of the North in matters musical, and the fact that the ambitious, wealthy St. Cecilia Society advertised on one occasion in northern papers for musicians, should not be construed to mean that Charleston was compelled to draw her musical forces from the North. It merely indicates that the managers of the society desired to attract the best talent available, no matter from which corner of our country. In opera, of course, the great distance would have interfered with any attempt to make the city a regular station on the circuit of either the Old Americans or Wignell and Reinagle's company. Hence, Charleston retained her independence even in opera. Not alone this, but, as the logical result of geographical conditions, she, in turn, became the theatrical centre of the South, supplying other Southern cities in competition with more Northern companies with theatrical entertainments and producing novelties simultaneously with or even prior to the great Northern companies. This much is certain. On the other hand, the gradual development of the theatre at Charleston during the last decade of the eighteenth century is not so easily traced as elsewhere.

After Mr. Godwin's failure in 1787, when Harmony Hall became a sort of Vauxhall, no tangible clues to theatricals appear until Messrs. Bignall and West, managers of the Virginia Company of Comedians, which flourished from at least 1790 on, turned attention towards Charleston. They started or were connected with a movement to erect a theatre there. The fame of the plans for this theatre travelled as far as New York, where in the September number (1792) of the *New York Magazine* the following communication from Charleston (dated Aug. 18) was printed, which I quote in full, as it seems to have escaped proper attention:

On Tuesday last the ground was laid off for the new theatre on Savage's Green. The cornerstone of the foundation is to be laid the 20th instant. The dimensions, we are informed, are as follows:

125 feet in length, the width 56 feet, the height 37 feet, with an handsome pediment, stone ornaments, a large flight of stone steps, and a courtyard palisaded. The front will be in Broadstreet and the pit entrance in Middletonstreet. The different offices will be calculated so as not to interfere with each other; the stage is to be 56 feet in length, the front circular, with three rows of patent lamps; the boxes will be constructed so that small parties may be accommodated with a single box; to every box there will be a window and a venetian blind; three tiers of boxes, decorated with 32 columns; to each column a glass chandelier, with five lights; the lower tier balustraded; the middle and upper boxes paneled; fancy paintings, the ground French white, the mouldings and projections silvered; in the ceiling there will be three ventilators. The frontispiece, balconies and stage doors, will be similar to those of the opera-house, London.

The theatre is to be built under the immediate direction of Mr. West. When it is considered that this gentleman has had near thirty years experience in many of the first theatres in England, that he is to be assisted by artists of the first class, Capt. Toomer and Mr. Hoban, we may expect a theatre in a style of elegance and novelty. Every attention will be paid to blend beauty with conveniency, and to render it the first theatre on the continent. The contractors have engaged to complete the building by the tenth of January next.

The Charleston Theatre in Broad street was opened on February 11, 1793, with Shield's 'Highland Reel,' in this cast:

Old M'Gilpin	Mr. J. Kenna
Sergeant Jack	Mr. West
Sandy	Mr. Courtney
Charley	Mr. J. Bignall
Capt. Dash	Mr. Kedy
Croudie	Mr. Hamilton
Laird of Racey	Mr. Dunham
Laird Donala	Mr. Andrews
Benin	Mr. Riffetts
Shelby (the laughing piper)	Mr. Bignall
Jenny	Mrs. Decker
Miss Moggy M'Gilpin (the little Highland soldier)	Mrs. Bignall

To these actors were added during the season principally the Sully family and the "star" Mr. Chambers. The price of admission was "Boxes, 6s.; Upper boxes, 6s.; Pit, 5s.; Gallery, 3s. 6d." which proves that the house actually contained several tiers of boxes and that it must have been of considerable capacity. The opening performance was honored with this report in the *City Gazette*, one of the most characteristic criticisms to be found in the old papers:

Monday evening the New theatre was opened with the *Highland Reel* and *Appearance is Against Them*.

Whilst we express our approbation of the zeal and activity exerted by the managers, in the rapid erection and fitting up this theatre— we must, at the same time, pay a just tribute of applause to the liberality and taste evinced by them in the scenery, decorations and embellishments, which, however they may be exceeded in gaudy glitter, can nowhere be surpassed in neatness and simple elegance.

The opera was well cast; and the principal parts performed with a spirit and truth of colouring which afford a pleasing presage of the elegant and refined enjoyment our citizens are likely to experience by an attendance on this most rational amusement.

To particularize the merits of *some* performers, may appear invidious; yet we are under the necessity of confining ourselves to a partial specification.

Mr. West, in *Sergeant Jack*, finely portrayed this artful and designing son of Mars, with a boldness and fancy which threw additional consequence on the character.

Old M'Gilpin, with all his unfeelingness of heart, his avarice, pride and ambition, was justly personified by Mr. Kenna.

Mr. Bignall was everything that the author could wish in *Shelby;* he gave his character with such original and native humour that the house was literally in a continued roar of mirth and hilarity.

Mrs. Bignall, in *Miss Moggy M'Gilpin*, displayed such comic powers, gaiety and *naivette* [!][1], that we may safely pronounce her the *Jordan* of America; and doubt not she will ever experience a continuance of that public approbation and applause which she so deservedly received on her first appearance.

The other performers were critically just and correct in their delivery and action.

The *Highland Reel*, like most of Mr. O'Keefe's productions, is wild and eccentric, and not to be judged by the strict rules of the

[1]Dr. Theodore Baker, to whom I am indebted for relieving me of much of the labor of seeing this book through the press, here made the following marginal remark: "Dear Author: Very likely 'naivette' was the local pronunciation! Up-State in New York, at the present time, they pronounce *décolleté* deck-o-*leet!!*"

drama. There is a romantic air through the whole, which, while it is not strictly reconcileable to sound reason, does not fail to interest and exhilarate the mind.

The music, the greater part of which consists in familiar Scottish airs, has in general strong claims to approbation. Several of the songs were *encored*. . . . .

West and Bignall's first season came to a successful end on May 31, 1793. The only obstacle was removed by the tact of the managers. Charleston was a peculiar city in those days; while as patriotically American as any other, yet the city, as a matter of tradition, retained a fondness for things English. At the same time she welcomed with fervor hosts of French political refugees and West Indian refugees, and it became a policy to offend neither. In the 'Siege of Belgrade' some hyper-tactful souls scented "many expressions and reflections injurious to the character of the English and French nations." Very cleverly Mr. Bignall denied this and referred to his "past conduct" as a guarantee that "he never would present any piece with a view of gratifying one part of the audience at the expense of wounding the feelings of any party whatever."

The second season opened in January, 1794, and closed the end of June, the managers having strengthened their company visibly by such acquisitions as Mr. Clifford, poet, composer and vocalist, and Mr. Edgar. That Mr. Edgar's name is mentioned particularly, is not so much because he was the inventor of an air-pump designed to keep the house cool in imitation of the pumps used on board ships, as because he soon was to try his hand as a manager at Charleston. Nor was this wonderful air-pump the main attraction of the season. It so happened that "some French play-actors" after a series of misfortunes had found their way to Charleston and under the heading "French Play" they announced on February 8, that Messrs. West and Bignall had generously given them the use of the Charleston Theatre for one night.

If the kind-hearted managers entertained a hope that these newcomers would soon leave town, they were mistaken. The French comedians had come to stay, and soon established themselves at the City Theatre in Church Street, which apparently was not identical with the surburban Harmony Hall, as Mr. Seilhamer would have us believe. Messrs. West and Bignall could not oust the French comedians, but they calculated that a combination of the two companies might be to the advantage of both. Accordingly they engaged the French company bodily for the ensuing season of 1794-95, with the understanding that the plays were to be performed by the English actors and "the pantomimes, etc.," by the French. On August 4 they first notified the public of this arrangement, together with plans for "cheaper and more convenient terms than ever were offered on this continent." These terms consisted in the first attempt in our country at an imitation of the European *abonnement* or *en location* system. They proposed to issue 458 shares, "208 of which to be subscribed for by ladies and 250 by gentlemen at the very low sum of £9, and the last £12, besides £1 entrance for both sexes, which will carry them to the plays the whole year through; and at three plays a week in winter and but two plays a week in summer, [would] be only 1s. 6d. each representation to the ladies and 2s. each to the gentlemen, for 125 representations in the year and as the shares [could] be transferred or lent, it [would] be great accommodation to such as may reside part of the year in the country." The only disturbing feature of this scheme to the historian is, that the calculation was based on the seating capacity of the Church Street or City Theatre, whereas the American-French alliance actually took effect, beginning with Oct. 6, at the Charleston Theatre in Broad Street. The alliance lasted until the end of April, 1795, when the French company, headed by our enterprising friend Alexander Placide, continued in command of the

Charleston Theatre until early in August. Similar arrangements apparently were resorted to during the following years. These condensed data will have made it clear that the advent of French opera and pantomimes was more than a negligible incident in the theatrical life of Charleston. The joint efforts of the two companies could properly be recorded jointly, but as I have reserved a rapid survey of French opera in America for a special, final chapter, I prefer to weed out the French performances and to consider here only the attention paid to opera in English.

When the Charleston Theatre opened again after a hiatus of nearly a year in February, 1796, theatrical affairs had assumed a very different appearance in the meantime. The City Theatre in Church Street had again been thrown open to a strong company of which Mr. Sollee of New York and Boston became the manager. This competition proved to be very much more serious than that of the Frenchmen had been before they entered into the curious alliance mentioned above. Indeed, as far as I can see, the Charleston Theatre remained closed from June 1796 until January 1798. That it was no longer managed by West and Bignall would appear from the fact that in 1797 the West family had joined the City Theatre Company.

On how treacherous ground the historian is now treading, may be further demonstrated by the fact that towards the end of the season of 1796, after the disbandment of Mr. Sollee's City Theatre Company, part of his contingent evidently joined the rival company, including Mrs. Pownall, who, to repeat it, died in August, 1796, of a broken heart, the cause of her untimely end being the elopement of Alexander Placide with one of her daughters, who thus replaced the former Mrs. Placide. This shifting process was repeated several times until the century closed, and it is therefore difficult to keep track of the managerial summersaults. For instance, "Mr. Jones and Company," that is to say, Sollee's cohorts from Boston, played at the City Theatre from November 7 until the end of December, 1797. Suddenly, beginning with January 1, 1798, the announcements of the very same company are headed "Charleston Theatre." The patient historian is about to breathe a sigh of relief when on February 13 the advertisements again begin to read "Charleston Theatre." The explanation is simple enough if one happened to notice in the *City Gazette* of February 12 a card by "the Proprietor of the City Theatre" in which he announces his removal to the Charleston Theatre in Broad Street for the remainder of the season.

Logically, these performances given until March 29, 1798, by the City Theatre Company at the Charleston Theatre cannot be credited to the latter. Otherwise the utmost confusion would ensue, as less than a fortnight later the Charleston Theatre was reopened by a totally different company, called "The Charleston Comedians." The members had in part drifted South by the way of Wilmington, names like Tubbs and Arnold being familiar to the reader. Headed by Mr. and Mrs. Edgar, the Charleston Comedians cannot be said to have contributed much to the cultivation of opera at Charleston. Their short-lived career at Charleston is recorded here as a kind of intermezzo. They performed, allowing for a few probable postponements:

```
1798, April 21; 23:  Deserter
      April 18:  Flora
      April 21:  Mysteries of the Castle
      April 28; 30:  Rosina
```

Why Mr. Sollee, the proprietor of the City Theatre in Church Street, should have left his own house in favor of the Charleston Theatre in Broad Street, would be rather puzzling were it not for some communications to the papers when his successors Messrs. Williamson, Jones, and Placide repeated the shift of gravity in 1799. From January until the middle of March they played at the City Theatre, which had been considerably enlarged and "beautified, surrounded by a brick wall and secured by a terrace on each side of the roof." Then, until about April 19, they moved their company to the Charleston Theatre "by the advice of many respectable friends" (*City Gazette*, March 13). This advice was undoubtedly due to apprehensions as to the safety of the City Theatre, for when on July 20 the managers acquainted the public of the renewal of their lease they spoke of "the accident last season," mentioned that the building had been strengthened and thoroughly examined, and also corroborated this statement over the signature of seven architects who pronounced "the house much stronger than it ever was and consequently safe for any audience." Notwithstanding this formidable array of expert opinion, the managers, after having performed in the supposedly safe City Theatre from Oct. 28 1799 until the end of March 1800, found it safer to again lease the Charleston Theatre from April to the end of the season, about the middle of May. Therewith ends the career of the Charleston Theatre during the eighteenth century, and as a kind of odd epilogue the fact may be mentioned that the managers of the ill-fated institution in the summer of 1800 opened on Sullivan's Island "a spacious and well ventilated saloon . . . . to be distinguished as the South Carolina Lyceum," where for twenty nights plays, readings, concerts and assemblies were dispensed "for utility, amusement and instruction."

From what has been said, it is clear that all performances at the Charleston Theatre, excepting those by Mr. Edgar's "Charleston Comedians," are to be accredited to the City Theatre Company; the following table therefore records the career of the Charleston Theatre only until 1796, that is, as long as it was managed by West and Bignall. These gentlemen emphasized the competition

Table I

TITLE OF OPERA	1793	1794	1795	1796
Agreeable Surprise	Mar. 23	Feb. 10; Nov. 21		
Battle of Hexham		Oct. 24		Apr. 00
Beggar's Opera ("the exceptionable passages of it obliterated")	Apr. 13	Dec. 24, 31	Feb. 16	
Castle of Andalusia		Feb. 28; June 28		Feb. **
Cymon and Sylvia		June 30	Jan. 12	
Day in Turkey; or, the Russian Slaves (pant., based on Mrs. Cowley's comedy, 1791)		May 23		
Death of Captain Cook (pant.)		Apr. 9, 11, 23; Oct. 17		Mar. **
Death of Major André (pant.)				May
Deserter	Apr. 12		Feb. 19	June 9
Devil to Pay	May 10	Apr. 24	Mar. 25	
Don Juan (ballet-pant.)		Mar. 5; June 25; Oct. 10		Feb.; Mar.
Duenna		June 16	Feb. 21; Mar. 13	Mar.
Fairy Gambols; or, Harlequin's Restoration (pant.)		May 23		
Farmer	Feb. 15; Apr. 15	Jan. 22; Dec. 3		
Flitch of Bacon		Jan. 24; Feb. 26; Oct. 6		Feb.; Mar.
Fontainebleau (Shield, 1784)			Mar. 9	
Forêt Noire (pant.)		Dec. 1, 5		
Harlequin Balloonist (pant.)		Oct. 22	Feb. 14	
Hartford Bridge				May 2
Haunted Tower (Storace, 1789)	Apr. 24		Mar. 4	Apr.
Highland Reel (Shield, 1788)	Feb. 11; Mar. 18	Jan. 31; Mar. 24; June 9; Dec. 22	Feb. 14	Feb.

Maid of the Mill...				
Midas...	Apr. 19	June 6		Mar.
Mirza and Lindor (pant.)...			Mar. 6	Apr. 30
Mysteries of the Castle...				
No Song, no Supper...	Feb. 27; May 1	Apr. 21		Apr.
Oscar and Malvina...				
Padlock...	Mar. 4; May 27	Jan. 27; Oct. 27	Feb. 21	Apr. 30
Peeping Tom of Coventry (Arnold, 1784)...	Feb. 18	Feb. 21		
Poor Soldier...	Mar. 15; May 8	Feb. 7; Nov. 24	Apr. 11	
Poor Vulcan...	Feb. 22			
Prize...				Feb.; Mar. 18, 25 Apr. 9; May
Quaker...	Feb. 14; Mar. 6	Mar. 26; Feb. 14 Nov. 12		Feb.
Rejected Fool (pant.)...			Jan. 24; Mar. 20	Mar.
Rival Candidates...	Feb. 16	Dec. 31		
Robin Hood (Shield, 1784)...		May 7, 9, 14 Oct. 24		
Robinson Crusoe (pant.)...				May
Romp...	Feb. 13; Mar. 11	Feb. 19; June 11		Feb.
Rosina...	Feb. 25; Apr. 6	Feb. 5 May 19; Oct. 8	Apr. 22	Mar.; May
Son-in-law (Arnold, 1779)...	Mar. 8	Feb. 3	Jan. 28	
Surrender of Calais (Arnold, 1791)...	Apr. 29	Apr. 4	Jan. 22, 28	Apr.
Thomas and Sally...		June 23		
Waterman...	Mar. 1	Feb. 15	Apr. 20	
Wedding Ring (Dibdin, 1771)...	Mar. 20			
Woodman (Shield, 1791)...	May 13	June 11, 25		

in 1796 to the point of performing the same operas on the same nights, but unfortunately the precise dates are missing in my notebooks and they will have to be supplied by local historians from the files of the *City Gazette.* [See *Table I.*]

It remains to round out the history of the City Theatre in Church Street. A company brought by Mr. Edgar from Savannah opened it on Dec. 19, 1794. Practically consisting only of the manager and his wife, Mr. and Mrs. Henderson, Mr. Francis and Mr. Spinacuta, ordinarily a tight-rope walker and general acrobatic utility man, but who was pressed into service for minor parts, the company was not a match for West and Bignall. The efforts of Mr. Edgar's comedians in opera were restricted to such easy works as

1795, Jan. 15: Romp
Feb. 7: Romp
Feb. 3: Thomas and Sally
Jan. 31: Virgin Unmasked

Then, as stated, Mr. John Sollee—the name occurs also as Solee—drove a wedge into the property of the Charleston Theatre people by transplanting from Boston into Southern soil a rather strong company, including Mrs. Pownall, her daughters the Misses Wrighten, Mrs. Hellyer, Mr. and Mrs. Jones and others, several of whom had seceded from the Old Americans. The cast of the 'Castle of Andalusia' as given on December 5, 1795, will display the merit and distribution of Sollee's company in opera at a glance:

This evening . . . the comic opera of the *Castle of Andalusia,* with new scenery, dresses and decorations.

Don Scipio	Mr. Turnbull
Don Cæsar, or, Ramirez . .	Mr. Collins
Don Fernando	Mr. Fawcett
Don Juan	Mr. Watts
Don Alphonso	Miss M. Wrighten
Pedrillo	Mr. Jones

Spado	} Banditti	{	Mr. Hipworth
Sanguino			Mr. Patterson
Calvette			Mr. Heely
Philippo	. . . . . .		Mr. Bartlett
Valquez	. . . . . .		Mr. Miller
Victoria	. . . . . .		Mrs. Hellyer
Lorenza	. . . . . .		Miss C. Wrighten
Isabella	. . . . . .		Mrs. Miller
Catalina	. . . . . .		Mrs. Pownall

The manager requests that no gentleman will smoke in the boxes or pit.

With this company, of which Mr. Turnbull, just from London, was the poet-laureate, Sollee began operations on Nov. 10, 1795, and closed his first season early in May, 1796. A conflagration which destroyed several blocks and a number of prominent buildings on June 13 interfered with his plans for a summer season, and only a few performances from June 29 to about the middle of July are on record. It deserves to be noticed that the proceeds of this short season were offered by John Sollee and his associates to the victims of the conflagration. We are not told if this generosity was reciprocated when the company returned for the first season of 1797, which lasted from January until the end of June. However, Monsieur Sollee must have felt encouraged, as he sent the following characteristic letter from Boston to the *City Gazette*, Aug. 16, 1797:

THEATRICAL INTELLIGENCE.

Copy of a letter from Mr. Sollee, dated Boston, 25th of July, 1797.

Dear Sir:

I am very happy to announce to you that my exertions to procure to the city of Charleston the first company in America, have been crowned with the most compleat success. You will see by the newspapers of Boston, that I have settled a very important piece of business for the theatrical entertainment of this place and Charleston. The two companies already fixed upon are of equal strength, and by exchanging them every winter, it will bring a very satisfactory novelty to the public . . . .

AUTHENTIC.

Boston, July 25.

The citizens of Boston are assured that for five years to come their amusements will not be disturbed by any opposition between the two theatres. A formal agreement has taken place between Mr. Hodgkinson, manager of the New York Company, and Mr. Sollee, proprietor of the City Theatre in Charleston, who have engaged the two theatres in town. The Haymarket will be reserved for summer exhibitions, the Federal Street for winter. The plan for the winter theatre is to have one company for Boston and one for Charleston to be exchanged every season. The persons already fixed upon and partly engaged are:

For Boston: Mr. and Mrs. Barrett; Mr. and Mrs. Marshall; Mr. and Mrs. C. Powell; Mr. and Mrs. S. Powell; Mr. and Mrs. Harper; Mr. and Mrs. Graupner; M. and Mad. Lege; M. and Mad. Gardie; Messrs. Villiers, Kenny, Dickinson and J. Jones; Mrs. Allen and Miss Harrison.

For Charleston: Mr. and Mrs.Williamson; Mr. and Mrs.Whitlock; Mr. and Mrs. Jones; Mr. and Mrs. Cleveland; Mr. and Mrs. Hughes; Mr. and Mrs. Placide; Mr. and Mrs. Rowson; Messrs. Chalmers, Williamson, Downie and M'Kenzie; Misses Broadhurst and Green.

We know, at least as far as Boston was concerned, that these ambitious plans miscarried, but the news must have filled the theatre-loving folk of Charleston with considerable joy. To these Mr. Edgar surely did not belong. He had leased the City Theatre for September and October, 1797, and when towards the end of the latter month information reached the city that the "winter company" was really approaching, Alexander Placide promptly went on a strike and poor Mrs. Edgar saw herself obliged to relinquish her benefit. Nevertheless, she respectfully tendered "her acknowledgements to the public for the very flattering prospect they gave her of a good house." With the further career of the City Theatre, and of the company engaged for it, the reader has been acquainted by the cursory data on the odd shifting process between the two theatres Charleston boasted in those years.

As I have tried in previous chapters to show by quotation what "public opinion"—*alias* critics, amateur and

professional—thought of the companies which put drama
and opera on a firm and comparatively high footing in the
respective cities, it is but fair to record the impression
made by Mr. Sollee's company on a "correspondent" of
the *City Gazette*. "Philo" had expressed his surprise at
the "so curious—so unaccountable procedure" of the
managers in depriving the audience of "the pleasure of
hearing the French popular tunes," and he added some
further strictures. Thereupon said correspondent on
Nov. 21, 1795, had this to say:

"Much has been said against the present Company of Comedians
in Church Street. The subject has not, as yet, been taken upon
the general grounds it ought to be considered; for it is not certainly
in Charleston that we ought to expect to see, at the theatre, the
first of the profession; the emoluments are not sufficient to pay the
salaries of the first rate actors—this observation has entirely escaped
Philo. In every profession mediocrity is more than half the world
arrives at; if, then, the present company of comedians exceeds the
generality, they are certainly entitled to consideration; they are
entitled to more. Mr. Jones is certainly possessed of great abilities
in the comic, and (which is rarely found) does not overact his part,
the strict observance of which entitles him to much commendation,
and pronounces him a good judge of propriety. The abilities of
Mrs. Pownall are well known; it may be truly said that she is a
perfect actress. Mr. Hipworth has merits in genteel comedy, and
if he was to confine himself to the author would certainly be much
better. Mr. Turnbull shows a perfect idea of the characters he
represents which entitles him to the rank of a perfect actor. Mrs.
Jones is equal with Mr. Turnbull, perfectly at home on the stage,
places the emphasis where it ought to be, which, joined to a good
voice, entitles her to a place much above mediocrity. The other
performers make a very decent appearance. Upon the whole, the
present company is the best we have had in Charleston. Mr. *Philo*,
by the terms he makes use of, shows a dislike to theatrical amusements, forgetting that it is not the profession that disgraces, but the
professor. He would do well when he intrudes again on the public,
to divest himself of prejudice and ill nature; for whoever reads his
criticisms, must be convinced that it is the profession he writes
against and not the performers.

Before submitting Mr. Sollee's operatic record, a few
further remarks are necessary on something quite

peculiar to Charleston. I do not mean by this the city regulation that no person of color could be admitted into any part of the house, nor other odd data of this character, but the frequency with which the public was prepared for novelties by a more or less detailed synopsis of the plays, operas or pantomimes. In my monograph on 'Early American Operas' I quoted the elaborated description of the "new musical and allegorical masque, never yet printed or performed, entitled Americania and Elutheria." This was perhaps the most striking instance of the kind, but it is by far too long for quotation here. It may therefore suffice to remark that a similar treatment was accorded, though not at such length, to several other works. Amongst these figured prominently (see *S. C. State Gazette*, April 22, 1796) the

. . . grand allegorical finale, called the *Apotheosis* of Franklin; or, His Reception in the Elysian Fields. The paintings and machinery executed in a masterly manner by Mons. Audin.

The above pantomime, of which Mr. Audin is the author, is a beautiful one, such as never was performed on the Continent for the honor and dignity of Americans, and to the glorie, energie, and virtue of Franklin. From scene to scene the Company will be more and more surprised by a new set of decorations made on purpose for this pantomime, with new dresses and new musical grand overture, agreeable to the subject, executed by the first musicians.

We are not told by whom the music to 'Franklin's Apotheosis' was furnished, but probably this duty fell to Mr. Bergman, leader of the orchestra and the accredited arranger of the orchestral accompaniments to such works as Storace's pasticcio 'Doctor and Apothecary.' That Mr. Bergmann, if the manager intended to make the 'Apotheosis' a big affair, could depend on a full orchestra for adding ear-dazzling colors to the enchantment of the eye, goes without saying, as the theatre orchestra, even if it contained only the usual dozen or dozen and a half pieces, could easily have been strengthened by the forces of the St. Cecilia Society.

Furthermore, readers of my book on Early Concert-Life in America will perhaps remember that the versatile and cultured Mrs. Pownall was assisted in her "musical festival" in 1796—at which was performed among other classic works Haydn's 'Stabat Mater'—by an orchestra of more than thirty musicians. However, though the regular theatre orchestra certainly was smaller than this, it is safe to say that it was formed of really capable musicians.

Mr. Sollee's record at the City Theatre was this [see *Table J*].

It is comparatively easy to trace the beginnings of opera in New England, because the primary sources for any historical investigation of our early musical life are still accessible there. I mean the old newspapers. By far more annoying are the difficulties if an insight is desired into the musical life of the South. It is one of the caprices of history that where, from the very nature of social conditions and instincts, one would expect to reap a harvest of data, the access to our sources has been obstructed and partly destroyed by indifference, carelessness, and the Civil War. When this does not apply, then usually distance interferes with the efforts of the historian not at leisure to visit and revisit the libraries of the South. Furthermore, next to nothing has been done by local historians to clear the underbrush. The reconstruction of the historical edifice will therefore for a long time to come and possibly forever remain fragmentary at best, as far as the South outside of Charleston is concerned. Still, these fragments will retain their value, for they indicate, as it were, the historical skyline. To fill in gaps may properly be left to local historians with sound methods. Without their painstaking enthusiasm no comprehensive and accurate history of music in America will ever become possible, particularly for a later period.

This last remark applies with peculiar force to New Orleans. In 1800 the population of the city was only about 10,000 souls, at least half of them negroes. In other words, New Orleans' white population was merely that of a hamlet, and with all due respect for the artistic instincts of the Latin race, New Orleans remained until 1800 a negligible quantity in opera. Pertinent information to be gleaned from the books on New Orleans is exceedingly meagre. Moreover, it is contradictory. For instance, Miss Grace King on p. 149 of her well-known book on "New Orleans" (1895) says:

> In 1791, among the first refugees from San Domingo came a company of French Comedians. They hired a hall and commenced to give regular performances. The success they met, it may be said, endures still, for the French drama has maintained through over a century the unbroken continuity of its popularity in the city . . .
> The hired hall in course of time became the "Théâtre St. Pierre" or "La Comédie" on St. Peter street, between Bourbon and Orléans streets, and barring a two month's respite, regular performances were given on its boards winter and summer for twenty years— classic drama, opera, ballet, pantomime. . . . . "

Of this theatre W. H. Coleman wrote, in his "Historical Sketch Book and Guide" (1885):

> In 1802, New Orleans possessed a theatre—such as it was—situated on St. Peters Street. . . It was a long, low, wooden structure, built of cypress and alarmingly exposed to the dangers of fire. Here, in 1799, half a dozen actors and actresses, refugees from the insurrection in San Domingo, gave acceptable performances, rendering comedy, drama, vaudeville and comic operas. But owing to various causes the drama at this place of amusement fell into decline, the theatre was closed after two years, and the majority of the actors and musicians were scattered. Some, however, remained and these, with a few amateurs, residents of the city, formed another company in 1802.

In his admirable "Historical Sketch of New Orleans" (1880, U. S. Census Report on Social Statistics of Cities; 1887) George W. Cable says:

> In 1793. . . The Marseillaise was wildly called for in the theatre which some French players from St. Domingo, refugees of 1791, had opened, and in the drinking shops was sung defiantly the song "Ça ira, ça ira, les aristocrates à la lanterne."

In Mr. Henry Righton's "Standard History of New Orleans" (1900) we first read the same account of the San Domingo refugees of 1791, and then:

The first theatre in New Orleans was erected in 1808, the Théâtre St. Philippe on St. Philippe street.   The building was afterward turned into the Washington Ball Room. . .

The newspapers of 1810 make mention of a theatre on St. Peter street, but very little is known of it and the writers upon the history of New Orleans of that period make no mention of it.

. . . Both grand opera and opera bouffe existed in New Orleans long before it was established in any other city of America.

It would serve no useful purpose to show wherein these accounts contradict each other; and until definite data are put before me, extracted perhaps from *Le Moniteur de la Louisianne* (founded in 1794) or other contemporary sources, I am inclined not to exaggerate the extent of "classic drama, opera, ballet, pantomime" at the Creoles' "sorry little theatre," as George W. Cable elsewhere called it, before 1800.   The fact is, nothing definite appears to be known either about the repertoire or the company.   At any rate, Gayarre in his famous History of Louisiana has nothing whatever to say thereon.   He merely dates the "origin of regular dramatic exhibitions in New Orleans" from 1791, tracing it to the San Domingo refugees.

Although Mr. David Barrow Fischer in his interesting article on "New Orleans's Rise as a Music Centre" (*Musical America*, 1914, Vol. 19, No. 19, pp. 3-5) has a photograph of the "Théâtre St. Pierre," he unfortunately forgot to inform us of the age of the print from which the photograph was taken.   Or did he merely photograph a "sorry, little" house now standing, which rightly or wrongly bears the inscription "Théâtre St. Pierre"?   Mr. G. Cusachs, President of the Louisiana Historical Society, informed me that this theatre, "built during the end of the 19th century"—I take it that he meant end of the 18th century—"is still in existence. The house has been altered to make residences out of it."

Mr. T. P. Thompson of New Orleans lately drew my attention to Berquin-Duvallon's account in his "Travels in Louisiana. . . . in the year 1802." This is at least fairly contemporary with the period here under discussion and carries more weight than later stories. Berquin-Duvallon speaks of conditions in 1802 as follows:

Nearly in the centre of the town is a small theatre, where on my arrival, I saw several dramas performed with considerable ability. The company was composed of half a dozen actors and actresses, refugees from 'the theatre of Cape Français, in the island of San Domingo.

John Davis, the translator of Berquin-Duvallon's Travels, added this foot-note:

This little theatre is built of wood, and consists of one row of boxes only, with a pit and gallery. The inhabitants of New Orleans are musical, and gentlemen often perform in the orchestra of the theatre.

The reader, I think, now knows the source of all the more modern accounts from Gayarre down; and he will agree with me, I trust, that nothing of importance has been added to the remarks of Berquin-Duvallon and John Davis by local historians.[1]

With reference to Savannah, Ga., I am merely prepared to say that theatrical performances took place there in 1794, as Mr. Edgar invaded Charleston, S. C., by way

[1]While the above paragraphs were in proof, Mr. G. Cusachs sent me the following letter under date of Nov. 19, 1914, but unfortunately neglected to mention his source of information:

"In answer to your inquiries about the theater in N. O. prior or up to 1800.

"A troop of comedians under the direction of Mr. Louis Tabary appeared for the first time in N. O. in 1791. Their representations were given in one house, then in another, under a tent, even in the open air. Tired of that wandering life a theater was opened on St. Pierre Street between Royal and Bourbon on the second story of a house which bears to-day the number 716. The lower floor was used as a dance hall.

"In 1807 the theater was rebuilt. It is the theater that Mr. A. M. Barrow Fischer has photographed. This same building is still in existence with some changes in the building.

"Up to 1800 the St. Pierre Street theater was the only one in N. O. I know of no play-bills or of newspaper prior to 1800. The only name we have of the first company in N. O. is that of Louis Tabary. He was the director of the troupe."

of Savannah.   Fortunately, local papers of that period
have been preserved, and it might be an easy matter to
follow this clue.   Indeed, the theatrical life of Savannah,
after the War for Independence, began with performances
by Messrs. Godwin and Kidd's company in 1785, but
beyond this Mr. Seilhamer, too, was forced to keep a re-
spectful silence.   That Mr. Edgar was not the last
manager to visit Savannah appears from the *Augusta
Chronicle*, Augusta, Ga., Nov. 26, 1796, when Mr. Godwin solicited "patronage in favor of a dramatic piece
to be published by him, called 'A School for Soldiers; or,
the Deserter.' "   In this appeal he speaks of "the New
Theatre erecting at Savannah by subscription," and
ends by "proposing to give intuition in fencing and
dancing *during the period of his acting at Augusta and
Savannah*."

At Augusta these performances, which may have included ballad-operas, took place at the Court House, and
to judge by the same paper (Nov. 19) were made possible
"by the members of the Dramatic Association."

Equally meagre is the information which I have to
offer on opera at Columbia, S. C.   There, on Aug. 30,
1799, Messrs. Williamson and Jones performed the
'Devil to Pay.'   From the *South Carolina State Gazette* of
the same day it would appear that this was the first in a
series of a "few nights."

The Kenna family was responsible for the theatricals
at Newbern, N. C., and Wilmington, N. C., in 1788.
Nine years later, on Feb. 9, Mr. Edgar gave Wilmington
another taste of drama and opera.   On that evening the
"theatre" was opened with 'Inkle and Yarico,' and
the *season* lasted until March 2.   In the *Wilmington
Gazette*, Mr. Edgar expressed his hope "that after the
conclusion of the farce no songs or other amusements not
mentioned in the bill, will be called for. Any lady or gentleman desirous of particular songs, and will honour Mr.
Edgar with their commands on the morning of the play

day, shall be obliged in rotation, as far as the abilities of the company can extend." This ultimatum evidently did not offend Wilmington, as Mr. Edgar, when announcing on April 15 a performance of the 'Poor Soldier' at Newbern, N. C., notified the public that he would leave Newbern in a few days for Wilmington. In March 1798 he returned again with what he called "a part of the Charleston Company" for "nine nights," on the first of which, March 8, he presented the ballet 'Lisette and Annette; or, the Bird Catchers,' and the 'Poor Soldier.'

On approaching Virginia, the data flow somewhat more generously. Richmond, the capital, may have precedence over Fredericksburg, Petersburg, Norfolk, Alexandria, for chronological reasons, if not for any other. It was here that Alexander Quesnay, pedagogue, dancing-master and promoter, erected in 1786 a theatre with a seating capacity of sixteen hundred persons as part of his ambitious Academy, and for which he engaged Hallam and Henry's Old American Company. They opened on Oct. 10, 1786, with the 'Poor Soldier,' but it is not known when the first season of this curious enterprise closed. Indeed, a good deal of mystery surrounds this attempt to introduce an esthetic culture course into the curriculum of Quesnay's Academy. However, during November and December of the following year Richmond was again treated to some theatricals, this time at "The New Theatre, Shockoe Hill." The fact that the performance of Nov. 17 was given "for the purpose of finishing the Academy" would indicate that Monsieur Quesnay again was the promoter. The performances included on Dec. 6 the 'Beggar's Opera,' and the names mentioned in the cast, such as Mr. Kidd, Mr. and Mrs. Rankin, Mr. Bisset and others, make it clear that the Old Americans had no part in the exhibitions. Then, from the middle until the end of October, 1790, the same theatre was occupied by the "Virginia Company." This was managed by

Messrs. West and Bignall and was the nucleus of the company that later moved its headquarters to Charleston.

To enumerate the members of the company, most of whom disappeared from the theatrical horizon as suddenly as they appeared, is hardly necessary. Still, to judge by the few casts printed in the *Virginia Gazette*, it was strong and capable enough to present Shield's '*Farmer*' (Oct. 18, possibly the first American performance) and 'Poor Soldier'(Oct. 28). The same company, though with considerable changes in its personnel, reappeared at Richmond from the middle of October until the end of December, 1795, presenting on Oct. 12 Arne's 'Cymon and Sylvia' and the ballet-pantomime 'The Bird Catcher' under the supervision of "the celebrated Monsieur Placide from Paris," who also indulged in some dancing on the tight rope, playing the violin at the same time. He was followed on Oct. 15 by "Mr. Francisquy from the Opera House, Paris" in his "ballet pantomime comic" the 'Two Hunters and the Milkmaid,' based on Duni's opera 'Les Deux chasseurs.' The same gentleman was responsible for the grand pantomime '*American Independence; or, the Fourth of July, 1776*,' given on Dec. 24 as afterpiece to the 'Maid of the Mill.' The Charlestonians reappeared at Virginia's capital during December, 1796, and part of January, 1797, again laying particular stress upon the inevitable pantomime-ballets, such as 'Oscar and Malvina' (Dec. 14). Of the operas performed I noticed the 'Son-in-law' (Dec. 28), 'No Song, no Supper' (Dec. 28), 'Peeping Tom of Coventry' (Dec. 23), 'Love in a Village' (Dec. 26), the 'Romp' (Jan. 6, 1797). Mr. Turnbull was the star of the company and on Dec. 26, his benefit night, Richmond had occasion to admire him in his triple capacity of actor, vocalist and poet, as on this evening his 'Ode to Columbia' was sung, in which he took part "as a philosopher patriot." The composer of this scurrilous piece is not mentioned.

Even such insignificant Southern villages as Lansing-
burgh—where Mr. Hammer's Long Room had been "fitted
up in a theatrical manner" for the 'Poor Soldier' (May 13,
1795)—and Dumfries, had their share of strolling talent.
Though the performances here and in similiar places
would come under the head of what is called in German
stage-slang *Schmiere*, it is worth noticing, as a proof that
everywhere in our country at least an interest was taken
in drama and opera, that a "Theatrical Society" existed
at Dumfries in 1796. The members, presumably together
with some professional comedians, performed among other
things on May 5 of this year the 'Waterman.'

At Fredericksburg, Va., less primitive conditions must
have existed, as, nothwithstanding the difficulty of access
to Southern papers of the period, theatrical entertainments may be traced there from 1788 until the end of
the century. The "Olio of theatrical entertainments"
given in June 1788 by Mr. and Mrs. Lewis "to discharge
some few debts," were the beginning. Then came the
Kennas (end of October, 1789), and remained until about
the middle of November, and though I found no operas
mentioned it is safe to say that one or the other of the
easier English works of the kind were included in their
repertory. They were followed by Godwin and M'Grath's
Company, who gave some performances beginning with
April 29, 1790, at "The Theatre Fredericksburg, elegantly fitted up at the Market House." On May 6 they
presented the 'Agreeable Surprise,' and on the opening
night "a musical farce" (taken from the comic opera of
the Duenna) called the *Elopement;* or, Cunning Outwitted,
evidently a simplified version of Sheridan's witty libretto.

In August, September and October of the same year
another company made its appearance with the 'Poor
Soldier' (Aug. 20) and the 'Virgin Unmasked' (Oct. 7),
and then Messrs. West and Bignall, "viewing with regret
the imperfect state of dramatic exhibitions in this part
of the world, are determined from motives of duty as

well as that of interest, to exert themselves in the service of their generous patrons and the public at large, by augmenting their company with characters of real merit." After some further clever remarks in this vein they "offer very liberal salaries to young gentlemen of figure and education who may incline to make the stage their profession." This curious document, which, by the way, served as stock in trade in several other towns, appeared in the *Virginia Herald*, Nov. 4, 1790, but I do not know if Messrs. West and Bignall found the desired "characters of real merit" in that year. However, their "Virginia Company" gave a series of noteworthy performances at Fredericksburg in August and September, 1791, including '*Romp*' (Aug. 5), 'Inkle and Yarico' (Aug. 12), the 'Farmer' (Aug. 26), 'Love in a Village' and the 'Poor Soldier' (both on Sept. 2), and Dibdin's '*Quaker*' (Sept. 16).

Whether or not West and Bignall returned regularly thereafter, I am not prepared to say, but it is not at all unlikely. At any rate, a company, made up of their Charleston contingent, occupied the New Theatre at Fredericksburg from the middle of August until the end of October, 1797. The cast of the 'Highland Reel' "with the original music, and Scotch medley overture," as offered on Sept. 11, will show that the company was not without merit:

M'Gilpin	Mr. Turnbull
Sergeant Jack	Mr. West
Charley	Mr. T. West
Sandy	Mr. Bartlett
Captain Dash	Mr. Radcliffe
Laird Donald	Mr. Heely
Laird Raasey	Mr. Ashton
Groudy	Mr. Hamilton
Berim	Mr. Morton
Selby (the Scotch bagpiper)	Mr. Bignall
Jenny	Mrs. Green
Moggy M'Gilpin	Mrs. J. West

Operas which I was able to trace "on the days of playing, Monday, Wednesdays and Fridays," were

Aug. 16: No Song, no Supper
Sept. 4: Adopted Child
Sept. 6: Romp
Sept. 13: Poor Soldier
Sept. 25: { Fontainebleau
{ Devil to Pay
Oct. 14: Mountaineers
Oct. 21: Farmer

and the pantomimes

Sept. 20: Death of Captain Cook
Sept. 30: Don Juan ("The fireworks by Mr. T. West")
Oct. 7: *Castle Besieged*

Part of the same company returned in Aug., 1798, with 'Cymon and Sylvia' (Aug. 3) and the 'Poor Soldier' (Aug. 31), and then Messrs. Radcliffe and McKinzie occupied the "Temporary Theatre in the Hall of the Market House" during April and May, 1799, though it does not appear if they ventured into the realm of opera. That they were not the last to invade Fredericksburg during the eighteenth century is certain, as a performance of the 'Flitch of Bacon' is on record for Oct. 8, 1799.

Another important station on West and Bignall's circuit was Norfolk, Va. A Mr. Heard is credited with performances there in the eighties; but not until the arrival of West and Bignall did Norfolk receive substantial theatrical nourishment. As they remarked of a performance in 1796 "for the first time these three years," it follows that they visited the town as early as 1793. This season I have not be able to trace otherwise, and my data on that of 1795 are not much fuller. They presented in this year "by authority" at the Norfolk Theatre the 'Quaker' (May 15), the 'Rival Candidates' (May 18), the 'Agreeable Surprise' (May 29), and probably some other works. They returned in 1796 for a comparatively long season (middle of July until Sept. 20), when they occupied the New Theatre. The announcements during this year were lengthy, descriptive of the plots, and the managers did not avoid the expense of printing full casts in the *American Gazette* and *Norfolk Herald*. This may serve as a clue for those who wish to elaborate on my data in the interest of local history. It will suffice here to trace the operas and pantomimes presented:

July 20: Don Juan (pant.)
Aug. 1: Mountaineers
Aug. 3: Farmer
Aug. 5: Robinson Crusoe (pant.)
Aug. 8: Inkle and Yarico
Aug. 8: Forêt Noire (pant.)
Aug. 27: Honest Yorkshireman
Sept. 5: Beggar's Opera
Sept. 12: Doctor and Apothecary (for the benefit of Mrs. Graupner, assisted in some incidental numbers by her husband, Gottlieb)
Sept. 19: Quaker

and for Mr. Edgar's benefit on Sept. 21 the masterpiece of Monsigny, to wit:

. . (for the first time these three years) the justly admired Entertainment of the *Deserter*. Translated from the celebrated French opera, called *Le Deserteur*, one of the most favourite Musical Pieces on the French stage.

Henry	Mr. King
Russet	Mr. Turnbull
Simkin	Mr. Bignall
Flint	Mr. Watts
Soldiers	
Skirmish	Mr. Prigmore
Louisa	Mrs. Graupner
Margaret	Mrs. Turnbull
Jenny	Mrs. Edgar

Part of the same company, to judge by the beneficiaries mentioned, reappeared at Norfolk in December, 1796, and may be traced there also in April, 1797. Though in the newspaper files accessible to me I found only the announcement of 'No Song, no Supper' for March 29, it goes without saying that the usual operas must have been performed. During October and November of the year 1796 the company visited Petersburgh, Va., assisted by some French actors. They gave among other works Turnbull's 'Recruit' (Oct. 28), the 'Purse' (Oct. 24), the 'Highland Reel' (Nov. 2), and on "the last night till January, 1797," 'Rosina' (Nov. 4). The company kept their promise and returned from Norfolk in time to open the Petersburgh Theatre on Jan. 18, and remained there until March 7. During this *season* were heard the 'Romp' (Jan. 20), 'Peeping Tom of Coventry' (Feb. 3), 'Adopted Child' (Feb. 17), 'Purse' (Feb. 24), 'Robinson Crusoe' (Feb. 28), 'Oscar and Malvina' (Feb. 23). Toward the end of April some further performances must have been given, as I found 'Lock and Key' announced for April 27, and for May 8 Matthew Locke's disputed music to 'Macbeth' and Arnold's 'Children in the Wood.' Finally, the Petersburgh Theatre was again opened "for Race week" on May 29 of the same year with performances on every evening. They included the 'Poor Soldier' (May 29) and 'Lionel and Clarissa' (May 30). Probably this same or virtually the same company took advantage of "Race week" during subsequent years, an event of particular social exertions, entertainments and jollification in all Southern cities; but references to such visits have escaped me except for the year 1797, when the fall races took place in October. On the last day of this month, for instance, the 'Quaker' was presented, but as Lailson's Circus was also in town it may seriously be doubted that the actors were successful financially.

Mr. Seilhamer, in a chapter on "American Strollers," credits a Mr. Fitzgerald with performances at Alexandria, Va., in November, 1793. This is only partly correct. He overlooked that this gentleman was under the management of Mr. McGrath, king of American strollers, in

whom Mr. Seilhamer takes a very lively interest. The
performances, *e. g.*, on Nov. 16 with the 'Poor Soldier,'
were given "at Fullmore's Long Room," and to accom-
modate families, children under ten years of age were
admitted upon one ticket. Two years later, in October,
Mr. and Mrs. Henderson "from the Theatre Charleston"
occupied Mr. Fullmore's Long Room, and they evinced
their civic interest by giving a performance "for the
benefit of the streets." Probably, though the heading
"Theatre Alexandria" was used, the same long room was
pressed into theatrical service when McGrath revisited
Alexandria from the middle of June to the middle of
August, 1796. His star performance occurred on July 4
with "the civic prelude called 'The *Fourth of July; or,
American glory,*' " and as a tribute to the favorite sons of
Alexandria and vicinity he introduced "the republican
song of Mount Vernon and the Land of Freedom,"
written by himself.

By this time theatrical entertainments must have
aroused sufficient interest in Alexandria to warrant the
desire for a real theatre, because I find that in July, 1797,
a share in the theatre "now building" was offered for
sale. It is therefore strange that the longest and most
substantial theatrical season of Alexandria before 1800,
namely from January to May, 1798, was again offered
at "the theatre in Mr. Fullmore's Long Room . . . .
fitted up in as commodious a style . . . as its size
will permit." Mr. Hamilton, apparently the manager,
Mr. Bartlett, Mrs. Decker, Mr. Radcliffe and several
other comedians took particular care "to prevent im-
proper characters intruding themselves into the boxes,"
and on April 19 informed the public that "several gentlemen of the town, *Amateurs*, have politely offered, as on
similar occasions, to assist the music, which will add
much to the entertainment of the audience." With the
help of these enthusiasts they ventured on a rather ambitious operatic repertory, as it included:

Feb. 1, 6:	Purse
Feb. 9; March 24:	Rosina
Feb. 13; March 21:	Farmer
Feb. 2; March 2:	Quaker
Feb. 14; April 10:	Son-in-law
Feb. 16:	Devil to Pay
Feb. 19; March 7:	Padlock
April 14:	Padlock
Feb. 21; March 5:	Inkle and Yarico
March 19; April 21:	Inkle and Yarico
Feb. 26; March 9:	Romp
March 16; April 3:	Poor Soldier
March 31; May 5:	Mountaineers
April 17:	Sicilian Romance
April 20:	No Song, no Supper

On June 12 of the same year the 'Mountaineers' were to form part of a *season* "of three nights only," but were postponed to the following evening "on account of the very disagreeable weather." Simultaneously, Lailson's Circus with his full "band of musicians" had arrived in town and it probably was well for the Thespians that they did not compete with wild animals, mountebanks, clowns, etc. In December of 1798 Fullmore's Long Room was occupied by a "society of Gentlemen." This is a further instance of the frequency which theatrical companies formed by amateurs for their own pleasure and incidentally for the benefit of the poor are met with in the South. This company was hardly identical with the one that announced on Feb. 19, 1799, for "the last night of the company's performance in town," the double bill of the 'Mountaineers' and the 'Purse,' as two professional actors, Mr. Hamilton and Miss Miller, are mentioned by name. These performances took place at the Old Theatre, presumably at Fullmore's, whereas a number of performances which may be traced in June, 1799, including the 'Prize' (June 5), the 'Mountaineers' (June 13), and "a new ballet, composed by Mr. Warrell, junior," called 'A *Trip to Curro*,' were presented at the just completed "New Theatre."

Mr. Warrell's name connects us again with Northern companies. When outlining the career of Wignall and Reinagle's Philadelphia company, it was remarked that these gentlemen repeatedly ventured as far South as Annapolis, Md., preferably during the races. It is hardly necessary to go into details, the less so as Annapolis was installed on the circuit more to keep the company busy than for pecuniary considerations. Indeed, inasmuch as "Messieurs" Reinagle and Francis in July 1799 were "desirous of employing their leisure time in attending a few scholars" with "music and dancing," it would seem that the theatrical business alone did not pay. Possibly the people of Annapolis were more interested in Mr. Salenka and "his sagacious dog," who visited the town in 1797, than in a season of twelve nights in 1798 by the best company in America. This they could easily verify by comparison, as Hallam and Henry's Old Americans came to town in 1790; the so-called "New American Company" in Feb., 1791; in November of the same year "The French Company from Paris"; McGrath's strollers in May, 1798; and, in May, 1799, "Messrs. Hamilton and Co."

This chapter, I believe, has fully corroborated by independent research Mr. Seilhamer's statement that the Virginia towns of this period were overrun with strolling players; though Mr. Bignall, the poet-actor-manager, thought:

> Too many Madisons in them are found
> Instead of fun, who study now the nation,
> And talk of politics and reformation.

Exception must be taken to Mr. Seilhamer's view in so far only as they were not strollers. It has become clear, I think, that Messrs. West and Bignall's stock company controlled the theatrical destinies of the South in those years, and this company was far from being inefficient. Nor is this point essential. Strollers in the deprecatory

sense of the term or not, these actors gave the small
towns in our country, like Newark, N. J. (1797, Oct.,
'Highland Reel' and 'Poor Soldier,' 1799, August,
'Agreeable Surprise') and even such embryonic settlements as Harrisburg and York, Pa., their first or second
taste of the stage. They prove that a surprising surplus
of histrionic talent had been accumulated which had to
spread into every corner of our country to escape starvation. They paved the path which their successors
travelled and still travel. They prepared the foundations
for—what might have been. The conditions of opera in
our country are peculiar, but these peculiarities have their
history, and their roots lie in the eighteenth century.
If history really means explanation, then much that is
strange in our present operatic situation may be explained
by just reading now and then between the lines of history.
If we look below the surface, we must observe that opera
was cultivated in our country in olden times in very
much the same manner as it was and still is cultivated in
England, France and Germany in such towns as do not enjoy a regular subvention from courts or municipalities.
The American who visits Germany, for instance, usually
knows next to nothing of her artistic (and inartistic)
life outside of musical centres and sub-centres. Many
towns larger than those of Virginia in olden times exist
in Germany which to this day have not been honored
by theatrical companies half as capable as West and
Bignall's, not to mention the Old Americans or Wignell
and Reinagle's company. Indeed, I know it to be a fact
that a certain German town, of about the size of Alexandria in 1800, depended for years on operatic efforts
culminating in a murderous assault upon 'Lohengrin,'
in what Americans would have called a Long Room, by
pupils of a near-by conservatory who could neither
sing nor act and who were merely supported by a pianoforte, recalling to our mind the orchestral "Besetzung"
of the Virginia company of 1752. Municipal and court

subvention has made Germany an operatic country; and it would be interesting to know if this supposedly "unconstitutional" artistic doctrine ever occured to any of our politicians and statesmen in the interest of American art and art in America when Wignell and Reinagle in the year 1800 extended their sphere of influence to Washington, D. C., remodelled Blodgett's Inn for their purposes and gave it a name so full of suggestion: The United States Theatre!

EPILOGUE : FRENCH OPERA

A short but not wholly accurate title, as it is meant to comprise less French operas given in English than French operas given in French. The title is also intended to include the exceedingly few Italian operas performed on American soil until 1800. That they were not sung in the vernacular is certain, and consequently, unless evidence to the contrary is discovered (*which would not surprise me in the least*), the year 1825 may still be considered the birthyear of Italian opera in Italian with the Garcia family at the cradle.[1] The German Singspiel had no place in our early repertory. True, Mr. Krehbiel in his fine article on opera in the United States in the revised Grove says: "there are even traces of a German *Singspiel*, Benda's 'Ariadne,' being on the New York list of 1791"; but these traces can hardly be verified. In fact, Mr. Krehbiel relied on my authority. I had included Benda's melodrama in some notes hastily compiled from my materials for Mr. Krehbiel when he was collecting the latest data for his excellently comprehensive article. However, the point is immaterial. As to the French operas in French, their appearance in our early repertory was a mere episode. The very fact that towards the end of the century the French comedians gradually but steadily, not to say, suddenly, vanish from the horizon, proves this. It is also clear that the shortlived French invasion which began in 1790 was wholly due to the French Revolution and its aftermath in the West Indies. Then

---

[1] It should constantly be kept in mind that such English pasticcio operas as 'The Contrivances,' 'Love in a Villiage,' 'Lionel and Clarissa,' etc., etc., were full of music by Italian opera composers. By compiling a list of composers pressed into service for the English librettos, it can be shown that American audiences knowingly or unknowingly got a taste of many a famous Italian opera composer of the eighteenth century, from Porpora down.

suddenly thousands of French refugees poured into our country. Considerable French blood was infused into our orchestras, and suddenly French vocalists, professional either by training or from necessity, appear on our concert programs. They treated American audiences preferably to arias from French and Italian operas in vogue at Paris, indeed to such an extent as to acquaint Americans fairly well, by way of excerpts, with the works of Grétry, Monsigny and lesser masters. It is certainly not surprising that these same refugees went one step further and coöperated by forming theatrical companies which performed, as well as circumstances and their abilities would permit, some of the same operas in their entirety. These performances, of course, could not compare in merit with those given by the English companies, and when the novelty had worn off, the French episode came to its natural and logical end. Perhaps this end was hastened by the shrewd move of the English managers to absorb the French companies whenever they could. The instrumentalists would then naturally prefer to remain with the stable English companies rather than to live from hand to mouth, and the French vocalists, deprived of orchestral support, could not think of continuing their experiments with French opera in French for any length of time.

The language problem also militated against their permanency. This difficulty did not interfere with the enjoyment of ballets and pantomimes. Consequently, where the actors proper failed, pantomimists like Alexander Placide, Mons. Lege, Mad. Gardie and Mons. Francisquy flourished and they kept themselves busy either by reproducing ballets known to the European public or "composing" such for the American public, or turning French operas into pantomime pasticcios. The lists of operas, strewn through this book, contain a remarkable number of the latter species. To trace these works, which added indirectly to the French repertory, in every instance to their original source would be obviously impossible, and I have refrained from any such futile attempt.

As far as I can see, Baltimore was the first port of entry for opera given in French in America, an exotic weed at its best. There, on June 14, 1790, postponed from June 12, a "French Company of Comedians" added, to a comedy and number of ariettas,

An opera, called *The Mistress and Maid.* The music by the celebrated Italian Pere Golaise [sic]

Randolphe	Mr. De Lisle
Zerline	Mrs. De Lisle
Scapin	Mr. Musart

This was, of course, the English title for 'La Servante maîtresse,' *parodiée*, as the term then went, from Pergolesi's 'Serva padrona.' The other members of the company were Mrs. St. Firmain, Mrs. Floricourt and Mr. Beaufort who spoke "the German, English and Italian in French Gibberish" on June 21 in a skit called 'The Useless Resolution.' This remained the first and last attempt of these French strollers at opera and their further, like their previous effort, consisted at Baltimore and Philadelphia of concerts with really fine French programs.

The second attempt at French opera was made in the fall of 1790 at New York. Here, on October 7, the City Tavern saw the American *première* of Audinot-Gossec's

Le *Tonnellier*, with proper scenery, machinery and decorations.

Le Tonnellier	Mr. Cammas
Colin	Mr. St. Aivre
Fanchette	Mrs. St. Aivre

At the end of the opera, the favourite song of 'O Richard! O mon Roi!' by Mr. St. Aivre.
After which there will be a Grand Ball.

Other arias by Grétry figured prominently on the program when "*Le Devin du Village*, an opera of one act by the celebrated John Jacques Rousseau, ornamented with beautiful new decorations," was introduced to an American public on Oct. 21. From the tenor of the announcement we are almost led to infer that Mr. St. Aivre made the desperate effort to interpret these and subsequent operas in English. Said he on Oct. 14 in the *Daily Advertiser:*

> The public will excuse his not being able fully to satisfy their expectations at the last opera, as he was very much fatigued, and laboured under the disadvantage of not understanding the language of this country.

That the performances did not even cover the expenses appears from St. Aivre's appeal to the generosity of the public when he announced that at the request of several gentlemen 'Le Devin du village' and 'Le Tonnellier' would be repeated on Oct. 26 with Henri Capron as leader of the orchestra. Then came on Nov. 9, after some postponements, Duni's *'Les Deux chasseurs'* and Rousseau's "lyric scene," *alias* melodrama, *'Pygmalion.'* As Mr. St. Aivre remarked that he would have the latter "translated into the English language," it stands to reason that, notwithstanding the possible inference allowed by the above quotation, the works really were, as a rule, given in French. 'La Servante maîtresse' was to have followed together with 'Les Deux chasseurs' on November 24, but was postponed to December 9 on account of the Subscription Ball at the City Tavern.

After this, silence reigned in the French camp until January 28, 1791, when Mr. St. Aivre announced in the *Daily Advertiser* that he had opened a subscription for

> Four new operas and dances of character to commence on Tuesday the 15th of February next, the second the 1st of March, the third the 8th and the fourth the 15th do., at the City Tavern. The Price to subscribers One Guinea . . . . The four operas . . . . under the direction of Mr. P. A. Van Hagen, Sen., late Director of the Concerts in Holland.

Subsequently he changed the dates to Feb. 28, March 14, 27, April 4 "at Corré's Hotel" and offered as special attraction "Peter, the Indian, lately arrived from his own country," in a genuine war dance and other more legitimate incidentals. St. Aivre actually carried his *season* to a successful end, though with the usual postponements. On February 28 he performed 'La Servante maîtresse' and 'Les Deux chasseurs'; the second night escaped me; but as the third of the series came on March 28, postponed from March 21,

Arianne abandonnée in the Island of Naxos, a new dramatic opera, which was performed with great success in Paris, and (when translated into English) in London.

Mr. St. Aivre has neglected nothing to embellish the scenery of the sea and the rock from which Arianne precipitates herself; he hopes that ladies and gentlemen will be pleased to honor with their presence a performance which will be very expensive to him.

The composer is not mentioned. Without the meagre details of the announcement before me, it is now clear how I became guilty of misleading even Mr. Krehbiel. That this was *not* Benda's famous and revolutionary melodrama 'Ariadne' appears conclusively from the announcement. Its tenor leaves no doubt that Mr. St. Aivre presented French *opera*, and we need not hesitate in connecting the work performed at New York with the opera 'Arianne dans l'île de Naxos,' composed, and brought out at Paris in 1782, by Joh. Fr. Edelmann, the Alsatian who was guillotined at Paris in 1794. The last "subscription opera" on April 4 was divided into three "acts," each with a different opera. This curious triple bill consisted of 'Le Devin du village,' 'Le Tonnellier' and 'La Laitière,' subtitle of Duni's 'Les Deux chasseurs.' Therewith ended Mons. St. Aivre's dream of transplanting French opera to American soil, and he continued, perhaps with greater encouragement, in his profession of dancing-master. Possibly he would have renewed his efforts as manager, had not Mr. Cammas, the star of this enterprise, returned to the West Indies in 1791.

The French dancers connected with the Kenna family during the season of 1791-92 at the Northern Liberties Theatre, Philadelphia, do not seem to have gone beyond Harlequinades. We may therefore safely turn our attention towards Boston, where Alexander Placide and his associates occupied the New Exhibition Room from January until the middle of May, 1793. The repertory, as stated in the chapter on Boston, was a mixture of English and French works. The latter consisted mostly of ballets, such as 'Mirza and Lindor' and the 'Bird Catcher,' original title 'Les Oiseliers.' None of these deserve special consideration here, except the "heroic pantomime entertainment in two acts, called, *Richard the First*, sur-named Cœur de Lion," presented for the benefit of Mad. Placide on May 29. Unless all signs deceive me, I am inclined to believe that this was a ballet-adaptation of Grétry's masterwork 'Richard Cœur de Lion,' detached arias from which had already become standard concert pieces in our country. For this reason, it is curious that Alexander Placide did not attempt to perform the opera as an opera, inasmuch as his pantomimistic tendencies did not extend to the adaptation of '*The Blacksmith*,' "a French opera for the first time in America" (March 25)—Philidor's 'Le Maréchal ferrant,' of 1761?—'The Cooper,' *alias* 'Le Tonnellier' (April 3, 29), and (April 24, May 1) his most important contribution so far to the history of French opera in America:

. . . . In three parts, a grand French opera, called *The Deserter*. With original overture, by Monsigny. All the favourite Songs, Duets, etc.

Alexis (the Deserter)	Mons. Douvillier
Jean Louis (an invalid) . . .	Mons. St. Poll
Bertrand (a clown) Courchemin (guard of the camp) } .	Mons. Mallet
Crie (keeper of the prison) . .	Mons. Trouche

Montaucil (a soldier)   .   .   .   M. Placide
Louisa .   .   .   .   Mme. Douvillier
Jeannette   .   .   .   .   .   .   Mme. Placide

In Act third, a Military Procession to the execution of the Deserter. (Plans of the opera delivered at the doors of the Exhibition Room, gratis).

Probably the meteor of French opera would have vanished very soon after its appearance at Boston, had not the black insurrection in the West Indies given it a fresh impetus a few months later. Thus two terrible revolutions were required to establish French opera temporarily—New Orleans permanently—on a solid basis in our country, and it is a noteworthy touch of the times that the combination of Placide's forces with the newcomers from the West Indies was effected not in the North, but in the South, at Charleston, S. C. As a human and historical document their first manifesto may follow here as printed in the *City Gazette*, Feb. 8, 1794:

FRENCH PLAY.

This evening, February 8. Some French play actors, lately from St. Domingo, after having been plundered by privateers, and conducted to Providence, where they experienced a number of misfortunes, have at length arrived at Charleston, this hospitable city, where the French have been for several months welcomed and treated as brothers. These play actors, notwithstanding the difficulties they foresee in exercising their profession in a country where their language is not generally understood, think they can, however, venture this resource, the only one which is left to them to alleviate their distress, in hopes that, being French and unfortunate men, these two titles will be sufficient to recommend them to the public benevolence. In consequence, they applied to Messrs. West and Bignall for the use of their house for a night, to give a representation for their benefit. Those gentlemen, whose hearts are always open to the relief of the distressed, willingly and humanely granted their request: under which circumstances should they be honoured by the benevolent attendance of the public, their utmost efforts will be exerted to meet their suffrage.

1st. *Pygmalion*

Scene lyrique of the celebrated John James Rousseau, with the interludes in music by the same author; in which piece Mr. Dainville will perform the part of Pygmalion and Mrs. Val that of Galatee.

2d.   *Two Pastoral Dances*
will follow, by Mr. Francisquy.
3d.   *The Plebeian become a Man of Consequence*
A comedy full of disguises, in which Mr. Dainville will personate seven different parts, and Mr. Val that of the Plebeian.
4th.   The English Dance or Hornpipe, by Mr. Francisquy
5th.   The *Two Chasseurs;* or, Hunters and the Milkmaid
A grand ballet comic, in which Mr. Francisquy will personate the part of Guillot, Mr. Dainville that of Colas, Mrs. Val that of the Milkmaid and Mr. Val that of the Attourney.
Tickets at the usual prices . . . . The same regulations will be observed as have been adopted by Mrs. West & Bignall at their performances.

On the strength of this performance the French actors forthwith announced (on March 26) their intention to open a "French Theatre." The proceeds of the first performance were intended for the benefit of their unfortunate brethren, the American prisoners in Algiers. The fact that "the musicians which [would] compose their orchestra," also offered their services gratis goes to show that the orchestra was not imported from San Domingo but recruited from among the musicians of Charleston. Three performances a week were planned and the prospective subscribers were notified that the performances would consist

Of dancing, pantomimes, ballets or dances, Harlequin pantomimes, rope dancing, with many feats and little amusing French pieces and to satisfy many who wish it, the grand pieces of the French Theatre.
Being willing to offer to those who are learning the French language, a sure way of perfecting themselves, the theatre being a place where the French language is spoke in its purity, they propose to the admirers of the French language, a fourth representation, weekly, by subscription, to be composed of tragedies, dramas and the first comic pieces.

It will have been noticed that opera was not mentioned in this prospectus and indeed no attempt at opera was made until May 17, 1794, when Duni's 'Les Deux chasseurs' was given. After this until the end of August opera continued to be on an equal footing with drama, comedy, ballet, pantomime, rope dancing, etc. It is a very odd glimpse into this exotic enterprise that the announcements were printed both in French and English under the respective headings 'Le Théâtre Français' and 'French Theatre,' but, whereas the explanatory remarks in French were very brief, those in English were very long for the obvious purpose of permitting an American audience to know beforehand what all the dialogues, monologues, arias, etc., in French signified.

It was after this first season that Messrs. West and Bignall engaged the Frenchmen for their Charleston Theatre, and the very fact that they did so would seem to prove conclusively that Placide and Francisquy had managed their Théâtre Français too successfully to allow further independent competition. During the next two years, as stated in a previous chapter, the career of the French actors is linked with that of their English colleagues, and this combination of English and French opera under one management may safely be said to have been the first serious instance of the kind in our country. The French repertory during these three years was approximately this:

1794, April 11:⎫
           29:⎭ Bird Catcher (pant., French title 'Les Oiseleurs')

April 21:⎫
      26:⎭ Robinson Crusoe (pant.)

April 25:⎧ *Rose and the Bud* ("grand ballette pantomime
May 3:⎨   in two acts," very probably based on Monsigny's
     ⎩   opera 'Rose et Colas')

April 26:⎧ *Anonymous Disguises;* or, the Useless Resolution
       ⎩ ("comedy . . . intermixed with singing")

April 29:⎫ Harlequin Doctor; or, the Power of Magic
Aug. 13:⎭ (pant.)

May 1: *Harlequin; or, Supposed Conjuror* (pant.)

May 6:⎫ *Milliners* ("La Marchande de mode," "comic
    17:⎭ pantomime")

May 8:⎫ Old Soldier; or, the Two Thieves ("historique
Aug. 1:⎭ pantomime with dances")

Aug. 10: Harlequin a Supposed Nobleman (pant.)

Aug. 15:
29: { Wood Cutters; or, the Militia man ("grand military pantomime," based on Philidor's 'Le Bûcheron; ou, le Milicien')

May 17:
July 12:
14: } Two Hunters and the Milkmaid (Duni's 'Les Deux chasseurs et la laitière')
1795, May 20:

1794, May 20:
Dec. 13:
1795, July 27: } Three Philosophers; or, the Dutch Coffee house ("ballet-pantomime," also called the 'Three Quakers,' the 'Two Quakers,' etc.)

1794, May 22:
24:
June 3: } Harlequin ballooniste. (pant.)

June 27:
31:
Dec. 19:
23: } Belle Dorothée ("heroic pantomime in 4 acts")

June 14:
July 8:
28:
1795, May 25:
July 24:
1796, June 9: } Deserter (Monsigny's 'Déserteur')

1794, June 17:
July 2:
Oct. 11:
1795, May 28: } *Speaking Picture* (Grétry's 'Tableau parlant')

1794, June 24:
Aug. 1:
Oct. 27: } *Orpheus and Eurydice* ("An heroic drama . . with the music and original overture by the celebrated Paisielo." [But P. is not known as the composer of such an opera. Was it perhaps Gluck's?] Mr. Dainville sang the *Orpheus* and Mrs. Val the *Eurydice*)

July 8: Mirza and Lindor (pant, in 3 acts)

July 16:
Aug. 4:
Dec. 13: } *Annette et Lubin* (comic opera by Blaise)

July 16:
18:
1796, May 15: } Pygmalion (Rousseau)

1794, July 21:
Aug. 1: } *Fusiliers;* or, the Clown outwitted. (Dibdin; Mrs. Placide's "first attempt in an English character")

July 21:
Dec. 6: } Devin du village (Rousseau)

July 23: | *Nina;* or, the Distracted Lover ("a celebrated
30: | opera, in two acts, with the original overture"
Oct. 20: | by Dalayrac, first perf. at Paris in 1786. The
| cast was this:

Count, father of Nina . . .	Mr. Dainville
Germeuil, lover of Nina . . .	Mr. Douvillier
George, foster-father of Nina . .	Mr. Placide
Several peasants of the village, with chorus	
	Messrs. Val, Spina-cuta, Latte
Nina	Mrs. Douvillier
Elisa, governess of Nina . . .	Mrs. Val
Country women with chorus . .	Mrs. Placide, Miss Scully, Miss Du-the, etc.

The subject of this much admired opera is so well known that Mr. Francisquy thinks it unnecessary to give an explanation of it; everybody is well acquainted with the beauty of its music and the various affecting scenes which frame the whole of it.

1794, July 23: | *Blaise and Babet* ("grand pantomime ballet in 2
28: | acts . . . . the subject . . . . is
Nov. 1: | extracted from the celebrated opera of that
| name and Mr. Francisquy, anxious to give
| it all the beauty it is susceptible of, hath pro-
| vided himself with its delightful music and ori-
| ginal overture, composed by Monsieur Dezède")

July 30: | American Independence; or, the 4th of July 1776
1795, July 4: | ("grand patriotic pantomime in three acts")

1794, Aug. 4: | *The 28th of June;* or, the Attack on Fort Moultrie
| ("patriotic pantomime" with fireworks)

Aug. 6: | *Zémire and Azor* ("much admired opera, in 4 acts,
8: | composed by the celebrated Grétry, with the
1795, June 9: | original overture, and decorated with new
| scenery." Cast:

Azor	Mr. Douvillier
Sander	Mr. Dainville
Aly, Sander's servant	Mr. Placide
Zémire	Mrs. Douvillier
Fatime } daughters of Sander . . {	Mrs. Val
Lisbe	Mrs. Placide

1794, Aug. 12: |
Oct. 13: | *L'Amant statue* ("composed by the celebrated au-
1795, June 6: | thor Mr. Dalerac," first perf. at Paris, 1785)
12: |

1794,   Aug. 12:   *Genevieve of Brabant;* or, Virtue triumphant ("new historic pantomime in three acts")

Sept. 20:   *Pyrame and Thisbe* ("lyric drama with the original overture," probably not Rebel and Francœur's opera, but possibly Baudron's lyric scene, perf. at Paris, in 1783)

Oct. 11: ⎰ *Whims of Galatea* ("pastoral pantomime ballet,"
15: ⎱   perhaps adaptation of André J. Rigade's ballet 'Acis et Galathée,' Paris, 1768)

Nov. 5: ⎧ *Four Valiant Brothers;* or, the Clemency of Charlemagne ("grand historic and military panto-
1795,   April 15: ⎨ mime . . . with new music, scenery, dresses, etc.")

1794,   Nov. 10:   *Merry Rustics;* or, Trick upon Trick ("grand French pantomime ballet")

Nov. 14: ⎰ *The 14th of July, 1789;* or, the Destruction of the
17: ⎱   Bastille ("new grand pantomime, in two acts . . . . with new music, etc.")

Nov. 19:   Le *Braconnier;* or, the Game Laws ("new grand French pantomime," perhaps based on Raymont's opera, Paris, ca. 1785)

Dec. 1: ⎫
5: ⎬ Forêt Noire ("domestic pantomime tale")
1795,   May 20: ⎭

1794,   Dec. 12: ⎰ Le *Déserteur Français;* or, the Supposed Marriage
15: ⎱   ("grand tragic comic ballet pantomime," probably based on Monsigny)

Dec. 17:   Le *Ballet des Provençaux;* or, the Sailor of Marseillois

1795, March 9:   *Lion with the Thorn;* or, Harlequin protected by Neptune ("entire new Harlequin pantomime")

April 15:   *Cupid's Revenge* (ballet-pant., based on Hook?)

March 28: ⎧ *Jupiter and Europa;* or, the Jealousy of Juno
April 17: ⎪   ("for the first time in America, an heroic pan-
June 6: ⎨ tomime, with new scenery, dresses, decora-
July 17: ⎪ tions, music, etc." This pant. had been in
24: ⎩   rehearsal for three months! Possibly based on Galliard's pant. of the same title)

April 6:   *Miller and Collier* (ballet)

April 17: ⎰ Cooper ("New pantomime ballet composed by
Aug. 6: ⎱   Mr. Francisqui," apparently based on 'Le Tonnelier')

April 29: ⎱ *Sampson;* or, the Treachery of Delilah ("favourite
May 29: ⎰ pantomime in three acts")

June 3:⎫
    18:⎪ *False Magic* ("grand opera in 2 acts," Grétry's
    22:⎬ 'La Fausse Magie')
July 27:⎪
1796, Sept. 21:⎭

1795,   June 9: Poacher; or, the Game Laws (apparently identical
                   with 'Le Braconnier') (pant.-ballet)

               ⎧ *Melomania;* or, Musical Madness (announced as
June 16:⎪ "a favourite opera of the celebrated Grétry;"
    27:⎨ but the one-act 'La Mélomanie' was by Stanisl.
July 27:⎪ Champein, Paris, 1781)
               ⎩

June 20:⎧ *Re-capture of Toulon* by the French army; or,
    22:⎨ The Young Female Soldier ("new pantomime
        ⎩ in three acts")

July 1: *Rose Bush of Salency* ("grand pastoral ballet
         pantomime"; probably based on either Grétry's
         or St. Amant's opera 'La Rosière de Salency,'
         possibly even on the older (1769) opera by
         Philidor, Blaise, Monsigny and van Swieten)

July 10:⎱ *Alexis and Justine* (2-act opera by Dezède,
    17:⎰ Paris, 1785). Cast:

Longpre, father of Alexis . .	Mr. Lavalette
Alexis, lover of Justine . . .	Mr. Douvillier
Thierry, foster-father of Alexis and father of Justine	By an amateur
Thomas (sylly man in love with Justine)	Mr. Placide
A Bailiff	Mr. Dubois
Country men (with chorus) . .	Messrs. Val, Spinacuta, Latte, Fayol, Duport, etc.
Genevieve (mother of Justine) . .	Mrs. Placide
Magdelaine (an old servant maid) .	Mrs. Val
Justine	Mrs. Douvillier

July 21: *Les Dettes;* or, the Way to Pay Debts (Champein,
         Paris, 1787)

July 21: American Heroine; or, the Cruel Return ("historical and military pantomime")

Aug. 3:⎧ *Caravan of Cairo* (Caravane du Caïre, Paris, 1784).
       ⎪ Announced as "opera in three acts, never performed here before . . . . with the ori-
       6:⎨ ginal overture, composed by the celebrated
1796, June 9:⎪ Grétry. Accompanied by the Recitatives at
       ⎪ the Theatre de l'Opéra at Paris with great success. Ornamented with new scenery and decorations")
       ⎩

St. Phar, son of Florestan and lover of Zelima	slaves of	Mr. Douvillier
Zelima, a princess	Husca	Mrs. Douvillier

Company of travellers and gang of slaves Messrs. Val, Dubois,
Fayol, Latte, Spi-
nacuta, Duport,
Mrs. Val, Miss
Duthe, etc.

French woman	Mrs. Placide
Troop of Arabians	
Chief of Arabians	Mr. Francisqui
Basha of Cairo	Mr. Lavalette
Florestan, commander of a French squadron	By an amateur
Officers of the squadron . . .	Messrs. Fayol, Du-bois, Val, etc.
Tamorin, confident of the Basha .	Mr. Latte
The Basha's retinue	
Almeida, favourite of the Basha .	Mrs. Placide

Then followed a minute description of the stage evolutions rather than of the plot. That of the first act may serve as a specimen:

A halt of the caravan on the bank of the Nile. Several groups of travellers, some free and the others slaves, the former chanting in chorus the pleasure they feel on their return to Cairo, the latter deploring the state of slavery which awaits them.

A dance in character, by Master Duport. The Arabians descend from the mountains and attack the caravan.—The travellers prepare for combat.—St. Phar requests Husca to release him from his irons and to permit him to fight the Arabians—his valour preserves the caravan from pillage and as a reward of his victory Husca gives him his freedom. St. Phar, whose only view in engaging in the combat was to ensure the safety of Zelima, requests of Husca to emancipate her instead of him; but Husca, who had great hopes of obtaining a large price from the Basha for Zelima, on account of her superior beauty, remains inflexible to all entreaties.

The caravan proceeds on its journey, and the camels cross the mountains.

In the performance of June 9, 1796, "Mrs. Pownall and the Misses Wrightens" gave "the public an opportunity of witnessing their theatrical abilities in a foreign language," a conclusive proof, if such still be asked for, that the French operas were actually sung in French. Mrs. Pownall took the part of Zelima.

1796, Feb. 16: *Brother Quakers* ("new comic ballet")
    April ?: - Maid of Orleans; or, Joan of Arc ("grand heroic historical pantomime in three acts . . . . new music")
    May ?: *Echo and Narcissus* ("speaking pantomime," possibly based on Gluck, or an American setting of Mrs. Cowley's unpublished dramatic pastoral)
    May 30: *Rinaldo and Armida* ("new heroic pantomime in three acts never performed in America," possibly also based on Gluck)
1797, May 15: *Princess of Babylon* ("pantomime in four acts," "to the different incidents of which [was adapted by Monsieur Lavallette, the author] a select choir of musical pieces taken from the celebrated French operas of Panurage [Panurge, Grétry], the Golden Fleece, Iphigénie [en] Tauride [Gluck?] etc., none of which has ever yet been performed in America")
    May 15: Servant mistress (probably the French *parodie* of Pergolesi's 'Serva padrona')

This record makes it clear that the era of French opera practically ended at Charleston in 1796; but it is also apparent that during the three years of its hot-house existence there, Charleston had a by far better opportunity than any other American town to enjoy exotic opera, not to mention the startling number of pantomimes re-boiled or "composed" to order. The weakest point in this by-product of two revolutions was, of course, the language question. Even in Charleston not enough précieuses ridicules apparently could be found to support this musical Berlitz school for any length of time, but when the handful of exponents of the purity of the French language as *spoke* on the stage, again ventured outside of Charleston, they were doomed to speedy failure, particularly so, as the enthusiasm for things French was rapidly giving way to resentment at the insults heaped on our government by Citizen Genet and his successors.

Independently of the Charleston Théâtre Français Madame Gardie, the fascinating balletteuse, gave for her benefit at New York on May 4 Duni's 'Deux chasseurs' together with a pantomime in one act, 'Jeanne d'Arc'; but the "French performers" whom the managers of the Old American Company engaged in March 1796 were none other than some of the Charlestonian Frenchmen headed by Mons. Francisquy. They were engaged for two performances only, and I find that they presented on March 3 Duni's 'Deux chasseurs' turned into a "grand comic pantomime dance" by Mons. Francisquy under the title of 'The Two Huntsmen and the Milkmaid; or, the Death of the Bear,' 'Le Tonnellier' (*alias* the Cooper) treated similarly and Rousseau's Pygmalion. The second performance escaped me, but Mons. Francisquy and Mr. and Mrs. Val were still thriving under the auspices of the Old Americans when on April 21 the 'Children in the Wood,' were followed by 'Les Deux chasseurs,' this time as an opera, in which even the genial, gentle-minded Victor Pelissier, erstwhile first French horn at Cape François, took a part as Colas. The performance closed with one of Francisquy's so-called compositions, the "comic ballet pantomime" *'Rural Waggish Tricks.'* Shortly afterwards, the several circuses turned their attention to French pantomime, and they appear to have offered the last haven of refuge to Francisquy and colleagues, who probably did not regret this change, as it was Mr. Lailson's ambition to surround with all possible splendor such ballet productions (Nov. 2) as 'The New Deserter; or, Supposed Marriage,' "got up under the immediate direction of Mr. Francisquy. The music and the original overtures by the celebrated Grétry," and (Nov. 14) this master's 'Richard Cœur de Lion' turned into "an historic pantomime with military evolutions."

Other cities fared even worse than New York. Baltimore, for instance, as far as I can see, had occasion to become acquainted after 1790 only with Duni's 'Les Deux chasseurs,' turned into a pantomime by Mons. Lege "from the Italian theatre at Paris," with the original music, the accompaniments by Mr. De Marque on Aug. 22, 1795, and with Champein's 'Mélomanie' on March 14 at the Théatre François. The announcement of the latter was printed both in English and French in the *Federal Gazette*, even to the extent of giving the price of admission in revolutionary French, to wit:

"On prendra un Gourde aux loges et 3 Gourdins au Parterre, les billets d'entrée se distribuent au Bureau à l'entrée de la Salle."

Richmond's invasion by the Frenchmen in 1795 has already briefly been recorded and it merely remains to trace Philadelphia's participation in French opera.

On Dec. 17, 1796, Messrs. Wignell and Reinagle, the managers of the New Theatre, "ever solicitous to vary and improve the exhibition at the theatre and evince their gratitude for the patronage they receive," respectfully informed the public that they had engaged a French Company of Comedians in addition to their present establishment. This company presumably was identical with our friends from Charleston. Their short career at Philadelphia was ushered in on the evening of the announcement with Grétry's 'Le Tableau parlant' and Duni's 'Les Deux chasseurs'. To this they added on Dec. 24 Al. Mar. Ant. Fridzeri's 'Les Souliers mordorés.' Their connection with Wignell and Reinagle apparently lasted into the following year, as on Jan. 7, 1797, they presented Dezède's 'Blaise et Babet,' attributing it here, too, incorrectly to Grétry. As far as I can see, their last attempts to conquer the public of Philadelphia were on Jan. 14 with Champein's 'La Mélomanie' and Dalayrac's 'Les Deux petits Savoyards' and on Jan. 21 with a repetition of 'Le Tableau parlant.'

When, after this, a French opera appeared on the repertory on March 25, 1798, it was an English translation and adaptation: Grétry's 'Richard Cœur de Lion' with accompaniments by Linley. But this was not the first rendition of the brilliant Belgian's masterpiece, nor was it the last. To Boston, where on Jan. 15, 1796, Mad. Gardie had selected for her benefit, evidently in French, Duni's 'Les Deux chasseurs,' belongs the credit of having greeted at the Federal Street Theatre on Monday, Jan. 23, 1797:

. . . . (for the first time on the continent of America) the grand historical Romance, called *Richard, Cœur de Lion*, with all the original music, songs, and choruses, composed by Grétry. The orchestra accompaniment entirely new, composed by Mons. Labarre. New scenery and decorations by Mr. Cullager.

Richard	Mr. Marshall
Blondel	Mr. Cleveland
Sir Owen	Mr. Rowson
Florestan	Mr. Downie
Sureschall	Mr. Hogg
Guillot	Mr. Villiers
Old Mathew	Mr. Kenny
William	Mr. McKenzie
Pilgrim	Mr. Clarke
Antonio	Mr. Williamson
Laurette	Mrs. Graupner (her first appearance these two years)
Julie	Miss Solomon
Dorcas	Mrs. Rowson
Collette	Miss Green
Matilda	Mrs. Marshall

A Pastoral Dance,
Incidental to the piece, by Miss A. Duport, Miss Solomon and Miss Hogg. First Shepherdess with a Pas Seul, by Miss Duport. The new scenery consists of a distant view of the Castle at Sunrise. An interior view of the fortifications, with the area, in which Richard is confined; and, the double parapet, from which Matilda endeavours to gain a sight of the King.

The whole to conclude with the *Assault and Taking* of the Castle, by storm; and the deliverance of Richard by the Cavaliers.

Evidently in this *première* the original score was adhered to except that Monsieur Trille LaBarre, the leader of the orchestra, furnished new, probably simpler orchestral accompaniments for the arias. This is the nearest the American public was allowed to approach the original, for when James Hewitt selected the same opera for his benefit at New York on May 21, 1800, as "never performed" there, he conducted a version for which Victor Pelissier had composed the accompaniments.

Simple as Grétry's music sounds to us to-day, it was not so considered in an era which looked aghast at the bold innovations and complications of *Papa* Haydn, not to mention the anarchist Mozart. If Grétry still held the reputation of a master of difficult music in Europe, very much more so, of course, in our country, where practically none but the easily understood, light English operas were known. The advent of his 'Richard, Cœur de Lion' was hailed therefore very much in the same spirit as we would to-day receive 'Pelléas et Mélisande,' but it is also characteristic of the innate musical commonsense of the public that they hailed this masterwork "with peals of applause." The criticism of the *première* in the *Columbian Centinel*, Jan. 25, 1797, which accompanied the announcement of a repetition on this evening is of a nature as to throw more light on the whole subject than any historical *post mortem* arguments:

THEATRICAL.

On Monday evening the grand dramatic romance of '*Richard, Cœur de Lion*,' was performed at the Boston Theatre, for the first time on the continent of America.—The audience was brilliant and crowded; the peals of applause, which were frequent during the performance, were instantaneous and unequivocal; and the success of the piece, attested by the general satisfaction, unprecedented in the novelties of this season. Its annunciation by the manager for a second representation this evening, was supported by a burst of approbation from every part of the house.

In the preparations, necessary for the performance of the opera, the respective talents of Mr. Labarre and Mr. Gullager evinced a decided superiority to any prior exhibition of music or painting; and we presume the amateurs of the fine arts have never known the orchestra accompaniments of any opera in this metropolis, composed with so much genius; nor the scenery and mechanism of a grand stage spectacle designed with so much elegance and invented with so much ingenuity.

The attention and industry of Mons. Labarre in perfecting the supernumerary vocal performers in their respective choruses also deserves much credit.

It has heretofore been invariably the attendant fatality of all operas, produced on our stage, that from the inability of the performers, either in the *science* or *numbers*, to execute compound music, they never have supported with success a musical dialogue, in which more than three voices were concerned. This imputation, however, was entirely removed by the performance of Monday Evening; for the choruses, with which the opera abounds, and all of them difficult and intricate music, were filled throughout with an ample power of voice, and given with a pleasing accuracy of execution . .

The merit of the performers in the characters of the piece was generally acknowledged to be of superior kind. Their respective *drafts* on the public patronage were all *honored at sight*, and paid in the *sterling ore* of genuine approbation. As the piece is given out for a second representation this evening, a particular critique on the performance is deferred.

This particular critique either escaped me or did not appear, nor was, to my knowledge, any critical comment made on the first performance in English (apparently with the original accompaniments!) of Grétry–Linley's charming *Selima and Azor* on March 31, 1797, "with new dresses, scenery, decorations and the original music," and in this cast:

Azor	Mrs. Marshall
Scander	Mr. Rowson
Ali	Mr. Cleveland
Lesbia	Mrs. Solomon
Fatima	Miss Rowson
Selima	Mrs. Marshall

Either for lack of encouragement or lack of scores and parts, which is perhaps more plausible, no further attempt at French grand opera in English was made at Boston. Only Rousseau's "interesting melodrama" 'Pygmalion' was brought out on May 10, 1797, and I have also already alluded in the statistical record under Boston to the performance of 'The Garden of Love' on April 21, 1800. To judge by the synopsis in the *Columbian Centinel,* April 19, this might be termed a pastoral pantomime pasticcio:

"A *Musical Interlude* from the most chaste compositions of the French, selected and got up under the direction of Mr. Audin, with entire new scenery and decorations. Entitled the *Garden of Love;* or, the Wounds of Cupid healed by Hymen.

Curtain rises and discovers a Shepherdess reposing on a bank of verdure, in the Garden of Hymen; Hymen sitting on a fountain of real water;—Harmonic music at a distance;—Cupid descends, throws his dart, and flies off—The shepherdess awakes and sings 'Sweet Echo'—during which the Shepherd appears; his countenance expressive of the tenderest love—they are joined by Hymen—Concluded with a duet.

Shepherd	Mr. Munto
Shepherdess	Mrs. Graupner
Hymen	Miss Graupner
Cupid	Miss C. Graupner

These performances at Boston, the production of Rousseau's 'Pygmalion' at Charleston, 1797, Monsigny's 'Deserter' at Norfolk, Va., 1793, the few stray performances of French works at New York, Baltimore, Philadelphia already recorded, constitute about all that would properly come under the head of French opera in English. Surely very little, but as much as one may reasonably expect to find in a country which borrowed its mode of conduct in matters operatic from England. How this tender root of French opera in English expanded until by force of circumstances and the inoculation of the polyglot system the whole aspect of opera in our country was changed into the supremacy of performances in foreign languages—another worthy pendant and sequel to conditions in England where, just as in America,

English opera and opera in English have been driven, generally speaking, into the abyss of operetta—how this tender root of French opera in English expanded I am not prepared to say. Yet the probabilities are that, if an earnest effort is made to follow the trail into the nineteenth century, strong connecting links will be found between the era which has been the subject of this essay and the era with which we all are familiar. More than this, it will appear that the standard French, Italian and German operas were sung in English and well sung and received with just as much pleasure as the English operas; and again the historian will sigh for—what might have been and still is bound to come, once our people see the folly of their ways, or at least the folly of their operatic purveyors.

During the eighteenth century, to repeat it, French opera was a mere episode and entirely subordinate to English opera. The latter, however, surely was cultivated in America to a very considerable extent, interpreted skilfully and enjoyed intelligently. This survey of early opera in America proves these three points beyond serious doubt and I hope has laid foundations solid enough for others to use for a reliable history of opera in America during the nineteenth century.

Of one thing I am absolutely certain: if opera in America is ever to attain to the distinction of being more than a sensational and exotic, though sincerely enjoyed, luxury of the relatively few in a few cities, it will have to be by the way of good performances of good operas in good English. Esthetically, of course, performances of operas in the original language as perfect as money and interpretative genius can make them will always be superior to those in translations, even with an equal investment in money and interpretative genius, but a decrease in esthetic value will be more than offset by the cultural value to the people, if they are *properly encouraged* to listen to musical dramas in a language which they understand. Even in matters of art, subtle esthetics cannot overrule the demands of common-sense for long without injuring the prospects of art and of native art in particular. I, for one, am heartily glad that these views are being shared by a steadily increasing number of sincere lovers of opera; and it is not a visionary prediction that sooner or later the glorious but gaudy, polyglot past of opera in America will be remembered with a sigh of relief by all except the foreigners. Let us wish a long life for the Metropolitan Opera House as an institution, unique and financially able to strive after model performances of foreign operas *au naturel*, but let us also wish that the operatic life of the rest of our country be based in the main on opera in English.

INDEX

N. B.   For titles of operas, pantomimes, etc., (indexed in italics)
consult also the Tables A-J